Invisible Darkness

Jean Toomer & Nella Larsen

Charles R. Larson

University of Iowa Press   Iowa City

University of Iowa Press,

Iowa City 52242

Copyright © 1993 by the

University of Iowa Press

All rights reserved

Printed in the United States

of America

Design by Richard Hendel

Printed on acid-free paper

97   96   95   94   93

C   5   4   3   2   1

97   96   95   94   93

P   5   4   3   2   1

Library of Congress Cataloging-in-

Publication Data

Larson, Charles R.

Invisible darkness: Jean Toomer

and Nella Larsen / by Charles R.

Larson.

p.   cm.

Includes bibliographical

references and index.

ISBN 0-87745-425-6 (cloth),

ISBN 0-87745-437-X (pbk.)

1. Toomer, Jean, 1894–1967.

2. Larsen, Nella.   3. American

fiction – Afro-American authors –

History and criticism.   4. American

fiction – 20th century – History and

criticism.   5. Afro-American

novelists – 20th century – Biography.

6. Afro-Americans in literature.

I. Title.

PS3539.0478Z73   1993

813′.5209896073 – dc20   93-15637

CIP

For Roberta, Vanessa, & Joshua

Contents

Acknowledgments

When you write an autobiography, you have only yourself to thank, although you can blame others for the mistakes of your life. A biography is a totally different matter. You would not be able to write it without the help of other people; you can blame only yourself for your mistakes. The errors in this book are solely my own. I would not have been able to write it without the generous support and assistance of dozens of people.

Arthur P. Davis, Bernth Lindfors, C. Barry Chabot, Eric Sellin, Frank Turaj, and John Collier gave initial support to the project itself. Bruce Kellner, a walking resource about the Harlem Renaissance, patiently answered questions about the period whenever I was stumped. Nancy Loughridge generously opened her files on Margery Latimer and filled in much of the background on the Toomer-Latimer marriage. Faith Berry and David Levering Lewis suggested numerous leads I would never have followed on my own. To these people I owe my respect and admiration.

As for interviews with people who knew either or both of the subjects, I want to single out Susan L. Sandberg for answering letter after letter about her mother, Margerie Content Toomer, as well as her stepfather, Jean Toomer. Alice Carper provided similar information about Nella Larsen. Without her help, as well as the support of Carolyn Lane and Mildred Phillips, I would probably have concluded that Nella Larsen actually did disappear. Interviews (both written and oral) with many other people were invaluable: William J. Welch, M.D., Carla Peterson, Hope Haley, Isaiah T. Creswell, and Richmond Barthe.

Shirley Rosenstock, interlibrary loan librarian at American University, spent hours tracking down books and periodicals for this project. Without her assistance, the entire project would have collapsed. Numerous other reference librarians at American University Library gave liberally of their time.

At Fisk University Library, I especially want to thank Beth M. Howse. At the Beinecke Rare Book and Manuscript Library at Yale University, David E. Schoonover was similarly supportive and always helpful. John D. Stinson helped me locate materials at the New York Public Library.

My thanks also to the following people, who answered queries and letters: Rosanne Pool, Victor Schmalzer, Irma D. Minott, William L. Lester, Waldemar A. Comas, Carl D. Brandt, Arnold A. Levin, Manford Byrd, Jr., Ejvind Slottved, Vera Joseph, Natalia C. Walter, Peter Howard, Franklin Davenport, Clifton Johnson, Joseph Foster, Judson Crews, Mike Ellis, Hugh Ford, Keith Fitzgerald, Sally Fell, Ann Allen Shockley, Frank K. Bjornsgaard, Lawrence Miller, Jr., and Peggy K. Lewis. Furthermore, I am indebted to Jean Toomer and Nella Larsen's earlier critics and biographers, who paved the road for much of the work in this book: Darwin T. Turner, John Griffith, Nellie Y. Mckay, Frank Durham, Brian J. Benson, Mabel M. Dillard, Cynthia Earl Kerman, Richard Eldridge, Rudolph P. Byrd, Thadious M. Davis, and Ann Allen Shockley.

For permission to quote archival materials, I would like to thank the following: the Yale Collection of American Literature, Beinecke Rare Book and Manuscript Library, Yale University, for quotations from the works of Jean Toomer and from the James Weldon Johnson Collection; the New York Public Library, Rare Books and Manuscripts Division, Astor, Lenox and Tilden Foundations, for quotations from the Carl Van Vechten Papers and from the Alfred A. Knopf, Inc., Records; the Amistad Research Center, Tulane University, for quotations from the Gorham B. Munson interview and the letters of Harold Jackman; and the Department of Serial Collections, Memorial Library, University of Wisconsin, Madison, for quotations from Margery Latimer's letters.

I would like to thank all those at the University of Iowa Press for their unabated support and confidence in my work. Special thanks to Mary Russell Curran, who made sense of my prose and greatly improved it.

Finally, I was able to undertake this project because of the generous support of American University, which provided travel money and release time from teaching, and the added assistance of the College of Arts and Sciences Mellon Fund for Faculty Development.

A research grant from the National Endowment for the Humanities allowed me to complete the project.

Introduction

Like most people of my generation, I grew up unaware of the existence of African American literature. There were no selections by black writers in the American literature textbooks I read in the public schools and at the university during the 1950s. Because of where I lived and where I was educated (Iowa and Colorado), I knew nothing about the lives of black Americans. Even the course I took in American literature at the University of Colorado, taught by a celebrated African American professor, contained no references to minority writing. Similar world literature courses taught in schools across the country limited their perspectives to Europe and America.

My initial exposure to African American writers, as well as to writers from the developing world, did not begin until 1962, when I joined the Peace Corps. What pleasures I had making those discoveries during the two years I taught in Nigeria. Back in the States in the mid-sixties, things had changed considerably, in the realms of both civil rights and education. The American literature textbooks were still white, though they were shortly to change. Since I was then living and teaching in Washington, D.C., it was possible to take an entire year's course in Afro-American literature, as it was then beginning to be called. I enrolled in Arthur P. Davis's two-semester graduate survey at Howard University, which for the first time exposed me to the historical scope of black American writing. It was in that course, during the 1965–1966 academic year, that I learned about the Harlem Renaissance and read Jean Toomer's *Cane* (1923) and Nella Larsen's *Quicksand* (1928) and *Passing* (1929).

These three novels had long been out of print and had to be read either on reserve in the Moorland Room at Howard University Library or by any other means the student could devise. As it happened, I was able to borrow them from the Library of Congress, though these and dozens of other works covered in the course were largely unavailable for the nonacademic reader. It was equally difficult to track down biographical information about Toomer and Larsen and a host of other black American writers. Even during the ensuing years, when I began to devote an increasing amount of my time to the study of black literature, much of the biographical information was sketchy at best.

Besides the power of their writing, what intrigued me initially about Jean Toomer and Nella Larsen was the common perception that they had "disappeared." This belief — or perhaps I should say misbelief — has persisted until recent times, though to a lesser extent with Toomer than with Larsen. Jean Toomer was known to have dropped out and to be living in Bucks County, Pennsylvania. There were speculations that he had chosen to pass as a white person after his second marriage (to a white woman) in 1934. It shouldn't have been very difficult to locate him, yet when he died in 1967, there were no obituaries except in local newspapers. It was months before the literary world was aware of his death, and even then there was a sense of surprise because many people assumed that he had died long ago.

If there were literary people who knew what had happened to Jean Toomer, almost no one knew the whereabouts of Nella Larsen. Personal friends of hers — Carl Van Vechten, Dorothy Peterson, Walter White, with whom she had ongoing communication and correspondence during the height of the Harlem Renaissance — had no idea what had happened to her. An article in Ms. magazine in 1980 described her as a "lost woman," as the "mystery woman of the Harlem Renaissance." This article, by Mary Helen Washington, mentions one of Larsen's biographers who "couldn't even bury"[1] her. There are no obituaries anywhere. Every published date of her birth and death that I found was incorrect. Richmond Barthe, another figure from the Harlem Renaissance, wrote me that "she disappeared and no one knew what had happened."[2]

One would assume that it would be easy to track down accurate information about Americans during the twentieth century, especially about people who have been public figures. I have learned, however, that this is not necessarily so. Documents of births, marriages, and deaths dating from the beginning of the century are often incomplete. More recently, one assumes, computers and bureaucracies (along with tax forms, Social Security records, passport applications, and so on) have made it impossible to avoid obscurity. Even the most reclusive figures must have had someone with whom they worked and communicated.

Jean Toomer was seventy-two years old when he died March 30, 1967. Fortunately, even though he had been in ill health the last decade of his life and had spent most of the time in a rest home, he had had the foresight to realize that sometime in the future his work would be rediscovered and people would be interested in learning about the fascinating activities and interests of his life. At the request of Arna Bontemps, another figure from the Harlem Renaissance, Toomer sent the bulk of his papers to Fisk University, where Bontemps held the position of university librarian. These papers, which were subsequently transferred to the Beinecke Library at Yale University, total nearly thirty thousand documents. Many of them were the letters Toomer had received from important literary and artistic figures throughout his life. There were also copies of his own letters and hundreds of documents pertaining to his publishing – contracts, rejection slips, pleas to editors to publish his work. Dozens of the manuscripts were his unpublished works, including book-length novels, plays, and several autobiographies, shorter essays and poems, and other essays he wrote for the Society of Friends during the last years of his life.

If anything, there is too much material about Jean Toomer. Scholars who have waded through the unpublished manuscripts of his creative works are in agreement that most of it deserves to remain unpublished. One of Toomer's most faithful critics and certainly the man who should be credited with restoring Toomer's literary reputation, Darwin T. Turner, edited a volume of excerpts from many of these works in 1980, *The Wayward and the Seeking: A Collection of Writings by Jean Toomer*. Nothing in this volume approaches the power of *Cane*, which has repeatedly been referred to as the swan song of Toomer's literary career. In the long run, a writer can be known only by what is published and not by what ends up in the file cabinet. Thus, I have limited my analyses and quotations in this book mostly to his published works.

What interests me as a biographer is why Jean Toomer failed as a writer after the publication of that one brilliant work. What diminished whatever potential there was in his later works? Why have the connections with the Harlem Renaissance (and with black culture in general) turned out to be so contradictory? What was Jean Toomer *doing* all those years after the publication of *Cane*?

Similar questions about Nella Larsen interest me, though the answers are much more problematic. In contrast to Jean Toomer, who seemed to be waiting patiently for that moment of rediscovery and carefully aiding the work of his future biographers, Nella Larsen appears to have sought obscurity and perhaps even the obliteration of her literary fame. She certainly went out of her way to distort the facts of her early life. When she was discovered dead in her apartment in 1964 (coincidentally, on March 30), she had been dead for a week. A coworker from whom she had become estranged was permitted to enter the apartment and found the place was in shambles — ransacked by other tenants or possibly the police. Letters and documents were strewn everywhere, though everything of value, including her books, was missing.

Nella Larsen left no will. There was no one in her immediate family with whom she had been in close contact for years. Her husband, from whom she had been divorced in 1933, had died in 1941. She had no children and few friends. She had lived a life of withdrawal for thirty years, letting the copyrights on her novels lapse into the public domain, apparently believing that no one would ever be interested in her life or her work.

Yet what dazzling lives Jean Toomer and Nella Larsen once lived. In the 1920s, the world was all before them. America was caught up in the fervor of an artistic renaissance soon to be called the Jazz Age. And the real fascination — for anyone in the know — was with black America.

In the Middle

Negro stock is going up, and everyone's buying.
— Rudolph Fisher, "The Caucasian Storms Harlem," 1927

Being a Negro writer these days is a racket and I'm going to make
the most of it while it lasts. . . . About twice a year I manage to sell
a story. It is acclaimed. I am a genius in the making. Thank God for
this Negro literary renaissance! Long may it flourish!
— Sweetie May Carr in Wallace Thurman, *The Infants of Spring*, 1932

Harlem certainly wasn't on everyone's mind in the 1920s,
though it must have been in the consciousness of many African Americans.
The great migration of the past several decades had brought thousands of
southern blacks to the North and many of them to New York City. Though
the rent they paid for apartments was often inflated, Harlem itself still had a
kind of newness to it, or freshness, nothing to make one think of it as a
dirty, sprawling urban ghetto. As James Weldon Johnson wrote in *Black Man-*
hattan in 1930, "It is not a fringe, it is not a slum, nor is it a 'quarter' con-
sisting of dilapidated tenements. It is a section of new-law apartment houses
and handsome dwellings, with streets as well paved, as well lighted, and as
well kept as in any other part of the city." [1] It was more than just a state
of mind.

It was a place that many black war veterans gravitated to after their return
to the United States, disillusioned at the enigma of having risked their lives
for a country that had little respect or place for them. Jim Crowism had
reached a kind of peak for black American soldiers in France with the publication of a government document called "Secret Information Concerning

Black American Troops." Briefly stated, that document said that the French should not regard black soldiers as equal to white ones. Returned home, these African American soldiers disseminated the contents of the document to the black community. Riots broke out in several American cities, triggered by a renewed questioning of what our country had to offer black people.

Some years later, in 1928, Claude McKay summarized the black soldier's experience in a few words in his best-seller, *Home to Harlem*, by having Jake, his hero, explain his reasons for going AWOL: "I didn't run away because I was scared a them Germans. But I beat it away from Brest because they wouldn't give us a chance at them, but kept us in that rainy, sloppy, Gawd-forsaken burg working like wops. They didn't seem to want us niggers foh no soldiers. We was jest a bunch a despised hod-carriers." [2] What was the reason for being in the armed services if black "soldiers" were limited to menial jobs?

Marcus Garvey was certainly asking similar questions. By the beginning of the decade, his Universal Negro Improvement Association had attracted considerable attention. He had begun construction of Liberty Hall, raised hundreds of thousands of dollars for establishing black businesses, and even launched the Black Star Shipping Line – all to give black people a sense of economic viability and racial pride. Hardly a Sunday passed without Garvey's followers parading down the streets of Harlem, proclaiming the sense of dignity and oneness which would unite them. In 1919, during his association's first convention, held in Carnegie Hall, Garvey had announced,

We are striking homeward toward Africa to make her the big black republic. And in the making of Africa the big black republic, what is the barrier? The barrier is the white man; and we say to the white man who dominates Africa that it is to his interest to clear out now, because we are coming, not as in the time of Father Abraham, 200,000 strong, but we are coming 400,000,000 strong and we mean to retake every square inch of the 12,000,000 square miles of African territory belonging to us by right Divine. [3]

Of course, not all blacks were wild about Garvey's back-to-Africa movement, but even his most outspoken critics – men like W. E. B. DuBois and James Weldon Johnson – privately had to admit that Garvey had done much to establish a new plateau of black consciousness, unequaled by such numbers at any earlier time. Reflecting upon Garvey's charisma at a much later date, Horace R. Clayton wrote, "Garvey organized a million black Americans and, although his goals were foolish, the pride he stirred in black hearts was very real."[4] Remembering a parade of thousands of black people, not in Harlem but in Seattle, Clayton wrote,

> In the parade were Negro women in the uniform of Black Cross nurses and others who wore wrapped puttees of the African Motorcycle Corps. Negro men were in the uniform of the Black Eagle Flying Corps and, in front, the Royal African Legions rode on horses.
>
> It was ludicrous and laughable, but the black washerwomen were deadly serious, and the black men, laborers and servants, had a pride that raised the demonstration out of the absurd and struck fear or admiration in the watchers. On the dark faces, for the first time, there was pride and joy and fulfillment. . . . For the Garveyites, he was a savior, a Messiah who promised to snatch them from the edge of the abyss and turn their grief into greatness. He had put steel in the spines of Negroes who had previously been ashamed of their color.[5]

Never mind that Garvey would eventually be deported, that black soldiers would experience similar humiliations in the next world war, that some of the glamor of Harlem would fade; black political consciousness was definitely on the rise during the 1920s. And with it came an attendant burgeoning of black culture, much of it centered in Harlem, though all of it left its mark across the nation.

This movement — called the Harlem Renaissance or the New Negro — was brought about by a handful of talented leaders who clearly understood the recent historical and sociological changes affecting the nation as a whole. Perhaps the most important of these, according to David Levering Lewis, was Charles S. Johnson, the director of the Urban League, who perceived his role as a kind of jump-starter for igniting the forces around him. Recognizing that blacks would not be accepted in most professions, Johnson identified the arts as an area with few restrictions. Artistic expression, he thought, would "redeem . . . the standing of his people."[6]

Thus Johnson worked behind the scenes, coordinating functions that would bring black artists together with wealthy white business owners and patrons as well as with other artists. The Urban League's publication, Opportunity, became a forum for the new black expression and sponsored several yearly artistic contests. The NAACP joined in the excitement by sponsoring an annual literary contest and publishing the winning works in Crisis, the organization's journal.

Walter White, assistant secretary of the NAACP, also entered the scene, supplying endless quantities of personal support for individual artists, with many of whom he carried on voluminous correspondence. Though he had been hired by the NAACP to investigate and keep abreast of lynchings, civil rights was only one of the areas that interested him. He would also turn his pen to creative expression by publishing two novels, The Fire in the Flint (1924) and Flight (1926).

Another founder of the movement was Alain Leroy Locke, a teacher at Howard University who had distinguished himself as a Rhodes Scholar and had earned a Ph.D. in philosophy from Harvard. It was Locke who orchestrated some of the major publications of the time, including a special Negro issue of Survey Graphic (March 1925). Many of the selections from that issue were reprinted, along with additional material, in a focal volume called The New Negro (1925). Like Walter White, Locke seemed to know every black artist of the time, and he took several of the more talented ones directly under his wing. Those he found most promising he helped financially by introducing them to his rich white patron, Charlotte Osgood Mason.

In his introductory essay for The New Negro, Locke stated, "The Negro is being carefully studied, not just talked about and discussed. In arts and letters, instead of being wholly caricatured, he is being seriously portrayed and painted. . . . Subtly the conditions that are molding a New Negro are molding a new American attitude."[7] Black artistry was being metamorphosed, and along with it there was a transformation of black people themselves.

Locke had stressed the fact that black culture was being examined not only by black artists but by their white counterparts. Nowhere was this more apparent than in literature. Some of the decade's most famous writers tried their hands with black subjects. These writers included Eugene O'Neill, Sherwood Anderson, Vachel Lindsay, William Faulkner, and Gertrude Stein, as well as a host of lesser writers who often wrote sensational works about black American life.

Of all of these white writers, Carl Van Vechten probably had as much to do with the promotion of black culture in this country as did Charles S. Johnson, Walter White, or Alain Locke. Van Vechten, a talented critic, novelist, and photographer, published *Nigger Heaven* in 1926 and immediately found himself in the midst of an uproar. Older black leaders and critics like W. E. B. DuBois were upset by the novel's picture of the seamy side of Negro life, though James Weldon Johnson, one of Van Vechten's close friends, admired the book.

Van Vechten was fascinated by black America. It was he who made it fashionable for whites to go slumming in Harlem, though to his credit Van Vechten perceived the relationship between black and white artists as a two-way circuit. He was present at many of the parties given by black people in Harlem, and they in turn were invited to the soirees that he and his wife, the actress Fania Marinoff, hosted farther downtown. Nathan Huggins has suggested that without the interest and support of Caucasian Americans, the Harlem Renaissance might have turned out quite differently. He admits, also, that Harlem was "therapy for deeper white needs. The most forbidden was most available: whiskey of course, but also cocaine and sex."[8]

By the midpoint of the decade, Caucasians made regular pilgrimages to Harlem to visit the cabarets and the nightclubs, to listen to jazz at rent parties, and to bump shoulders with black artists and intellectuals. Other black figures, like A'Lelia Walker, held sway in slightly different arenas. A'Lelia's mother, known as Madame C. J. Walker, had become a millionaire by manufacturing hair-straightening products. As a monument to her success, she built a thirty-four room mansion, called Villa Lewaro, in Westchester, which overlooked the Hudson River. Her daughter, however, preferred Harlem and set up shop there, hosting fabulous if somewhat funky parties and squandering her mother's wealth. Money appeared to flow freely from the booming postwar economy. Casper Holstein made millions with the numbers racket. Middle-class blacks lived better than they ever had before, even if many of the artistic figures of the Renaissance could just barely make a go of it.

Black visibility in the theater and the cinema also reached new heights during the Renaissance. The achievements of black performers during the decade were so frequent that they gave the impression of a string of firecrackers going off one after the other. Florence Mills became an instant celebrity, starting with her performance in the chorus line of *Shuffle Along* in

1921. Thereafter, for the next half-dozen years until her death in 1927, she dazzled Broadway in a series of musicals, culminating in *Blackbirds* in 1926. Paul Robeson created an equally impressive trail of successes, beginning with O'Neill's *All God's Chillun Got Wings* in 1923 and then following almost immediately with a revival of *The Emperor Jones* in 1924. (Charles Gilpin had starred in the original production in 1920, but by 1924 he was more in love with the bottle than with the theater.)

The careers of other performers and musicians, including Ethel Waters, Duke Ellington, Eubie Blake, Fats Waller, Bessie Smith, and Louis Armstrong, began in the same era. Some of these entertainers could be seen on Broadway and in the uptown Harlem theaters – the Lafayette, the Alhambra, and the Harlem Opera House – as well as in cabarets and nightclubs. Many of them would shortly gravitate to Hollywood, where the tinsel screen was undergoing its own revolution from silent to sound movies. One has only to recall the success of Al Jolson in *The Jazz Singer* (1927), although the throwback to minstrelsy was clearly unsettling for many black artists.

Black films by black filmmakers were also beginning to enjoy a measure of success during the twenties, though few copies of these works have survived. If the Harlem Renaissance was limited in scope by its geographical context, the black films of the era were nonetheless appreciated by many audiences across the nation, though they were almost unknown to most white viewers. All aspects of filmmaking and distribution were curtailed by Jim Crow restrictions, yet several black directors and production companies became famous during the period.

According to Thomas Cripps, two of the most famous production teams, Emmet J. Scott and George and Nobel Johnson, produced films which largely "embraced the American success myth brought to light by Horatio Alger."[9] These films presented "heroes, who promised blacks the hope of success and the conquest of despair."[10] At times, however, there were instances of cross-fertilization between blacks and whites. In his *Black Film as Genre*, Cripps cites the instance of *Black and Tan* (1929), a talkie starring Duke Ellington, on which Carl Van Vechten had collaborated.

It was Oscar Micheaux, however, who largely ushered in a more realistic view of black life, beginning with the filming of several of his own novels. *Body and Soul* (1926), starring Paul Robeson, stabilized Micheaux's career, even though he was always a kind of "one-man motion picture company"[11] fending off his creditors. Micheaux also adapted two works by black writer Charles Waddell Chesnutt, *The Conjure Woman* (1926) and *The House Behind the Cedars* (1927).

Film, theater, music, and art — as exemplified in the works of Aaron Douglas, Richmond Barthe, and Sargent Johnson — all these areas of expression underwent a vast upheaval during the Harlem Renaissance, leaving them remarkably different from the way they had been before. Yet nowhere is the black cultural explosion shown so completely as in the literature of this era, which broke away from the plantation tradition, with its stock characters and themes, and underwent a revolution both in content and form.

Prior to the Renaissance, the route many black writers followed forced them to accept a kind of schizophrenic identity necessitated by their dual audience. Charles W. Chesnutt (1858–1932), already mentioned, had succeeded in publishing short stories in important magazines such as the *Atlantic* before the turn of the century, yet his identity as a black writer was concealed from many of his readers until he was well into his career. Chesnutt's contemporary Paul Laurence Dunbar (1872–1906) became the most famous black poet of his time, although many white readers knew him only by his four sentimental novels, which were inferior to the stunning lyricism of his poems.

In the decade prior to the Renaissance, the novels of W. E. B. DuBois and Oscar Micheaux suffered in part because they were brought out by minor publishing houses. In 1917 when James Weldon Johnson published his singular novel, *The Autobiography of an Ex-Colored Man* — a hard-hitting examination of "passing" that many people believe helped to usher in the realistic novels of the Renaissance — he published the work anonymously. Somewhat earlier, Sutton E. Griggs had confronted the question of the dual audience by printing his novels himself and peddling them in black communities, without the aid of conventional publishing channels.

Much of this separatism was beginning to change during the 1920s, as one example will reveal. Paul Laurence Dunbar's last novel, *The Sport of the Gods* (1902), is the only one of the four he wrote that presents black people as main characters and frontally attacks the question of racism. This work is also the first novel written by a black American to make use of a Manhattan setting. In 1921, two white producers named Ben Strasser and Robert Levy, of the Reol Company, made a movie version of Dunbar's novel. It was praised by black reviewers and played to overflow houses in the East, although these were limited bookings. Posters for the film described Dunbar as "America's Greatest Race Poet and Author" and the story as "true to life" with an "All-Star Cast of Colored Artists." [12] Although the controlling financial interests in the film were white, here was material by a black writer presented directly for what it was: a race movie, made for black audiences, drawn from the work of a beloved black author.

A similar mixing of talents helped black writers of the Harlem Renaissance reach audiences they had only dreamed of before. Vachel Lindsay helped Langston Hughes launch his poetic career. Max Eastman hired Claude McKay to be the executive editor of *The Liberator*. Before he had graduated from college, Countee Cullen had poems accepted by *Harper's*, *Poetry*, *Century*, the *American Mercury*, the *Nation*, and the *Bookman*. Waldo Frank convinced Boni and Liveright to publish Jean Toomer's *Cane* in 1923. Carl Van Vechten helped any number of black artists, including Nella Larsen, whose first novel he took to Blanch Knopf. All of these black writers and others, such as Rudolph Fisher, Walter White, Jessie Fauset, George Schuyler, Wallace Thurman, and, somewhat later, Zora Neale Hurston, found themselves courted and published by major publishing houses.

What did all of this amount to? New hopes and aspirations, certainly, for the artists themselves, although difficult times would shortly arrive with the stock market crash and the subsequent depression. Still, for a time Americans were interested in black culture as they had never been before, and Harlem – the focal point of much of the activity – was an exciting place to be. To quote David Levering Lewis, Harlem was in vogue. [13] Or, in the words of another Renaissance scholar, Harlem became the "capital of the black world." [14]

Toomer

By the time the Harlem Renaissance was in full swing, Jean Toomer had already decided he wanted nothing to do with it. Nor did he want others to identify him with the movement. Rarely has a writer made such an about-face as Toomer did after the publication of *Cane*. The birthing of his masterpiece had not been particularly arduous or even painful. When the subsequent rejection began, it was not exclusively the fault of the author himself; the world had expectations the author of a "Negro book" had to meet.

When Jean Toomer arrived in New York City in the winter of 1919 determined to become a writer, he was twenty-five years old and still largely unformed. He had spent the previous five years of his life wandering around the country and had tried earlier stays in New York City. He had moved from university to university (without completing his degree), from job to job, and even from ideology to ideology. One of these was socialism, which gave him an immediate goal and a larger context for his first job.

It was a bitter cold December. Toomer would rise at five o'clock and leave his room on Ninth Street for the New Jersey shipyards. He wrote that the work was hard: "All day long I had to cramp myself under heavy plates, in small compartments, and work the holes so that bolts could be slid in from the top."[1] The pay was $22 a week, and Toomer stuck it out for only ten days. That quickly he had judged his coworkers and been disappointed by their lack of interest in his socialistic cure for their ills. They were more concerned, he later wrote, with "playing craps and sleeping with women."[2]

Cured of his own flirtation with socialism, he got a job in sales, moved to the East Side, and started reading Walt Whitman. Then a crucial event occurred. His grandfather, back in Washington, sold some property from Toomer's mother's estate and sent him $600. Liberated by the windfall, Jean quit his job and devoted himself to literary and musical interests. Yet it wasn't long before he put the music aside and turned his energies exclusively to reading and writing. During the days, he read at the library; at nights, he wrote in his room, unless he attended a lecture.

One of these lectures – on Romain Rolland's *Jean Christophe*, given by Helena DeKay at the Rand School – opened up the literary world for him. Toomer, whose given names were Nathan Eugene, had admired the book for years and may even have decided to call himself Jean because of the hero's namesake.[3] After the lecture, he was bold enough to ask DeKay if he could walk her home. She agreed and invited him to attend a party at Lola Ridge's. There he met a number of important literary figures: Edwin Arlington Robinson, Waldo Frank, Witter Brynner, and Scofield Thayer. Toomer felt that he didn't quite belong, yet with the bravado that was typical of much of his life he also concluded,

> There was not a person in the room whom I felt to be a better man or as strong a man as myself. As for writing – well, we'd see about that. That would depend upon how much talent I turned out to have, and upon what I could make of it. In terms of life, of experience and understanding of life, of overcoming difficulties, of struggles, and so on, I felt I had as much or more than anyone I saw.[4]

At Lola Ridge's, Jean was exposed to literary chitchat, particularly about what was happening in the little magazines. Ridge was the American editor of *Broom*, which three years later would publish some of Toomer's early writing, including the "Kabnis" section of *Cane*. It was Waldo Frank, however, who would prove to be most important for Jean's incipient literary career.

The two of them ran into each other in Central Park a week or ten days later, and Frank apparently remembered Jean from the party. Warm weather had returned, and they sat on the grass and talked. Jean told the older man about his interests in music and literature, and Frank promised to help in whatever way he could. The $600 legacy had nearly run out, and Jean had decided to return to Washington, to take care of his elderly grandparents, and to devote his remaining time to writing. Frank gave his address to the younger man, who promised to write to him.

The return to Washington, D.C., in the summer of 1920, was layered with unresolved anxieties. Toomer had spent most of his childhood and adolescence in his grandfather's house under the stern patriarch's rule. P. B. S. Pinchback had long been the authority figure in the young man's life, while Jean's attachment to his grandmother was on a more positive level. It was Pinchback who had largely paid for Jean's years of wandering, including his several attempts to complete a university degree. Money had long before become a difficult subject for the two of them, so touchy a topic that Jean had told Pinchback he had finished his B.A.

The arrangement struck by the two of them, grandfather and grandson, was that Jean would take care of his grandparents and be paid $5 as a weekly

allowance. His livelihood thus guaranteed, the twenty-six-year-old appren-
tice writer was determined to stick it out in Washington until he had legiti-
mized his literary career. As he later wrote in his autobiography,

> I was in the house with two old people whom, despite the continual
> struggle with grandfather . . . I loved. And they were dying. No, they
> weren't dying. Grandfather gradually declined – a tragic sight – and, one
> day he broke. After that, he was a dottering old man, not dying, not
> living, yet hanging on. He might hang on for years and years. But I had
> to take over whatever of his affairs needed attention. And I ran the house,
> even cooking meals and sweeping and cleaning.[5]

As the months advanced and 1920 gave way to 1921, Jean's closeness
to his grandmother increased, and her physical state rapidly deteriorated.
While Jean was caring for his grandparents, his uncle Bismark became ill
and remained so for more than a month, so Jean also took care of him. Still,
he had time for reading and writing, often with a sense of near frenzy. He
read all of Waldo Frank and many of the Russians, particularly Tolstoy and
Dostoevsky, as well as Flaubert, Baudelaire, Coleridge, and Blake. Of the
American poets, he was especially taken by the Imagists. Sinclair Lewis and
Theodore Dreiser interested him, and he singled out Frost's poems and Sherwood Anderson's *Winesburg, Ohio*.

Freud and psychoanalysis were subjects in his reading also, and – as the
months flowed on – Buddhist philosophy, the Eastern teachings, occultism,
and theosophy. Of the last few subjects, he wrote, "Much of the writing
itself seemed to be poorly done; and I was certain that the majority of the
authors of these books had only third or fourth-rate minds."[6] He also returned to the Bible, convinced that as "a work of literature . . . we had
nothing to equal it."[7]

As he assimilated and distilled the contents of this eclectic sampling,
Toomer formulated some of his early opinions about the ideal man: "a complete and whole individual who was able to function physically, emotionally, and intellectually."[8] In a way, this sense of unification was to become
his lifelong quest, the singular question behind all of his writing and searching. The turmoil of his present situation would, in fact, turn out to be little

different from that of the later stages of his life. The neophyte would continue his quest, flitting from one solution to another, yet never quite discovering what he sought.

There was another perhaps even more urgent question than the emotional distancing vis-à-vis his grandparents, the matter of his artistry, or even the quest for wholeness, and that was the issue of race. P. B. S. Pinchback, Jean's grandfather, who for all appearances was a white man, during Reconstruction had claimed to be black. It was a matter of political expediency, resulting in his election to the United States Senate from Louisiana. By the time his grandson was born, Pinchback had left politics and settled into a life of leisure in Washington, living in a white section of the city. In high school, Toomer had the shock of his life when his grandfather told him of his black ancestry. The question of race smoldered in Toomer for more than half a dozen years, surfacing from time to time as the young man attempted to grapple with the question of his identity. It manifested itself again during 1921, when Toomer was taking care of his aged grandparents, who had by then lost their fortune and were living in a black section of Washington.

Toomer's voracious appetite for reading inevitably returned him to the question of his heritage:

> During this period I read many books on the matter of race and the race problem in America. Rarely had I encountered the nonsense contained in most of these books. It was evident to me, who had seen both the white and the colored worlds, and both from the inside, that the authors of these writings had little or no experience of the matters they were dealing with. Their pages showed very little more than strings of words expressive of personal prejudices and preferences. I felt that I should write on this matter. I did write several fragments of essays. And I did a lot of thinking. Among other things, I again worked over my own position, and formulated it with more fullness and exactitude. I wrote a poem called, "The First American," the idea of which was, that here in America we are in [the] process of forming a new race, that I was one of the first conscious members of this race.[9]

Expressed another way, it was a matter of avoidance, of finding a way he could live with the question of his own so-called Negro blood. By saying that he was a member of a new race, the *American* race, he was also stating that he was not a Negro and that he wanted nothing to do with negritude, although he probably could not admit this to himself at the time. Then, too, there was the matter of curiosity, both emotional and intellectual (opposites he had tried to unify). He simply wasn't certain about his black heritage, yet he wanted to find out what it meant to be a black person in black America.

Late in 1921, the opportunity to test his blackness suddenly came about. Tethered as he had been to his grandparents for months and months, he had reached a state of physical exhaustion; yet he was afraid to leave the two old people alone. He had managed to get away for a week at Harper's Ferry, during the heat of the summer, after arranging for a woman to stay with his grandparents. Shortly thereafter he learned of a temporary position as the head of a school for black children in Georgia. As he wrote in his autobiography, "My situation was so desperate that any means of getting out of it appeared as a God-send. I accepted [the] offer. Besides, I had always wanted to see the heart of the South. Here was my chance." [10] He arranged for a woman to take care of his grandmother and placed his grandfather in a hospital.

The position at Georgia Normal and Industrial Institution, in Sparta, began in October and lasted for only a few weeks, yet Toomer felt the effects for a lifetime. In a letter to Alain Locke, written from Sparta and dated November 8, he expressed his elation at discovering his calling as a teacher. He also cautioned, "There is poetry here – and drama, but the atmosphere for one in my position is almost prohibitory." [11] Presumably, he was referring to his status as an educated Northerner and as a city dweller suddenly transported into the country.

Written during the immediacy of the situation, the letter to Locke expresses the duality of so many events of Toomer's life: the excitement of the moment, yet also the sense of foreboding. Never had he been so close to black life, felt the center of its vitality, as he did in the cane country of rural Georgia. The school was outside the village, and Toomer, as acting principal, had a little shack to himself. As he later reflected,

The setting was crude in a way, but strangely rich and beautiful. . . . There was a valley, the valley of 'Cane,' with smoke-wreaths during the day and mist at night. A family of back-country Negroes had only recently moved into a shack not too far away. They sang. And this was the first time I'd ever heard folk-songs and spirituals. They were very rich and sad and joyous and beautiful.[12]

If he had found something with which he could identify, he had also discovered a new fear of potential loss. The black people in the town objected to the folk songs and spirituals, which they referred to as "shouting," being sung by their counterparts in the country. Barely had Toomer felt the sense of connectedness than he was fearful of disunity. The blacks in the town had already been corrupted by player pianos and Victrolas. "I realized with deep regret," Toomer wrote, "that the spirituals . . . would be certain to die out. With Negroes also the trend was towards the small town and then towards the city — and industry and commerce and machines. The folk-spirit was walking in to die on the modern desert. That spirit was so beautiful. Its death was so tragic."[13] He had found the subject for his novel *Cane*.

On the trip back to Washington in November, the floodgates opened up, and what was dammed up inside of him burst forth, beginning the most fertile period of his life. Poetry, fiction, and drama spewed from his pen, almost all of it related to the unanswered question of his heritage. Was he a Negro, this man with lemon-colored skin like that of his persona Kabnis who had lived most of his life and thought of himself most of that life as a white man? Or was he a kind of primeval man, returned to his roots, the soil of the South, his black identity?

He wrote like a demon, first on the train taking him back north and then back with his grandparents at 1321 U Street, N.W., Washington, D.C. The trip to Georgia, according to Mabel M. Dillard, "gave him what he had been searching for to fulfill his 'growing need for artistic expression.'"[14] For the next twelve or fourteen months, he would be at the peak of his powers. During this period of time, until the end of 1922, he would also form the strongest network of friends within the literary world, and he would complete the manuscript for *Cane*.

As soon as he returned to Washington, Toomer was confronted with the ongoing question of his grandparents. He took his grandfather out of the hospital because, as he said, "His condition there was too pitiable for me to bear."[15] Jean nursed him until the end, which wasn't very long. P. B. S. Pinchback died two weeks before Christmas, closing an important chapter for Toomer: "Our almost life-long struggle and contest was finished, and all my love and gratitude for the once so forceful and dominant but now so broken and tragic man came to the fore." [16] The day before Pinchback's death, Toomer finished the first draft of "Kabnis," the surreal drama which would eventually become the third section of *Cane*. With his uncle Walter, Jean accompanied Pinchback's body to New Orleans for interment in the family vault – in an all-white cemetery, next to Jean's mother.

Toomer's writing continued, and as he gained confidence, he began submitting stories and poems to little magazines. By the end of 1922, his work had appeared in the *Crisis*, *Double Dealer*, the *Liberator*, *Little Review*, and *Broom*. Yet not all of these publications came with equal grace or ease. When he submitted "Karintha" and "Fern" to the *Double Dealer*, he received the following response from John McClure, the magazine's editor:

> We would have been glad to print them, but we were frankly afraid. The bigotry and prejudices do permeate our subscription list to a great extent. Also there are the guarantors on whom we depend for support. There would have been hostility which, in all probability, would have sent the *Double Dealer* on the rocks. We felt the existence of the magazine was more important than any single manuscript. [17]

In submitting material to the *Double Dealer*, Toomer had identified himself as a Negro and chosen two stories with obvious racial concerns. The works the magazine published later in the year – "Calling Jesus," "Storm Ending," and "Harvest Song" – were largely devoid of that issue, as were a number of the other sections of what would become *Cane*, particularly the poems. Toomer had encountered the hard awakening that every African American writer repeatedly confronted, and he was no exception. It did not take very long for him to realize that being a black writer would be much more difficult than being a white one. Still, he addressed the issue of his blackness in the majority of his prose and dramatic pieces written during 1922, letting the inspiration from his teaching in Georgia take him where it would.

One of these works of limited success was a one-act play called *Balo*, written during the winter of 1921–1922 and presented by the Howard University Repertory Company during the 1923–1924 season. There is little dramatic tension in the episodic piece but more a sense of mood and wonder and perhaps even love and care for the characters, who often appear as if they have been viewed anthropologically by an outsider. The latter quality is particularly true in the detailed stage directions, which compose almost a third of the play's brief text. Thus, when the black sharecroppers sing "Steal Away," Toomer remarked, "At each repetition the emotional excitation becomes greater. . . . yet the rhythm and the tune are maintained. Thus is achieved one of the striking, soul-stirring effects of Negro melody." [18]

Balo demonstrates a strong sense of community and brotherhood, particularly in Will Lee's strength and fortitude. Instead of squandering the profits gained from the previous year's plentiful harvest, Will has banked his money and therefore prepared himself for the current year's dismal crop. He aids his friends and relatives who have had less foresight and gains continued solace from his religion and the respect of his grown sons. Will's son Balo undergoes a quasi-mystical transformation in the last episode of the play, and the explanation is that he has found Jesus.

More than anything else, *Balo* adumbrates other works that Toomer was writing simultaneously or would write somewhat later during this creative year. The religious concern parallels certain incidents in "Esther" and "Kabnis," as do several of the characters. Uncle Ned, a prophet from the days of slavery, bears a close affinity to Father John in "Kabnis." Even Toomer's title for the work appears to be a variation on Barlo, the name of a minor character in *Cane*. Interestingly, the racial question in the play is stripped of any dramatic potential because Jennings, Will Lee's white neighbor, shares many of the latter's moral qualities. When he wrote *Balo*, Toomer's move toward darkness was still an unresolved question in his mind.

In his correspondence throughout the year, Toomer appears to have been constantly redefining that sense of darkness, working out just what it was to be called a Negro writer. In his frequently cited August 19 letter to Claude McKay, one of the editors of the *Liberator*, Toomer wrote,

Racially, I seem to have (who knows for sure) seven blood mixtures: French, Dutch, Welsh, Negro, German, Jewish, and Indian. Because of these, my position in America has been a curious one. I have lived equally amid the two race groups. Now white, now colored. From my own point of view I am naturally and inevitably an American. I have strived for a spiritual fusion analogous to the fact of racial intermingling. Without denying a single element in me, with no desire to subdue one to the other, I have sought to let them function as complements. I have tried to let them live in harmony. Within the last two or three years, however, my growing need for artistic expression has pulled me deeper and deeper into the Negro group. And as my powers of receptivity increased, I found myself loving it in a way that I could never love the other. It has stimulated and fertilized whatever creative talent I may contain within me. A visit to Georgia last fall was the starting point of almost everything of worth that I have done. I heard folk-songs come from the lips of Negro peasants. I saw the rich durk [sic] beauty that I had heard many false accents about, and of which till then, I was somewhat skeptical. And a deep part of my nature, a part that I had repressed, sprang suddenly to life and responded to them. Now, I cannot conceive of myself as aloof and separated.[19]

Yet that separation is even a part of the statement itself, suggesting that Toomer was far from certain about his blackness. Living as he had amidst both cultures, it would have been impossible for him not to be familiar with the adage that one drop of Negro blood makes one a Negro. Thus he tosses out that vague term American, as he had already done before and would continue to do throughout the rest of his life. It was a laudable attempt to move beyond color, but, unfortunately, few other Americans were willing to be so casual about ethnic matters.

Toomer's correspondence with Sherwood Anderson later in the year also demonstrates his tendency for fence straddling. Anderson had written to Toomer first, in September, prompted by reading some of the material that Jean had sent to the Double Dealer. Of "Nora" (later retitled "Calling Jesus"), Anderson said, "It has a note I have been wanting to hear come from one of your race."[20] Curiously, Anderson had spoken to John McClure, who told him that Toomer was a Negro. Toomer responded to the letter by expressing his admiration for Anderson's Winesburg, Ohio and The Triumph of the Egg and commenting only briefly about his heritage by referring to his recent trip to Georgia: "My seed was planted in the cane and cotton fields, and in the souls of the black and white people in the small southern town."[21]

Anderson began his second letter to Toomer, written in late December, by stating, "Your work is of special significance to me because it is the first negro work I have seen that strikes me as really negro."[22] Anderson offered to help Toomer find a publisher for the book he was writing and even to write an introduction for the volume. Returning to the question of race, Anderson's letter mentions a black woman he had met in London who was a "bit too negro . . . inclined to overestimate everything done by negroes because a negro had done it."[23]

One wonders how anyone could have responded to a statement such as that, though in an odd way Anderson's comment was at the core of the dilemma Toomer would shortly confront as a published writer. How black could his writing be and still be accepted by the white literary world? What if he chose not to write "black" at all? Toomer responded, however, with an equally revealing remark: "The Negro's curious position in this western civilization forces him into one or the other of two extremes: either he denies the Negro entirely (as much as he can) and seeks approximation to an Anglo-Saxon (white) ideal, or, as in the case of your London acquaintance, he over-emphasizes what is Negro."[24]

Sherwood Anderson might have become Jean Toomer's mentor, were it not for the fact that Toomer met Waldo Frank first. The relationship with Waldo Frank, which was at its closest during the early part of 1922, typifies all the confusions and subsequent reversals that Toomer would later manifest about his black heritage. Drawn to Frank in part because of *Our America*, Frank's study of the nation's cultural and ethnic diversity, Toomer proclaimed his blackness forcefully and directly in his first letter to the famous writer:

> In your "Our America" I missed your not including the Negro. I have often wondered about it. My own life has been about equally divided between the two racial groups. My grandfather, owing to his emphasis upon a fraction of Negro blood in his veins, attained prominence during Reconstruction politics. And the family, for the most part, ever since, has lived between the two worlds.[25]

The letter, written in March 1922, concludes with a request that Frank read some of his sketches and poems, which he describes as "attempts at an artistic record of Negro and mixed-blood America."[26]

The novice writer certainly must have known what he was doing when he wrote this letter. There's the gentle nod toward one of Frank's popular books, hinting at a kind of oversight on his part. That error can be corrected, however, if Frank will take the time to read what the younger man (who, even if he is a Negro, comes from good stock) has written. The letter appears to have been written and sent to Frank as a provocation. How could anyone refuse?

Frank responded ten days later, and although he did not agree to read the younger writer's works, Toomer had managed to get his foot in the door. As John Griffin has pointed out, it is one of the ironies of the relationship that Waldo Frank also had his reasons – perhaps even his needs – for developing the friendship with Toomer. Horace Liveright, Frank's usual publisher, had declined his most recent novel, City Block, because of fears of possible obscenity charges. Frank decided to publish the novel himself, which meant that there would be problems with distribution. Frank wrote to Toomer, and presumably to other friends, to ask if he could help distribute the book.

Soon Frank had other requests to make of Toomer. His novel-in-progress, Holiday, concerned itself with Negroes, yet Frank was astute enough to comprehend that his familiarity with black life was limited. It wasn't long before Frank realized the benefits of having Toomer join him in a planned trip to the South, where Frank could observe a little local color. Their correspondence developed, as Toomer critiqued his own writing in his letters to Frank and became a local distributor of sorts for City Block in Washington, D.C.

The trip to the South for Frank began with a stopover on September 1, 1922, in Washington. John Griffin suggests that Frank underwent a kind of shock staying with Toomer and his grandmother, but the two of them departed the next day for their destination, Spartanburg, South Carolina. Interestingly, both men passed themselves off as Negroes, traveling for two weeks by Jim Crow trains and experiencing other segregated facilities.

The trip was enough of an eye-opener for Frank that he realized he needed assistance with his novel. He asked for Toomer's help with the dialogue – not just the usual proofreading of the galleys that one writer might ask of another but actual rewriting of those passages which he considered unfaithful to black life. Toomer agreed. He had designs of his own. He was completing the manuscript to Cane, and Frank, he knew, had the right contacts to get the book published.

The pressures of writing – and perhaps even of accommodating himself to Frank's requests — must have been overwhelming for Toomer during the late part of 1922. At the end of September, he worked as an usher at the Howard Theater for a short time, probably in order to improve his finances, although it may have been equally important for him to get away from his writing and from his grandmother. He suffered bouts of insomnia and gastric pains, which would recur later in his life; yet somehow he completed the manuscript to *Cane* on December 12 and sent it off immediately to Waldo Frank with the following letter:

> *Cane* is on its way to you!
>
> For two weeks I have worked steadily at it. The book is done. From three angles, *Cane's* design is a circle. Aesthetically, from simple forms to complex ones, and back to simple forms. Regionally, from the South up into the North, and back into the South again. Or, from the North down into the South, and then a return North. From the point of view of the spiritual entity behind the work, the curve really starts with Bona and Paul (awakening), plunges into Kabnis, emerges in Karintha etc. swings upward into Theater and Box Seat, and ends (pauses) in Harvest Song.
>
> Whew!
>
> You will understand the inscriptions, brother mine: the book to grandma; Kabnis, the spirit and the soil, to you.
>
> I believe that before the work comes out, Little Review, Dial, and Seccession will have accepted certain of its pieces. The ones I mention are the certain ones. Between each of the three sections, a curve. These, to vaguely indicate the design.
>
> I'm wide open for criticism and suggestion.
>
> Just these few lines now.[27]

Frank received the manuscript a day or so later and read it almost immediately because of a meeting with Horace Liveright on the fifteenth, when he gave the manuscript to his publisher. With remarkable speed, Liveright accepted the novel January 8, 1923. The contract was a standard one, as far as royalties and a second book option. The advance was $150. Yet what should have been a triumph for Toomer quickly turned into a state of deflation. Although no revisions were mentioned in Liveright's acceptance letter, they were shortly asked for. With Frank's help, Toomer cut several sections and reshaped others. The revised manuscript went back to Liveright in March, by which time Toomer had developed reservations about his "blackness."

What Toomer had slowly begun to realize was that Frank had orchestrated the acceptance of his book by stressing the fact that the author was a Negro. The problem for Toomer was that he had decided that he wasn't a Negro. He had used his heritage for more than a year in almost all of his correspondence and contact with Waldo Frank and had achieved what he had wanted all along, the acceptance of a book. Now that that book was under contract, he no longer wanted to be identified as a black person.

A week after Liveright accepted *Cane*, Toomer agreed with Frank that the question of his blackness should be emphasized: "Sure, feature Negro,"[28] he wrote, concerning the introduction to the book. When he read what Frank had written, however, Toomer again reversed his decision. John Griffin says that the matter was so upsetting for Toomer when he read Frank's foreword, that he became ill.

In that introduction, Frank, though frequently oblique – "the artist, hard, self-immolating, the artist who is not interested in races, whose domain is Life"[29] – nevertheless managed to make it absolutely clear that the author of *Cane* was a Negro. One suspects that it was the kind of introduction that Toomer might have written himself, emphasizing art rather than ethnicity, if the situation had been reversed: "A poet has arisen in that land who writes, not as a Southerner, not as a rebel against Southerners, not as a Negro, not as an apologist or priest or critic: who writes as a *poet*. . . . The gifted Negro has been too often thwarted from becoming a poet because his world was forever forcing him to recollect that he was a Negro."[30]

The obfuscation of Toomer's identity, collaborated upon by both Toomer and Frank, troubled Horace Liveright enough that he wrote to Toomer during the summer, before the publication of *Cane*, and asked for a clarification of the matter. Liveright, who clearly had one eye on promotion and profit, was chagrined because he felt the exotic quality of blackness needed to be emphasized if *Cane* was to be successful. At Liveright's request, Jean had written a brief autobiographical sketch of himself, and it ignored the question of race. Liveright wanted the sketch to be rewritten: "I feel that right at the very start there should be a definite note sounded about your colored blood. To my mind this is the real human interest value of your story and I don't see why you should dodge it."[31]

Toomer's response to Liveright's letter didn't help the matter. "My racial composition and my position in the world are realities which I alone may determine,"[32] he wrote. "I do not expect to be told what I should consider myself to be. Nor do I expect you as my publisher, and I hope as my friend, to either directly or indirectly state that this basis contains any element of dodging. In fact, if my relationship with you is to be what I'd like it to be, I must insist that you never use such word, such thought, again."[33] Yet the forceful beginning quickly became wishy-washy, as if the about-to-be-published novelist still wanted to have it both ways:

> As a B and L author, I make the distinction between my fundamental position and the position which your publicity department may wish to establish for me in order that Cane reach as large a public as possible. In this connection I have told you, I have told Messrs Tobey and Schneider to make use of whatever racial factors you wish. Feature Negro if you wish, but do not expect me to feature it in advertisements for you.[34]

What should we conclude from this letter – that Cane was black but its author wasn't? That appears to have been Toomer's stance by September 1, the publication date of his novel. Whatever Jean Toomer's exact feelings, one fact is evident: by the time Cane was published, the author had decided that he could no longer identify with the material that had inspired the book. As recently as April of the same year, Toomer had responded to a letter from Claude Barnett, a black journalist, by defending his blackness and stating, "In so far as the old folk-songs, syncopated rhythms, the rich sweet taste of dark-skinned life, in so far as these are Negro, I am, body and soul, Negroid."[35] Yet the texture and richness of black life was a thing of the past, as Cane shortly became more of a burden than a liberation for its author.

Reflecting on the matter of the novel's publication some years later, when he wrote the essay "Outline of an Autobiography," Toomer gave a slightly different version of the incident, though one equally revealing:

> I answered [Liveright] to the effect that, as I was not a Negro, I could not feature myself as one. His reply to this did nothing else than pull my cork. He said he didn't see why I should deny my race. This made me mad, and I was all for going to his office and telling him what was what in no uncertain terms, even at the risk of losing him as my publisher. Friends

dissuaded me, and I let the matter drop, but not without having explained to them the facts of my racial actuality.[36]

In "Outline of an Autobiography," when he discusses the events surrounding the publication of *Cane*, Toomer also misspells the title several times, changing it to *Cain*, as if that is what the book finally became for him.

Although tensions between Jean Toomer and Waldo Frank reached a crescendo by the fall of 1923, they had been fraught with increasing turmoil for most of the summer. Inasmuch as each man had been using the other for his own particular needs, the relationship was probably fated to disintegrate from the beginning. One senses from their correspondence that Frank was slowly losing his patience with the younger man and that he worried about a more direct confrontation. Since their trip to South Carolina the previous year, all communication between the two of them had been via the mail.

Toomer had become particularly anxious to return to New York City, no doubt in part because of the continued emotional strain caused by his grandmother's decline. The attraction of New York City also must have increased after *Cane* was accepted. There were other literary figures with whom he had been corresponding – notably Gorham Munson, another one of Frank's literary disciples – and he desired more direct contact with them. In short, Toomer was itching to get back into the literary world, which – no matter what the status of his own identity quest – was still aglow with Waldo Frank's fire.

Frank kept giving excuses, postponing Toomer's visit for some weeks, until Toomer finally decided that it would be best to begin his reentry into New York life via the Munsons. Yet even those plans were complicated because the Munsons, who lived at No. 4 Grove Street in the Village, already had another house guest, a young man named Hart Crane, who for months had been staying in their cramped quarters. Finally Crane found a job and left, which made it possible for Toomer to stay with them.

Toomer arrived in June and soon found a place of his own on Gay Street, a center of black activity in the Village. Interviewed in 1969, Munson recalled Jean's lounging in a deck chair in the backyard, where he read during the summer months. When the Munsons left New York for a vacation,

Toomer moved back into their apartment, though by that time he had also visited Waldo Frank and his wife, Margaret Naumberg, a psychologist, at their place in Darien, Connecticut. All of these events took place during the months before the publication of *Cane*.

During those summer months, Jean Toomer and Margaret Naumberg fell in love. The attraction was almost immediate, beginning the moment Toomer visited Frank and his wife in Connecticut. The affair began during the hours that Frank secreted himself from his unavoidable house guest, and it continued, rather flamboyantly, in New York City. Critics of the two writers have analyzed the motives for Toomer's indiscretion by claiming that Frank had become a surrogate father for the younger writer, which would imply a kind of incestuous relationship with Margaret Naumberg. When he was questioned about the affair, however, Munson said that the "Frank-Naumberg marriage had already headed for the rocks. . . . I don't feel that Jean did anything more than precipitate the situation that already existed."[37]

Nevertheless, one has to agree that it was an unusual situation. If it was not exactly a matter of metaphorically destroying the father in order to sleep with the mother, it was at least a question of artistry being liberated at the expense of the previous generation. Although they were not so far apart in years, Frank was, after all, an influential writer/intellectual, while Toomer was still virtually unknown. On the other hand, perhaps there was nothing in the affair to suggest such complex dynamics; it may have been simply a matter of chemistry.

Still, Gorham Munson suggests a number of reasons that may have contributed to the Toomer-Naumberg affair. The first was Toomer's sexual attractiveness: "His sex nature was sweet and pure and, I imagine that he was a genuine lover and a genuine person in his sex contacts."[38] Munson speculates also that white women were attracted to his swarthy complexion. During the same summer, while he was staying in the Munsons' apartment, Toomer had conducted a brief affair with Rosetta Herewitz, Gorham's sister-in-law. After the liaison with Margaret Naumberg ended, Toomer would have a string of affairs with other women, several of whom would subsequently become quite famous.

Munson provides a reason for the length of the Toomer-Naumberg affair, which lasted until the summer of 1926, by attributing it to Jean's depressed finances: "The Naumbergs were a wealthy family, and Margaret was pretty well-heeled. Waldo Frank had been pretty fairly well-heeled too. Jean had nothing."[39] Margaret financed Toomer's spiritual quest during the next couple of years, until he found someone else who would indulge his whims. All his life, in fact, Jean Toomer was "successful in getting people to support him."[40]

Perhaps the strongest attraction between Toomer and Naumberg was the sense that each had discovered a kindred spirit, a soul mate embarked upon a similar vision quest. Margaret's spiritual journey had already lasted several years. She was famous — as well known as her husband — as a progressive educator and as the founder of the Walden School. She had certainly read some of Toomer's "visionary" writings in manuscript form and had heard her husband talk about his new disciple. Moreover, it was Margaret who introduced Jean to her own guru, George Ivanovich Gurdjieff, whose teachings Toomer would follow throughout most of the rest of his life. By the end of the summer, unable to deceive his mentor any longer, Jean told Frank about the affair. Margaret moved into the city, and in October Frank left for Europe, where he remained for nearly a year. By that time the initial reviews for Cane had appeared, and they were followed by several curious events.

One of these had begun somewhat earlier, in August, when Toomer was spending some time in the Catskill Mountains. On the nineteenth of that month, Boni and Liveright ran an advertisement for Cane in the New York Times Book Review, describing the work as "a book about Negroes by a Negro." The announcement caught the eye of John Bennett, one of the founders of the Poetry Society of South Carolina in 1920. Toomer had joined the Society as a nonresident. Believing that a Negro had been admitted, Bennett had a fit, since he feared that Toomer had joined the society intentionally to embarrass it and, worse, that promotion for Cane might identify the author as a member of the society. Frank Durham, however, says that Bennett was able to save face. In the annual Year Book, which usually listed members' publications, the decision was made to omit those titles, and Toomer was listed as "Mr. Jean Toomer of Washington, D.C.," the "Mr." being deemed an adequate disguise.[41]

When the reviews for Cane appeared, Toomer was living at 429 West 23d Street, and was being supported by Margaret Naumberg. Most of the initial reviews, regardless of whether the reviewer was Caucasian or black, emphasized the fact that the author was a Negro. Several of the reviews were racist, as might be expected given the time, but almost all the reviewers praised Toomer's talents. John Armstrong stated in the *New York Tribune* that "the Southern negro . . . has found an authentic lyrical voice in Jean Toomer," admitting "it has always been felt that there are negroes in America with genuine poetic feeling, intellect and discrimination approximating the standards of the more civilized whites."[42] An anonymous reviewer in the *Boston Transcript* developed the same theme of Negro inferiority, concluding, "Probably this volume is a daring overflow, for it presents the black race as we seldom dare represent it, mournful, loving beauty, ignorant, and full of passion untutored and entirely unconnected with the brain."[43] In the *New Republic*, Robert Littell concluded, "*Cane* is an interesting, occasionally beautiful and often queer book of exploration into old country and new ways of writing."[44]

In the December issue of *Opportunity*, Montgomery Gregory hailed Toomer's debut: "Few books of recent years have greater significance for American letters than this 'first' work of a young Negro. . . . Fate has played another of its freakish pranks in decreeing that southern life should be given its most notable artistic expression by the pen of a native son of Negro descent."[45] Gregory compared Toomer to West Indian novelist René Maran, whose novel, *Batouala*, had won the Prix Goncourt the year before. W. E. B. DuBois, in the *Crisis*, felt that "the world of black folk will some day arise and point to Jean Toomer as a writer who first dared to emancipate the colored world from the conventions of sex"; he also praised the "strange flashes of power" in Toomer's writing.[46] Other reviews that appeared somewhat later, such as a second piece in *Opportunity* in May 1926, described *Cane* "in respect to content and form, [as] an audacious book, stamped all over with genius."[47]

Almost uniformly, reviewers underscored the author's Negro heritage. If Toomer was unsettled by these references, he must have been even more upset by comparisons to Waldo Frank and *Holiday*. The two novels, which had been published within days of each other, were reviewed together by Bruno Lasker in the *Survey*, in November; not only was *Cane* described as the lesser book — "Compared with *Holiday*, *Cane* is fragmentary"[48] — but Lasker went so far as to suggest that there was no real Jean Toomer, that Frank had written both books: "In this medley of poems, sketches and short stories,

Frank — for is not 'Jean Toomer' a polite fiction — exhibits the methods of his workshop rather than his finished product."[49] Robert Littell, in the *New Republic*, had also drawn a related conclusion: "In many respects, Mr. Toomer recalls Waldo Frank. They seem curiously to coincide at their weakest points."[50]

There were, of course, certain compensations. By the time that Toomer read these reviews, Frank was well out of his way in Europe, and Frank's wife was his mistress. Still, it must have troubled him when he received his first royalty statement from Boni and Liveright, dated December 31, 1923, and discovered that the book had sold only 429 copies, adding up to $85.20 of the $150.00 advance.[51]

What was this unusual book that Jean Toomer published in 1923?

Seventy years after it appeared, *Cane* continues to perplex readers who come across it for the first time. The confusion is largely a matter of categorization, of immediate accessibility. Readers have difficulty in understanding the book because it appears to defy the traditional unities of time, place, character, and plot. In 1971, in one of the first and most important studies of Jean Toomer, Darwin T. Turner described *Cane* as "a collection of [Toomer's] works."[52] And yet, in *The Negro Novel in America* (1958), Robert A. Bone featured *Cane*, describing it as "an important American novel. By far the most impressive product of the Negro Renaissance, it ranks with Richard Wright's *Native Son* and Ralph Ellison's *Invisible Man* as a measure of the Negro novelist's highest achievement."[53]

In addition to the novel's three-part structure, what initially surprises most readers is *Cane*'s unusual mixture of poetry and prose. Though these individual "selections" may appear to be randomly ordered, they are, in fact, the basis of its interlocking structure. Although Toomer himself apparently did not regard *Cane* as a novel, there is little reason to consider it anything else. All of the traditional unities can be identified within the work. *Cane* is as much a novel as Sherwood Anderson's *Winesburg, Ohio* (1919), which certainly had an influence upon it, or William Faulkner's *The Unvanquished* (1938) or *The Hamlet* (1940). *Cane* is a radically experimental novel, as densely packed and intellectually challenging as the works that would follow it by John Dos Passos, Gertrude Stein, and William Faulkner. As an innovator in novelistic form, Toomer is in every way their equal or their better. Cane is, I believe, one of the major American novels of this century.

Cane has three major sections. The first two are composed of prose and poetic subsections, varying in length from as few as seven or eight lines in the short imagist poems to a dozen or more pages in some of the longer stories, though Toomer often includes snatches of verse in the prose sections. The third section of Cane is a long prose narrative, which often slips into dramatic form complete with stage directions, almost suggesting a scenario for an expressionistic movie. Along with a mixture of narrative, poetic, and dramatic forms, Toomer employs stream of consciousness, particularly the internal monologue, and literary surrealism. Throughout the entire work, the traditional literary forms tend to blur and overlap. One way of labeling Cane is to call it a lyrical novel, unified by a core of central images.

Parts 1 and 3 are set in the South, during and after World War I. The episodes in part 2 take place in the North during approximately the same time. By contrasting the two locales, Toomer makes his position clear. The black American's roots are in the agrarian South. In the urban North, he is essentially displaced. Like sugar cane stalks, black Americans derive their nourishment from the soil.

Part 1 is composed of six prose sections or stories and ten poems. All six of the stories are about women who live frustrated and unrewarding lives. Women's names are used for the titles of five of the six stories. Men always wanted Karintha – even as a child – though once they had her as an adult, they were left unsatisfied. Becky, a white woman, bore two Negro sons, estranging her from both the black and white communities. In spite of her masculine qualities, Carma's attractiveness was not diminished; her husband was so jealous of other men that he ended in the chain gang. The men who have taken Fern have had no joy in their encounters. In "Blood-Burning Moon," Esther's white seducer, Bob Stone, is killed by her black lover, Tom Burwell, who is subsequently lynched by the white community.

Tension, frustration, sexual dissatisfaction, and silent rage typify the male-female relationships described in these six episodes, culminating in the violent murders in "Blood-Burning Moon." For the most part, the events in these stories take place outside after dusk, often in the cane fields, in the haven of darkness. In the counterpoint presented in the poems, the primary images are darkness, barrenness, and despair brought about in part by the end of the yearly agrarian cycle.

Of the seven prose sections in part 2, three are mood pieces — "Seventh Street," "Rhobert," and "Calling Jesus" — and four are short stories. The mood pieces set the scene for much of the subsequent activity. Blacks, particularly males, are displaced in the North, alienated and whitewashed, largely because their roots are severed from the earth. The events in most of the seven prose sections take place within the confinement of houses and other structures or on the hard pavement of the streets.

Like the women in the first part of *Cane*, the men Toomer describes in the prose sections of part 2 are equally frustrated, sexually unfulfilled, longing for some kind of human contact. When the narrator of "Avey," who has lusted after Avey for years, finally believes that he will be able to spend a night with her, she falls asleep on him. In "Theater," John is similarly repulsed by Dorris. In "Box Seat," Dan Moore makes no headway with Muriel because of her frigidity. In "Bona and Paul," the last section in this part, the white girl Bona is similarly repelled by Paul, who cannot come to terms with his blackness.

The poems in part 2 are brief images of equally harsh life. In "Beehive," the drone may be lying on his back and drunk on silver honey, but still he wishes to escape the confinement of the hive where a million bees swarm. In "Prayer," the narrator seeks similar liberation from his condition, a unity between body and soul, each of which is opaque to the other. The narrator of "Harvest Song" cries out in hunger ("My throat is dry"[54]) and pain, which brings no understanding of his situation.

"Kabnis," part 3 of *Cane*, replicates many of the themes of parts 1 and 2, yet it achieves a sense of symbolic unity or wholeness in spite of the fragmentation of Ralph Kabnis himself. As a Northerner teaching in rural Georgia, Kabnis is alienated and displaced, as much from his home turf of Washington as he is from his own people, who are black. Fear is the dominant emotion of his life because of his estrangement from the earth itself ("The earth my mother"[55]) as well as from most of the black people around him. Kabnis copes by escaping into a dream world.

By contrast, Lewis, who is Kabnis's double and "what a stronger Kabnis might have been . . . [,] seems to be issuing sharply from a vivid dream."[56]

It is Lewis who identifies with Father John, who is confined to Halsey's basement, because the old man as the embodiment of slavery must never be hidden away. For better or for worse, the black American's roots reach back to slavery, which must be understood instead of forgotten. Lewis understands this, as does Halsey's younger sister, Carrie K.

What unifies all of these seemingly disparate sections and literary forms are not only the opposing tensions — North-South, male-female, black-white, and urban-rural — but Toomer's use of image clusters or leitmotifs and his creation of a central dramatic persona, who wanders in and out of the narrative itself. Images of dusk, night, darkness, and the setting sun permeate the novel, beginning with the fragment of poetry that opens the first section "Karintha":

> Her skin is like dusk on the eastern horizon,
> O cant you see it, O cant you see it,
> Her skin is like dusk on the eastern horizon
> . . . When the sun goes down.[57]

Toomer repeatedly connects his characters to these images, suggesting a cyclical phase in their lives, a period of dormancy or decline.

That periodic decline is related to harvest in "Reapers," to the return of harsh weather in "November Cotton Flower," and especially to the aftermath of slavery in "Song of the Son," where Toomer makes his statement that slavery must be comprehended instead of repressed. The use of the setting sun continues in the prose sections in part 1, and the implication is clear: these women are bound up in a new form of slavery that not only emasculates the men around them but results in no satisfying erotic-romantic encounters. The stories mostly depict an unhappy, childless world that can only lead to violence and despair.

That world is barely altered in the stories and poems of parts 2 and 3, where most activities continue after nightfall, which never quite brings the expected sense of liberation. Fern falls asleep; Bona walks out on Paul; even the men carousing with the prostitutes in Halsey's cellar in "Kabnis" appear singularly frustrated by their lot. Yet Toomer alters this tension and implies a sense of rebirth in the concluding paragraphs of "Kabnis," though not through his main character in that section or even through Lewis. Rather, it is Carrie K. who represents the hope of the future, born out of an under-standing of the past. As she kneels before Father John, dawn breaks forth:

> Light streaks through the iron-barred cellar window. Within its soft circle, the figures of Carrie and Father John.
>
> Outside, the sun arises from its cradle in the tree-tops of the forest. Shadows of pines are dreams the sun shakes from its eyes. The sun arises. Gold-glowing child, it steps into the sky and sends a birth-song slanting down gray dust streets and sleepy windows of the southern town.[58]

The climax of the novel is muted, to be sure, yet subtly hopeful in a symbolic rather than literal way. Other than a "portly Negress"[59] briefly mentioned in "Box Seat," Carrie K is the only female character in the novel presented in such positive terms. From her fusion with the past, represented by Father John, a new life will be born. It makes little difference whether that new life manifests itself in her unborn child or, more likely, in a new lifestyle that unites black people with their heritage. In either case, the future must be connected to and nourished by the past.

One of the major ironies of this richly textured work is that the dramatic persona who narrates much of the novel is unable to bridge that gulf between past and present. Expressed another way, Jean Toomer was unable to apply directly to his own situation what he preached so emphatically in *Cane*. The unnamed observer is not synonymous with the author, who seemingly discovered his heritage during those few weeks he taught in Sparta, Georgia, but, rather, with the about-to-be-published writer, who decided that he was an American and not a Negro.

That narrator-witness is present in twelve of the twenty-eight sections of parts 1 and 2 of *Cane*: "Reapers," "Becky," "Carma," "Song of the Son," "Fern," and "Evening Song" in part 1; and "Avey," "Beehive," "Her Lips Are Copper Wire," "Calling Jesus," "Prayer," and "Harvest Song" in part 2. In two other major sections of the novel, "Bona and Paul" and "Kabnis," the observer-narrator has disguised himself as the light-skinned Negro who cannot decide whether to be black or white. Given such an interpretation, *Cane* can be regarded as the expression of Jean Toomer's unresolved struggle to accept his racial origins – not just his blackness, but his whiteness also.

At times, such as in "Reapers" or "Calling Jesus," the observer merely relates an individual section of the novel in the first person. More often, however, he becomes a participant in the episode recorded. In "Becky," for example, he becomes a spokesman for the community. In "Fern," the observer attempts to become involved with the woman whose story he is relating. In "Avey," his involvement is ineffectual, resulting in a symbolic jilting or rejection.

One early poem, "Song of the Son," defines the observer's role as the "son," a poet-writer who must record the lives of black people before their histories are forgotten, connecting them to the light imagery so central to the novel: "Now just before an epoch's sun declines / Thy son, in time, I have returned to thee." [60] Both the pun on son/sun and the time are crucial here, "for though the sun is setting on / A song-lit race of slaves, it has not set." [61] One seed remains for him,

> An everlasting song, a singing tree,
> Caroling softly souls of slavery,
> What they were, and what they are to me,
> Caroling softly souls of slavery. [62]

The sense of urgency bespeaks the poet-observer's role: as horrendous as the institution of slavery was, the poet has an obligation to chronicle his people's past before it becomes forgotten.

Although "Esther" introduces the theme of the Negro light enough to pass for white, it is in "Bona and Paul" that the issue becomes one of true rejection. The story prefigures Toomer's personal dilemma with racial matters. Bona makes it clear that she is attracted to Paul because of his olive color. When the two of them, along with another couple, go to a segregated nightclub, even the black doorman does not realize that he has let a Negro enter. Paul feels the icy stares of the other people at the club, fearing, of course, that someone will realize that he is passing. When Bona and Paul begin to dance, Bona asks him directly: "Since when have men like you grown cold?" [63] In her frustration with Paul, who cannot accept his blackness, Bona runs out of the nightclub, with Paul at her heels. At that moment, the doorman realizes that Paul is passing and smiles at him, a knowing sign of recognition, but Paul says he's wrong. In his denial, Paul not only loses his heritage but Bona also.

Kabnis (cannabis?), who represents an older version of Paul, has seemingly come South in order to test his feelings about race, yet at the beginning of the narrative, they appear to be confirmed. He feels uncomfortable with Negroes; he rejects black religion; he fears for his life because he knows that Southern whites will not tolerate an educated, Northern Negro. Not only does he reject Lewis and Father John, but when the former asks him about his ancestors, Kabnis responds,

> And besides, he [Father John] aint my past. My ancestors were Southern blue-bloods –
> Lewis: And black.
> Kabnis: Aint much difference between blue an black.
> Lewis: Enough to draw a denial from you. Cant hold them, can you? Master; slave. Soil; and the overarching heavens. Dusk; dawn.[64]

By identifying with Southern blue bloods (Negroes whose skin was light enough that their veins shone through), Kabnis has made the ultimate decision of his life. He has observed black life at first hand and decided he wants nothing to do with it. His descent into Halsey's cellar and into the past has convinced him that his decisions have been correct. Blackness is not for him. It is a thing of the past. He is free to return to the North and live beyond color.

The greatness of *Cane* resides in its haunting lyrical beauty, in Jean Toomer's ability to capture powerful images of strength and unity, to lay out a map for the future. It is not Kabnis or Paul or the narrator-observer who provides us with models of black life but, rather, the lesser mortals, the common folk – Carrie K. Lewis, the portly woman in "Box Seat," even the displaced Dan Moore, who fully understands his sense of uprootedness. Most readers down through the years have probably had little knowledge of Jean Toomer's uneasiness about his race. They have identified instead with the novel's strong assertion about heritage, the need for keeping those roots intact, not suspended above the soil that would nourish them but firmly entwined in the land.

Ironically, though Toomer was unable to accept his own thesis, there can be little doubt about *Cane's* subsequent influence upon writers and artists who followed him. Summing up the period at a later date, Charles S. Johnson had this to say of the novel's appearance: "Here was triumphantly the

Negro artist, detached from propaganda, sensitive only to beauty. . . . More than artist, [Toomer] was an experimentalist, and this last quality has carried him away from what was, perhaps, the most astonishingly brilliant beginning of any Negro writer of this generation." [65]

In spite of what Jean Toomer chose to do with his own life, Cane took on an identity of its own, becoming a quasi-underground classic among black artists and intellectuals. Of the 1,265 copies of the first printing, 197 were sent out for review and 350 were eventually remaindered. Still, the novel was in sufficient demand to merit a second printing (with corrections) of 500 copies in 1927, though 100 of those were never bound. Liveright continued to hold stock of the book until 1938, when the last copy was sold and the book was officially out of print.

Well into the mid-sixties it was possible to purchase copies of Cane in used book stores for quite reasonable prices, though often they were tattered, appearing as if they had been pored over by dozens of readers. There was hardly a black writer who was not familiar with the book. I remember seeing a well-read copy with Paul Robeson's name written in it. In 1967, Cane was reprinted by the University Place Press. Two other editions soon appeared, and once again Toomer's masterpiece was readily available.

Perhaps the most accurate statement that can be made about Jean Toomer at the time he published Cane is that he perceived himself as a divided person. He had made one attempt at unification (for what is Cane other than an inchoate blueprint of Toomer's lifelong quest for identity?) and the results were unsatisfactory. Perhaps it was time to make another. "The question was," he later wrote, "how to bring man together into an integrated complete whole. . . . because of my personal experiences, my disorganization of parts, I was convinced that the parts of man – his mind, emotions, and body – were radically out of harmony with each other. But how to bring them into harmony? I did not have a means of doing this." [66]

Enter Gurdjieff. Throughout the early months of their affair, Toomer and Margaret Naumberg shared an interest in Eastern philosophy, often reading it together. At about the same time, Toomer and his friends learned about the writings of P. D. Ouspensky and A. R. Orage, two of Gurdjieff's disciples. In January 1924, Toomer met Orage, who had come to New York to arrange for the subsequent arrival of his mentor. Then in February, as if by magic,

Jean Toomer, circa 1932. Photo by Marjorie Content. Courtesy of Susan L. Sandberg.

Gurdjieff himself arrived, along with a motley group of followers who appeared to shadow him wherever he went.

Perhaps Gorham Munson best described the excitement that met Gurdjieff's arrival:

The sensation in New York for the past month has been the visit of Gurdjieff, Orage, and a troupe of pupils from Fontainebleau. They came unheralded, give out no addresses, assign no purpose for their visit, and put on quite suddenly demonstrations for invited audiences. It is the very devil to find out when and where they are demonstrating, and it is the very devil to get admitted. At last, however Lisa [Munson's wife, who was a dancer] and I were placed on their list. I have seen two demonstrations and heard three lectures. The dancing is quite undreamed of. Ritual dances from the East, temple dances of esoteric cults, monastic experiences: I have never seen so much complexity, contradiction, and detailed variety held together in an unaccountable unity. It is a dance of design (of complicated geometry) rather than of motion. Strictly impersonal. Also there are demonstrations of tricks, semi-tricks, possibly thought-transference, and these have been concentration tests. Gurdjieff is the most powerful man I have ever seen: God or Satan himself – almost. Everyone is talking – literati, society, little girls – amazing rumors spread.[67]

The suddenness of Gurdjieff's appearance in New York that winter had been paralleled eleven years earlier, in 1913, when the great man had appeared in Moscow – almost spontaneously, as if he were the by-product of some minor Big Bang. In that year, the Mystery Man, as he has been called by many people, had appeared seemingly out of nowhere and apparently with no past, though details of his early life, always in contradiction, were subsequently enumerated.

Though 1866 and 1869 are often cited, George Ivanovich Gurdjieff was probably born in Alexandropol in 1877, the offspring of a Greek father, who was a poet, and an Armenian mother. The young Gurdjieff was educated by Roman Catholic priests at the Kars Municipal School in northeastern Turkey. During his subsequent years of wandering and searching for hidden knowledge, he claimed to have traveled to Abyssinia, the Sudan, Egypt, Crete, and the Holy Land. When he began his practice in Moscow and Petersburg in the mid-1910s, he seemed as much a businessman as a mystic. For his livelihood, he sold oriental carpets, and there were other strictly economic ventures. By the early 1920s, when he had fled the Bolsheviks and settled in France, he set himself up as a physician, a "hypnotist, curing hopeless cases of alcoholism and drug addiction."[68]

Many of Gurdjieff's acolytes have spoken about the oddities of the man's life. His eyes, it was said, were so penetrating that he could look right through a person. His teaching, which has often been referred to as esoteric Christianity, was, according to P. L. Travers, "an uncovering of secret things."[69] Colin Wilson described him as "a psychologist of singular brilliance and insight, on a level with Nietzsche."[70] Though a master of many languages, his English was somewhat broken, with the result that quotations attributed to him often sound like gobbledygook: "God made an umbrella when he should have made an enema, and now he is idiot and like everyone else sits in galoshes."[71] He was cynical, often crude, yet unquestionably a great teacher. Furthermore, he had an amazing ability to promote his cause, to weasel money out of people.

Gurdjieff established a commune for his followers, the Institute for the Harmonious Development of Man, at Fontainebleau, outside Paris, late in 1922, after purchasing an old chateau with the assistance of a rich female patron. In his study of Gurdjieff's influence on Jean Toomer, Rudolph B. Byrd describes the situation as follows:

> The core of Gurdjieff's followers, comprised initially of his family and a small group of students who had been with him since the founding of the first institute some years earlier in the city of Tiflis in the Russian republic of Georgia, had now expanded to include a large number of new students from Europe and America. As many as one hundred fifty to two hundred students were at the institute at any one time. There was never a great deal of money in the institute's treasury, but as the institute was largely self-sufficient since food and other necessities were produced on the grounds, there were periods when the needs of the institute did not exceed its budget.[72]

Shortly after the institute was opened, there was a crisis. Gurdjieff faced the negative publicity surrounding the death of Katherine Mansfield. The celebrated short story writer was already in the last stages of tuberculosis when she arrived at the Chateau du Prieure and well beyond the possibility of survival by any known cure, yet her death unleashed an attack of invective that still threatens the objectivity of Gurdjieff's most open-minded critics. D. H. Lawrence, for example, wrote, "I have heard enough about that place at Fontainebleau where Katherine Mansfield died, to know it is a rotten, false, self-conscious place of people playing a sickly stunt."[73] Strong words, those, from a man not exactly known for his love or praise of the female artist.

Mansfield's prescribed cure – fresh milk, plenty of sunshine, and the breath of cows, which required her sleeping in the barn – seems ludicrous today, but it illustrates one of the fakir's primary tenets: the fusion of body and intellect, a not unknown goal for Jean Toomer and many of his fellow searchers in the early 1920s. As Nellie Y. McKay has written, "Gurdjieff's system is best described as a 'work' with philosophical and psychological bases that engage the physical, mental, and emotional centers of human activity."[74] Rigorous physical and mental activities were prescribed for attaining such unity or higher consciousness. In Gurdjieff's own words, filtered through P. D. Ouspensky in his book In Search of the Miraculous,

> The development of the human machine and the enrichment of being begins with a new and unaccustomed functioning of this machine. We know that a man has five centers: the thinking, the emotional, the moving, the instinctive, and the sex. The predominant development of any one center at the expense of the others produces an extremely one-sided type of man, incapable of further development. But if a man brings the work of the five centers within him into harmonious accord, he then "locks the pentagram within him" and becomes a finished type of the physically perfect man. The full and proper functioning of five centers brings them into union with the higher centers which introduce the missing principle and put man into direct and permanent connection with objective consciousness and objective knowledge.[75]

Wasn't this fusion of seemingly disparate factions what Jean Toomer had already attempted in Cane, without, of course, the paraphernalia of a formulated philosophical system? Wasn't Gurdjieff's "system," in fact, as old as the soul's quest for wholeness and understanding, complete with the cult of the modern individual and the flamboyant guru?

In Cane, Toomer had reached out and attempted to embrace his darkness, but what he had caught within his arms was the fear that if he continued to identify himself as a black man his life would always bear the stigma of restriction. Instead of expanding his perspective, blackness, he feared, would limit it. He had glimpsed the marketplace for the black writer and, in Nellie Y. McKay's words, realized that "it was offered to him on the basis of his 'Negro' blood."[76] What he wanted was something larger, bigger, wider: completeness.

And yet ironically, what a loss that quest produced. In *Cane* he had raised the question of his roots to the visionary level. "Time and space have no meaning in a canefield,"[77] he had written in "Carma," and somewhat later, in "Fern": "I felt strange, as I always do in Georgia, particularly at dusk. I felt that things unseen to men were tangibly immediate. It would not have surprised me had I had [a] vision. . . . When one is on the soil of one's ancestors, most anything can come to one."[78]

Those powerful mystical intimations – Barlo's understanding of slavery, Paul's momentary glimpse of a "pine-matted hillock in Georgia" when he looks out his dorm window in Chicago, the symbolic union of Father John and Carrie K at the end of "Kabnis" – those unforgettable moments of illumination, that is what would be missing from his writing in the future, though, of course, Toomer would argue that unification within his life was more important than in his art. Thus, he became a drone, caught in a beehive of his own construction, one more camp follower on someone else's mystical journey, instead of a prophet himself, his body and mind opaque to his soul, with no prayer to liberate him.

Expressed another way, Toomer gave up the possibility of immortality with the gods when he stopped identifying with blackness and became a fragmented and incomplete soul, like those mysterious circular arcs which have perplexed the readers of his novel for years:[79]

Toomer saw them as a unifying symbol for the novel's apparent open structure. In his letter to Waldo Frank announcing that the manuscript was on its way, he had referred to *Cane*'s design as a circle and suggested that black life would come full circle through the nourishment of its roots. Yet that sense of completeness or totality was missing from the lives of almost all of his characters, and no more tellingly symbolized than in Ralph Kabnis himself, sitting in Hanby's workshop and surrounded by broken wheels he is unable to repair. Ignoring his own message, Jean Toomer felt ready for bigger and better things: the search for the miraculous at the feet of the redeemer, who often appeared more like a carnival pitchman than a reclusive prophet.

Several of Jean Toomer's most persuasive critics have suggested that Gurdjieff became another father figure for the writer. There is much to support this theory, but there was also an immediate sense of identification on Toomer's part, as if he had tracked down a long-lost brother, or perhaps his own double, instead of his displaced father. Both were in a sense cultural half-castes, as much of their own making as anything else. Although in pictures the two men look remarkably different from one another, Toomer's physical description of Gurdjieff, after his first observation of the man, might just as easily be a description of himself: "His complexion was swarthy, his dark eyes wide-spread, his nose finely modelled and even delicate compared with the rugged four-square lower face, and he had a tigerish black moustache."[80]

Certainly, there is little question about the affinities that the men shared, especially for music and gymnastics. In "The Second River" – written much later in his life – Toomer described the electrifying effect Gurdjieff's dancers had on him, when he first observed them at a public demonstration in 1923.

There were demonstrations of gymnastic exercises. In past years I had practiced both Swedish and German gymnastics. More recently I had learned some of the exercises worked out by F. Matthias Alexander for the conscious control of the individual. Not anywhere at any time had I come upon exercises that, to my way of thinking and feeling, were comparable to those shown by Gurdjieff's pupils. These seemed to take hold of the body and literally re-create it. To see them being done made me want to do them. Nor was their appeal limited to the physical. To me they were strangely beautiful, and, in a way I could not explain, profound. No mere manual motions, these. They involved the whole man, I felt sure, and were means in the service of an essentially religious quest.[81]

The dance called "The Initiation of a Priestess" in particular attracted his attention. He described it as "simply marvelous. It was pure religion. I felt I would want to become a member of the Institute if for no other reason than to learn and take part in this dance."[82] But the music also appealed to him: "It was powerful, dynamic, deeply moving music that touched chords of my being and seemed to awaken an ancient memory of music I had once known, or a life I had once lived, a world that had been mine and that I had left and forgotten. It made me feel as a wayfarer who was being recalled to his rightful way and destiny."[83]

As for his response to the man himself during that initial encounter, Jean wrote, "There is a man, if ever I have seen one. He seemed to have everything that could be asked of a developed human being, a teacher, a master. Knowledge, integration, many-sidedness, power – in fact he had a bit too much power for my comfort."[84] The overall impression of the demonstration "evoked a life and a world that seemed utterly native to me. Here, without doubt, was a religion of training,"[85] a whole way of life, a complete system of living. Yet Toomer held back from Gurdjieff, even distancing himself from New York City for a time.

Before he decided to become a writer, Toomer had considered becoming a musician, and he was drawn to the musicality of the master's performers: "I did bring with me to the Gurdjieff demonstration the love of sound, a dynamic response to rhythm, the capacity to be touched and stirred by music."[86] The precision of Gurdjieff's dancers also reminded Toomer of the rigorous gymnastic training he had undergone in his student days and had briefly described in "Bona and Paul." Toomer was not only attracted to Gurdjieff but would in time assume the guise of the prophet's American counterpart. Cynics would say that a European charlatan had met his American equivalent – or was it the other way around?

The following year, Toomer made his move. He arrived in Fontainebleau in July 1924, just about the time Waldo Frank, his old mentor, returned from Europe. Toomer was almost too late, for shortly after he reached the Chateau du Prieure, Gurdjieff, speeding along at sixty miles an hour, crashed his automobile into a tree. Apparently saved by his higher consciousness, Gurdjieff recovered and, thereafter, according to James Moore, won a new title as the world's worst driver.

The rituals at Fontainebleau included physical labor, which mostly meant heavy farm work throughout the day, and intellectual stimulation in the evening, including the songs and dances which were part of the Gurdjieffian ritual. At times, Gurdjieff would read from *Beelzebub's Tales to His Grandson*, his work in progress. One cannot help noticing that some of these activities were similar to the chores and responsibilities shared by the participants at Fruitlands or Brook Farm by the American transcendentalists seventy-five years earlier. Nor can one ignore the streak of Emersonian self-reliance that formed a part of Gurdjieff's own teaching. Gurdjieff said, "Knowledge is one thing, understanding is another thing,"[87] and had even begun one of his lectures years earlier with the words "Know thyself."[88]

Whatever these similarities between Emerson and Gurdjieff, actual or real, Toomer considered himself an evolved consciousness by the end of his Fontainebleau stay, part of which was shared with Margaret Naumberg, who had arrived later in the summer, newly divorced. When he returned to New York City in October of that year, he announced his intent to follow his master's footsteps and set up his own discussion group.

Unquestionably, Jean Toomer was on an emotional high during the fall and winter of 1924, when he started his Gurdjieff study group. His feeling of elation, however, was not always shared by others. Orage, Gurdjieff's official spokesman in the United States, was upset by Toomer's chutzpa, since Toomer was considered a novice. Gorham Munson noted Toomer's cockiness, as well as his reservations about Orage: "Jean organized, on his own, a weekly class in the Gurdjieff . . . dances and movements. Jean had a lot of nerve to do that; he was really not qualified to do it."[89]

Toomer began to imitate Gurdjieff's worst excesses; according to Munson, "he used the Russian words that Gurdjieff used instructing in the dance, and he began to affect, as I said, certain mannerisms of Gurdjieff. The dance group collapsed after perhaps five or six meetings. Jean revealed his incompetence to direct such a group. I mention this, however, as an early example of Jean's great desire to be a leader."[90] Toomer saw himself as a teacher, aspiring to the profession he claimed to identify with so strongly when he had taught in Sparta. Munson says that Toomer shortly returned to the fold, worked with Orage throughout the year, and then in the fall of 1925 was appointed leader of several Gurdjieff groups in New York City, including one in Harlem. It is impossible to ignore the irony of the Harlem group, especially given Waldo Frank's later assessment of Toomer's need for aligning himself with Gurdjieff in the first place: "In his need to forget he was a Negro, he joined the transcendental pseudo-Hindu cult of Gurdjieff, whose psychological techniques aimed at obliterating in the catachumen the condition of being a man."[91]

Orage's remark about Jean Toomer's return to Harlem is also revealing: "This is really wonderful because Toomer goes to Harlem not as an exponent of black culture, not as an exponent of white culture, but as an exponent of human culture." [92] And who were some of Toomer's disciples? Wallace Thurman, Aaron Douglas, Arna Bontemps, Harold Jackman, Dorothy Peterson, and Nella Larsen, though some of these people quickly lost interest. The first meeting of the group was at the 135th Street branch of the New York Public Library, where Nella Larsen worked as a librarian. Subsequent discussions were held in private homes.

Arna Bontemps hints that Toomer's female acolytes may have been more interested in Toomer himself than in Gurdjieff, especially when "Jean surprised everyone by admitting that sometimes he liked to flirt." [93] Toomer's lecture notes from about this time are highly sexual in their imagery, and they also make it clear why so many women were attracted to him. His lecture for a new group of disciples began as follows:

> In sexual terms, the effort should be to impregnate and effect a conception. Since the terms that are familiar to those present are unknown, since the special type of ideas that appeal to each are likewise unknown, it is necessary to broadcast, to sow with many terms and ideas in the hope that conception will take place in all. I should hold clearly in my mind the attitude of the "I" that is to be conceived, this "I" being separable from, and capable of development separate from the organism, – the aim being to conceive it, develop it, in order that it may control the organism. [94]

The last word on "Gurdjieff in Harlem," however, belongs to Langston Hughes, who wrote in *The Big Sea* (1940) that

> the trouble with such a life-pattern in Harlem was that practically everybody had to work all day to make a living, and the cult of Gurdjieff demanded not only study and application, but a large amount of inner observation and silent concentration as well. So while some of Mr. Toomer's disciples were sitting long hours concentrating, unaware of time, unfortunately they lost their jobs, and could no longer pay the handsome young teacher for his instructions. Others had so little time to concentrate, if they wanted to live and eat, that their advance toward cosmic

consciousness was slow and their hope of achieving awareness distant indeed. So Jean Toomer shortly left his Harlem group.[95]

By leaving Harlem, Toomer missed the major years of the New Negro.

There were other significant events in Toomer's life during 1925. In the spring, he published a diffuse retelling of the Christ story called "Easter" in the Little Review. In the summer, he spent some time visiting Alfred Stieglitz and Georgia O'Keeffe at Tennant's Harbor in Maine, while working on Values and Fictions, an autobiography. At the end of the year, by which time his affair with Margaret Naumberg had cooled considerably, he had become involved with Mabel Dodge Luhan, or at least she had become involved with him.

Mabel Dodge Luhan had first learned of Gurdjieff the year before. Another searcher like Toomer, she thought she had discovered the answer to her questions about life, though she may have confused her attraction to Toomer with her search for higher consciousness. Her passion for her most recent husband had already dissipated. Lois Palken Rudnick, her biographer, has written that while her "passion for Toomer did not last more than a few months, it was one of the most intense of her life."[96] In an undated letter to him, Luhan said that her husband, Tony, "awakened my heart & my altruism, & kept it alive so that it is alive for good – & he made me maturer and stronger"; but Jean, Luhan believed, was able to "transmute" her fire "to another centre where it is no less fire but is burning somewhere else, – & in this more lofty region – every cell is filled with light & no more weight remains in matter."[97]

To say that Mabel Luhan fell madly in love with Jean Toomer is a bit of an understatement. At the age of forty-four, she had already gone through several husbands – including her most recent, Tony Luhan, a Taos (Tiwa) Pueblo Native American – and numerous other lovers. Her life was characterized by erratic swings of temperament and interest. First she invited Toomer out to her place in Taos, New Mexico, where he arrived in late December. Then, realizing that her passion was largely one-sided, she "lent" Toomer $14,000, in hopes that he would open up a Taos branch of the Institute for Harmonious Development. Meanwhile, Tony Luhan recognized the signs of her infatuation and threatened suicide. At this stage Toomer may have gotten cold feet. He returned to New York, where Mabel shortly followed.

Other activities impinged upon Toomer's busy life, including his return to Fontainebleau in the summer. Lois Rudnick states that Toomer gave a rather unflattering picture of Mabel Luhan to Gurdjieff, yet by the end of the year Toomer was again considering a move to Taos. When that plan did not materialize, communication between the two of them was left to the mails. By 1927, Mabel's letters to Jean had become pathetic, begging him to return the $14,000. In one of them, she revealed her guilt about Tony, stating that she had ruined him, totally alienated him from his culture. It wasn't until 1932, however, the year of Toomer's first marriage, that Jean sent her an apology, prompted in part by his knowledge that Mabel's money had long since disappeared into Gurdjieff's coffers.

In the summer of 1926, when Toomer made his second trip to Gurdjieff's fiefdom (perhaps in part to escape Mabel Dodge Luhan), he was again financed by Margaret Naumberg. During this visit, Gurdjieff began calling Toomer Mr. Half-Hour-Late, a term that other people also used to refer to Jean's slowness of speech. Still, Toomer apparently had nothing but admiration for the man whose teachings began to dominate almost all aspects of his life. Naumberg spent a part of that summer at Fontainebleau also, though by fall, Toomer confessed to Munson that he was in love with someone else, Edith Taylor. In his 1969 recollections about Toomer, Munson describes Edith Taylor as the wife of Caesar Zwaska, "a homosexual esthete known as the 'office boy' of The Little Review."[98] Munson describes his surprise at Jean's infatuation, since he thought that Edith was a lesbian. Nevertheless, the two of them were intensely involved with one another until Toomer proposed marriage.

In the fall of 1926, Toomer organized a Gurdjieff discussion group in Chicago. Munson, who remained one of Jean's friends for much of his life, cites the Chicago phase as a turning point in Toomer's life. Henceforth, Jean tried to pass himself off as an Eastern mystic or mystery man. In his strongest criticism of Toomer, Munson stated that

a good deal of Jean's life after he went to Chicago, set up as a leader of Gurdjieff, was the leading of a life of lying, lying, lying. . . . Jean pretended to be more than he was. He assumed the development and psychology beyond the point that he had ever reached; he ascribed to himself powers and knowledge which he had not really attained. Some would say he had a fantasy which he truly believed in, a fantasy about himself as a master of psychological teaching, psychological knowledge. It doesn't seem to me that he could have deceived himself to that extent. He play acts as a spiritual leader.[99]

A major event during 1926 solidified Toomer's bonding with Gurdjieff, both the man and his philosophy. It became the centerpiece of Jean's life. It may also explain Toomer's "play acting" as a mystic, though it may be little more than a strange coincidence. During the summer, after his return from Fontainebleau but before he went to Chicago, Toomer underwent an extraordinary mystical transformation. Standing on a subway platform in New York City, he suddenly felt transcended: "I was born above the body into a world of psychological reality. . . . In my private language I shall call this experience the Second Conception."[100] The significance of this event, for Toomer, cannot be underplayed. In his various autobiographies, written twenty or thirty years later in his life, Jean typically referred to the incident as the "experience" of his spiritual quest, describing and expanding the event again and again, as if he could relive the experience if he could only record it precisely.

In the fifth draft of From Exile into Being, written in the mid-forties, the experience is given full weight. Jean was standing on the platform of the 66th Street "L" Station, in New York City, at approximately ten o'clock on an April evening.

> I was startled by an uncommon inward event. It was as though I had been touched from within in an extraordinary quiet way that stilled my functioning and momentarily suspended me between what had been and what was to come. My very life had been stopped, so it seemed, and yet I was about to live again, live anew, and strangely. Somehow I understood I was going to be moved, regardless of my wish or will, into a nameless experience.[101]

His sensations, he wrote, "could not have been more strange had my body quietly left the ground and soared into the air."[102] He felt his entire presence was changing – "My body and my life were in the power of a Power."[103] He had the uncanny sense of separation, of another being entering his life as a stranger: "I was losing my life. It was being taken away by a noble creation. . . . There was Being, Consciousness, and Existence so large and deeply powered – that it would surely absorb me as a particle." [104] Using words such as "inner light" and "insight," Jean wrote of feeling "a second body, a body in addition to the physical, composed of subtler matters, having its own forces and appropriate functions." [105] He felt visited by grace.

The out-of-body experience continued with the sensation of watching himself standing at the railing of the station, while observing the people all around him. Everything seemed original, he wrote, "as if the world out there had just been created, as if I were beholding the newly finished work of the First Creator." [106]

> . . . when I looked at my body – how strange! It seemed removed from me, placed "out there," and below me, as though there were space between myself and it. Though I knew I was still attached to it, or it to me, I felt no relation to it whatsoever. It could have walked off and gone about its business, vanished, and I would not have missed it.
>
> I had been born above the body. To me the body was an object.[107]

The people on the street were "somnambulists," [108] unaware of the experience he was undergoing. He felt a sense of rebirth, that he had died, that he was the "only soul alive." [109] When the train arrived, he wondered if he would be able to get on it: "Body and I got on" [110] and then off at 23d Street, continuing home, as the experience continued. Jean wrote that he went to bed that night feeling the same way and slept "an unusually tranquil sleep." [111] The elation continued until the following morning when he awoke, yet "Body was more real to me, and in a sense, more 'mine.'" [112]

Was Toomer susceptible to such an experience because of his admiration for Gurdjieff, or is that an unfair reading of the experience? At the beginning of the incident described in From Exile into Being, he admitted, "As the Gurdjieff ideas were almost constantly in my mind, I doubtless reflected on the condition of man in the light of one or the other of them, as I stood there [on the platform]. Thoughts of the possibility of higher states of consciousness may have presented themselves." [113] The incident is fascinating not only because of Toomer's life-long quest for wholeness and understanding but also because of its reverberations with an earlier episode in Gurdjieff's life, an incident Toomer must certainly have known about. Early in February 1917, when Gurdjieff was departing from the Nikolaevsky station in Petrograd, his followers noticed a remarkable transformation within the man. Ouspensky, who describes what happened in In Search of the Miraculous, stresses that he and the others present thought that Gurdjieff was his usual self. He appeared as they had always known him. Then Gurdjieff entered the train and looked at them through the window.

> He was different! In the window we saw another man, not the one who had gone into the train. He had changed during those few seconds. It is very difficult to describe what the difference was, but on the platform he had been an ordinary man like anyone else, and from the carriage a man of quite a different order was looking at us, with a quite exceptional importance and dignity in every look and movement, as though he had suddenly become a ruling prince or a statesman of some unknown kingdom of which he was traveling and to which we were seeing him off.[114]

Gurdjieff had already informed his followers that "if one mastered the art of plastics one could completely alter one's appearance. He had said that one could become beautiful or hideous, one could compel people to notice one or one could become *actually invisible.*"[115] It can be argued that Gurdjieff's followers were ripe for believing in such an incident, which might be regarded as mass hysteria. Ouspensky, however, suggests not; moreover, a journalist who happened to be present at the time also noted the sense of calm that had transformed the mystic and later published an account of it. Toomer referred to his own similar transformation in various autobiographical writings. Although it is difficult to doubt his veracity, it does appear more than coincidental that the site as well as the nature of his own particular metamorphosis should be so similar to Gurdjieff's.

Throughout the rest of the decade, Jean Toomer's primary location was Chicago, where he continued to guide his flock of Gurdjieffian followers. Though he was paid for his efforts and apparently worked very hard at making the group successful, money was a continual problem, since he was expected to send what he raised to Gurdjieff in Fontainebleau. Toomer was forced to borrow from his friends, and the debts were extensive enough that after his second marriage, his wife had to replay them. His summers were spent mostly in residence at Fontainebleau. Gurdjieff made two more trips to the United States during these years, during one of which, in 1930, he visited Toomer in Chicago.

Gurdjieff's influence remained strong throughout these years, not only with Toomer but with numerous other Americans. Gorham Munson and his wife spent at least one four-week period at Fontainebleau, and even Waldo Frank eventually visited the Chateau du Prieure, though he must have departed in complete frustration. Arriving at the chateau in the summer of 1927, he did not meet Gurdjieff, as he had expected, but Jean Toomer. Munson says that Frank was fit to be tied. It was the final humiliation. There he was at Gurdjieff's estate, being guided around by his former disciple. Toomer was the example par excellence of kicking the gift horse.

Toomer's published writings during the late 1920s, during what can be called the heart of the Harlem Renaissance, include two short stories, "Winter on Earth," published in 1928 in the Second American Caravan, and "Mr. Costyve Duditch," published in the Dial in December of that year; a fragment from a novel, "York Beach," in the New American Caravan, for 1929; and two poems, "Reflections" and "White Arrow," both in the Dial in 1929. Balo was also published, in Plays of Negro Life in 1927.

In all of these works (with the exception of Balo, written earlier), Toomer attempted to explore his new way of life. Rudolph P. Byrd has noted that "during the ten years that Toomer was most active in the Gurdjieff work, he wrote more novels, plays, poems, sketches, and essays than at any other period in his life." [116] The two short stories published in 1928 and 1929 incorporate a number of Gurdjieff's ideas: namely, the individual's place in the universe vis-à-vis the earth itself and other human beings. In "Winter on Earth," Jean presents a rather sophomoric description of two opposing life-styles, a little as if he were writing a paper for an undergraduate assignment. Oddly, his description of the real world is much more convincing than his utopian vision of Gurdjieffian paradise.

The first part of the story (or polemic, as it might more accurately be called) is set in Chicago during a bitter winter. Bums are freezing to death while the rich go about their partying, oblivious to the suffering around them. The heavy-handed slice-of-life account describes a handful of isolatos trapped, one might say, by the harshness of urban living. Human contact has been reduced to something resembling the animal level, and people rarely communicate with one another: "most Americans . . . go down the streets each one shut up behind his own mask as if confined in solitary cells. . . . Should someone speak to another, the person who spoke would be fearful lest he be rebuffed."[117] This is American civilization as it is, depicted in a cold, naturalistic approach reminiscent of the writings of Stephen Crane.

In the second half of the story, the style and tone abruptly shift to that of a fairy tale. "White Island [was] a miracle of nature, a form so beautiful and wild and free that many on first beholding it doubted that their eyes had seen the real, and suspected it to be the work of instant magic."[118] On this island paradise, the people are hardworking, religious, and above all a part of a community with strong roots. Furthermore, they share a symbiotic relationship with their environment, yet why shouldn't they, given their origins?

> White Island, the legends ran, was so called because the Angels, long ago, had descended and dwelt there. They had been sent down to Earth by God, commissioned to teach and aid the men on Earth to improve their way of living. Everywhere over the broad lands men had departed from universal harmony. And as a result of this their bodies grew sick, and their souls became dis-eased. The Angels chose this spot from which to direct their ministrations because it was isolate from the mainland and the way between was washed with clean waters.[119]

Apparently feeling that his message was not clear, Toomer ended the contrast by returning to the snows of the mainland, the "cold white wilderness in which nothing grew or could ever grow."[120]

"Mr. Costyve Duditch" is not nearly so heavy-handed, though it is also inferior to the stories in *Cane*. Again using a Chicago setting, the story follows a bachelor wanderer, an "aimless globe-trotter,"[121] who spends his life traveling from one part of the world to another. His wandering is due in large part to his sense of inferiority, as if he were "a vagrant, a useless appendage."[122] The wanderlust also permits him to remain aloof, free from involvement with other human beings.

On the day that Toomer describes him, Duditch has returned to Chicago, where he encounters an old friend, J. Breastbuck Coleeb, who reminds him of a party to which both have been invited. After they separate, Duditch goes shopping at Marshall Field's and accidentally breaks an expensive cut-glass bowl. What Duditch has yet to understand is that the shattering of the bowl is a prefiguration of his own life. Later in the day, Duditch attends the party, which momentarily gives him a feeling of connectedness. As he becomes involved in describing his travels, "he began to regret that he was leaving so soon. Here in this company, in his own town, the purpose and end of his wanderings seemed about to receive not only recognition but fulfillment." [123]

When one of the guests asks him if he fears dying in a foreign land, away from his roots, Duditch asks what difference it makes. The guests are aghast and quickly leave the party, followed by Duditch, who realizes that he is "tense, fidgety, and miserable." [124] Duditch flees not only the party, "his world smashed to bits about him," [125] but Chicago, too. As he grabs his bags and departs for the train station, he comforts himself in the knowledge that soon he will be "speeding over some southwest region of the American wilderness," [126] lost among a crowd of unfamiliar faces.

Written in the style of Gurdjieff's own parables, "Mr. Costyve Duditch" imitated the master's allegorical form as well as his use of strange-sounding (and presumably comic) names. The result, however, is a pedestrian account of Duditch's failure to relate to the world around him, to any group of people or to any specific place. Because the story is so obvious a restatement of Toomer's own problems with connectedness, it demonstrates that he was far from resolving the issue he thought he had put behind him.

Part of the problem with these two stories and others that Toomer published after Cane is their sense of fragmentation. They often read as if they are unfinished, parts of something else. When sections of Cane are anthologized today, readers are similarly bewildered. What this suggests is that even though Toomer often wrote short works, it is the texture of the larger fabric – the counterpoint and balance – that gives Cane its majesty. In bits and pieces, the effectiveness is often lost.

The two short works that appeared in the Dial at the end of the decade are usually classified as poetry, though they bear little resemblance to the poems Toomer included in Cane. More accurately, they might be described as poetic aphorisms, foreshadowing Essentials, the book of sayings that Toomer would publish in 1931. "Reflections" is composed of four single-sentence statements that have a thematic unity but fail to cohere as a poem. The first of these, "A running man cannot take a new direction," [127] is open to question the same way that Toomer's later aphorisms were. (Why can't a running man take a new direction?) "White Arrow," more visibly a poem in its design, also suggests the possibility of contradictory interpretations:

> Your force is greater than your use of it.
> Existing, yet you dream that breath depends
> On bonds I once contracted for. It is
> A false belief induced by sleep and fear.
> In faith and reason you were swift and free,
> White Arrow, as you were, awake and be! [128]

Like most of these works, "York Beach" suffers from the same attempts to force idea onto, instead of expressing imagination through, creative form. The five-chapter excerpt (roughly 28,000 words) was written between the summers of 1928 and 1929, after Jean had spent a month at York Beach, Maine, with his friend Paul Rosenfeld. There can be little doubt that its appearance in The New American Caravan for 1929 was the direct result of the friendship between the two men, because Rosenfeld was an editor of the volume, along with Alfred Kreymborg and Lewis Mumford. Reading "York Beach" today, one wonders not so much about the reading taste of the era as about what could possibly have interested readers (except for Rosenfeld) in 1929. Rosenfeld appears in the story as Bruce Roalm, described as "a famous American literary figure" [129] unequaled by his peers: "few men in America contained the varied vivid materials of culture as Bruce did." [130] How could any editor resist such flattery?

Toomer is present also as Nathan (Toomer's father's given name) Antrum, upon whom the slight narrative focuses. There is also a young woman, named Alma Oliver, to give the story the semblance of a romantic triangle, though in the opening five chapters, very little ever comes of it. Instead, Toomer attempted to write a thesis novel, incorporating bits and pieces of Gurdjieff's philosophy.

What happens? Nathan Antrum leaves New York City for a vacation at York Beach, where he attempts to work on his new book. He is not very successful at this and instead engages in one-sided dialogues with Bruce Roalm. The writer's block in time is supplanted by Nathan's realization that he shares a natural affinity with the place itself. "For Antrum, York Beach came to exist as an entity, as much an entity, in its scale, as Bruce or Alma in theirs." [131] The place becomes more important for him than the people, since Nathan realizes that although Bruce has revealed his inner life to him, he "simply never mentioned his deepest experiences"[132] to Bruce. No man is an island except when he decides to become a part of the island itself.

As an engaging piece of fiction, "York Beach" fails throughout. The dialogue is stilted; the plot has been developed out of invisible ink; even the characters are secondary to the repeated philosophical meanderings, beginning with the opening lines:

> According to Nathan Antrum's philosophy, the pattern of his life led him through alternating phases of apparent fulfillment and apparent non-fulfillment. Sometimes the gifts of earth and of his fellow men more or less corresponded to his inner state; and at such times it was as if his active wishes had found and merged with their objects. At other times the substance of the exterior world seemed fragmentary, insufficient: its various forms and forces did no more than stimulate wishes and cause them to intensify themselves and grow more intense the more they manifested without tangible means of satisfaction.[133]

"York Beach" is also not without its free flights of Gurdjieffian double-talk. Early in the narrative, Nathan says to one of his friends,

> "It is an empty game we play with ourselves. We put ten pennies in a hat. We turn our heads and say: a hat is that which contains ten pennies. We rediscover the hat, and find that in fact it does contain ten pennies. Hurrah! We understand the hat. Ancient men understood ancient hats. Modern men understand modern hats. If asked: what are ten pennies? We answer: ten pennies are those things which are found in a hat. Sure enough they are just that!"[134]

The last word, however, belongs to Toomer himself, who describes Nathan at the beginning of the final scene of the narrative as follows: "One evening after a day of hard work which had made him intense, integrated, dynamic with brilliant life, clear thoughts, and vivid feelings, tensioned in himself and within life, Antrum, a force, entered the dining room."[135] The scene that follows is ludicrously comic, though I do not believe it is intended to be so. In "York Beach" it is impossible to determine whether Toomer is parodying himself or his mentor, George Ivanovich Gurdjieff.

The problem was that by the time his counterparts in the Harlem Renaissance were publishing their major works, Jean Toomer no longer knew who or what he was. The denials of his blackness were increasing, even though there were occasions when he permitted that identification to be continued. He was quite upset in the fall of 1925 when Alain Locke's *The New Negro* appeared because it included four selections from *Cane*, two stories and two poems. Prior to the book's publication, Toomer had declined Locke's request for unpublished material for the anthology. He had also instructed Locke not to include any material from *Cane*. Yet his commentary on the incident, illustrates his continued vacillation:

> He pressed. I thought of [an] article. I offered it to him. It turned out that he did not want it. My expressed attitude was — this article or nothing. I concluded that the matter was finished. Before Locke left he talked to me about Winold Reis, the artist. He said Reis was doing interesting things and had expressed a desire to do a portrait of me. He urged me to sit for Reis, never mentioning that he himself would use the portrait in his book.[136]

Thus the anthology included not only the material from *Cane* but a portrait of Toomer, prompting him to remark in his autobiography, "Locke tricked and misused me."[137] Toomer said he was furious, ill-treated: "My dear enemies, those who liked to misrepresent me, would have echoed Horace Liveright and said at once, 'Toomer wants to deny his race.'"[138] A paragraph later he added, "The label 'Negro' was of no more consequence than any other,"[139] yet he continued to contradict himself. He permitted Locke to include *Balo* in *Plays of Negro Life*, published two years later, probably believing that the title indicated that the plays were *about* Negroes and not necessarily by them (as was the case). When James Weldon Johnson wrote him and asked permission to include some of his poems in the *Book of American Negro Poetry* (1930), Toomer declined.

By the end of the decade, Jean Toomer's life had considerably altered. He was truly on his own, since his grandmother had died in September 1928. He was thirty-six years old, and although he didn't know it, the part of his life that had made him famous was already behind him. Except among black readers, *Cane* was already beginning to be forgotten. If his own questions concerning his blackness were unresolved, still he had managed to cloud the issue for others. People who met him for the first time had no reason to regard him as anything other than a Caucasian. He thought he had found his niche in the world, his home in Gurdjieff's bosom. Small wonder that he had missed the Harlem Renaissance. Smaller wonder that he didn't appear to care.

Larsen

The year that Jean Toomer decided to become a writer, 1919, was equally significant for Nella Larsen. On May 3, she married Elmer S. Imes, who must have been considered a good catch by any measurement. Elmer, who was eight years older than Nella (she was twenty-eight and he was thirty-six), had completed his doctorate in physics the year before at the University of Michigan at Ann Arbor. Ph.D.'s were rare enough in 1918, but for black Americans they were almost unknown. At the time of their marriage, Elmer was a research physicist for Burrows Magnetic Equipment Corporation in New York City, where he worked until 1926, when he became a research engineer for the Edward A. Everett Manufacturing Company. At the end of the decade, in 1929, he would return to Fisk University, his alma mater, to chair the physics department.

The wedding was conducted in the chapel of the Union Theological Seminary in New York City, and the ceremony performed by the groom's younger brother, William Lloyd Imes. Equally as talented as his sibling, William would in time become famous for his lengthy career fighting racial discrimination and segregation. Besides holding the position of minister at a number of famous churches (including St. James Presbyterian Church in New York City), William would serve on the NAACP's board of directors from 1925 to 1945 and become vice-president of the organization in 1945.

The Imes marriage must have been the envy of many of their friends, since Nella could boast of an equally illustrious string of accomplishments. Adah B. Thoms would include Nella in her book *Pathfinders: A History of the Progress of Colored Graduate Nurses* (1929) with this entry:

Nella Larsen (Imes), a graduate of the Lincoln Hospital School of Nursing, Class of 1915, served as an assistant superintendent of nurses of her school for one year. Further professional experience and preparation came with the responsibilities of ward supervision and teaching in the Lincoln School of Nursing, and at Tuskegee, Alabama, where she served as superintendent of nurses for two years.[1]

In 1918, she had returned to New York, where she worked for the city health department.

The exact date when Nella Larsen decided to give up nursing and pursue a career related to books and writing is unknown. It is certain, however, that Nella and Elmer moved in highly literate circles. They were part of what W. E. B. DuBois termed the "Talented Tenth," the Negro elite, whose education matched that of their Caucasian counterparts (and at times surpassed it). Sophisticated and urbane, and usually light skinned if not blue bloods, they assumed a kind of stewardship for their darker and less educated sisters and brothers. Among their friends, Nella and Elmer would shortly include the DuBoises, the Fausets (Jessie and Arthur), Charles Johnson, Walter White, and James Weldon Johnson. This social group would be greatly extended as the Harlem Renaissance burst forth, but as early as 1920, Nella must have decided that being a nurse was not equal to the talents and aspirations of her many friends.

Nella's first publications appeared the summer after her wedding in The Brownies' Book, the recently inaugurated magazine for African American children, edited by Jessie Fauset. Fauset was the literary editor of the Crisis, the NAACP publication edited by DuBois, which would shortly play such a significant part in the incipient black arts explosion. Although The Brownies' Book was DuBois's brainchild, it was "obviously Jessie Fauset's achievement."[2] Her biographer, Carolyn Wedin Sylvander, credits Fauset with most of the day-to-day work for the imaginative and handsomely produced publication: she "wrote hundreds of signed and unsigned stories, poems, dialogues, biographies, [and] articles"[3] for the twenty-four issues that appeared during 1920 and 1921.

Langston Hughes's first published work – travel pieces, unlike anything he would later write – appeared in The Brownies' Book. Nella Larsen's two appearances in the magazine were also removed from her subsequent work: "Three Scandinavian Games" (June 1920) and "Danish Fun" (July 1920). The first of these begins, "Dear Children: These are some games which I learned long ago in Denmark, from the little Danish children."[4] Thereafter follow the instructions for playing "Cat and Rat," "Hawk and Pigeons," and "Travelers." The second piece begins similarly with "Dear Children – These are pleasant memories of my childish days in Denmark"[5] and is followed by descriptions of "The Fox Game," "Hide the Shoe," "The King is Here," and "Danish Riddles." For both of these early publications, she identified herself as Nella Larsen Imes.

The following year, in 1921, Nella changed careers. She quit her job as a nurse in the Department of Health and began working as a librarian. New York City Public Library records indicate that she worked in this capacity from September 15, 1921, until January 1, 1926, most of this time at the 135th Street branch library in Harlem. On applications that she completed for positions later in life, however, she stated that she worked intermittently in this profession for eight years, beginning as an assistant children's librarian. She also claimed to have earned a diploma in 1923 from the library school of the New York Public Library, which later merged with Columbia University. Columbia University, however, cannot confirm that she was awarded this certificate.

Whatever the conditions under which Nella Larsen decided to become a librarian, they conjure up Helga Crane's similar inclination in Larsen's novel *Quicksand*. Unemployed and running out of funds, Helga thinks, "She would find work of some kind. Perhaps the library. The idea clung. Yes, certainly the library. She knew books and loved them."[6] Helga, however, is unsuccessful. Fleeing from her interview, she becomes aware of her lack of qualifications for the position: "'Library training' – 'civil service' – 'library school' – 'classification' – 'cataloguing' – 'training class' – 'examination' – 'probation period' – flitted through her mind."[7]

Midway through the decade, there were cracks in the Larsen-Imes marriage, though outwardly their public image was shaped by their active social life: parties, cabarets, theatrical events – all of the visible glow from the emerging New Negro movement. Unfortunately, little of Nella's correspondence exists for the years prior to 1926. It is difficult, for example, to determine the scope of her interest and participation in Jean Toomer's Gurdjieff group in the fall of 1925. Increasingly, however, Elmer's work was beginning to take him away from home to Ann Arbor and to Montreal. Nella was struggling with her writing, which she described somewhat later as "hack

writing." Their principal residence since their marriage had been 51 Au-
dubon Avenue in Jersey City, New Jersey, and Nella at least was anxious to
move to Harlem, into the eye of the storm.

Then 1926 arrived, and Nella knew that she was a real writer. The year
began auspiciously with the publication of two of her stories, though very
few people have ever realized that they were written by Nella Larsen. The
fact is, however, that she went out of her way to disguise her identity as the
author of the stories, as if already determined at this early stage in her career
to separate her personal and her public selves. Using an anagram of her
name, Allen Semi, she published both stories in *Young's Magazine*, "The Wrong
Man" in the January 1926 issue and "Freedom" in the April issue of the
same year.

In "The Wrong Man," a woman named Julia Romley attends a party and
encounters Ralph Tyler, who had once kept her as his mistress. When Julia
realizes that her husband and Ralph had known each other years ago at
college – and that Jim is anxious to renew their friendship – she has one of
the servants at the elaborate function deliver a message to Ralph, asking him
to meet her in the garden. When he arrives, she begs him not to tell Jim of
her sordid past: "when a girl has been sick and starving on the streets, anything can happen to her. . . . she's grateful for food and shelter at any
price."[8] Julia discovers too late that the man she has been talking to is another Ralph Tyler, not the Ralph Tyler who had kept her years ago.

Ignoring the somewhat melodramatic plot, there is much in "The Wrong
Man" that links it with *Quicksand* and *Passing*, starting with the source of the
conflict in a woman's hidden past. The setting reflects the glitter and glow
of the occasion: "The room blazed with color. It seemed that the gorgeous
things which the women were wearing had for this once managed to subdue the strident tones of the inevitable black and white of the men's cos-
tumes."[9] Julia is dressed in a "smoke-colored chiffon gown (ordered spe-
cially for the occasion)";[10] her red hair and beauty stand out even in this
remarkable crowd. In the background, an orchestra blares out "a primitive
staccato understrain of jazz";[11] everyone at the party appears to be happy.

Then Julia sees Ralph Tyler across the room and the mood abruptly shifts.
Images of destruction and enclosure are used to illustrate Julia's fear that her
marriage will be destroyed. Ralph, she feels, has "risen from the past to
shatter the happiness which she had grasped for herself."[12] When Jim asks

her if she is tired, she replies that she feels "sort of trapped," [13] by all the people at the party, though it is her terrible secret that has entrapped her. As the brief story moves to the final scene, however, the feeling of claustrophobia ends because — and this is certainly different from most of Larsen's subsequent work — Ralph Tyler, this second Ralph Tyler whom she has mistaken for the earlier one, is a gentleman. He tells her, "I can assure you that your secret is safe with me. It will never be from my lips that Jim Romley hears you have been — er — what you say you have been." [14]

The second story, "Freedom," is told entirely from the point of view of a man who is never named but through whose thoughts we observe all of the activity. At the end of a three-month separation from his wife while he has worked in another town, he reflects upon his marriage and decides not to return to her. "Her appeal for him was bounded by the senses," [15] and he leaves her because of her demands. He regards her as a parasite and even wishes for the finality of her death.

He travels for a year, and then another, until curiosity finally prompts him to inquire about her. He discovers that she died in childbirth, months after he abandoned her, and that his child also died. Soon he realizes that he has not escaped her, but, instead, their roles have been reversed: "It was she who had escaped him. Each time he had cursed and wondered, it had been a dead woman whom he had cursed and about whom he had wondered." [16] He sees that "she had spoiled his life; first by living and then by dying." [17] As his sense of guilt becomes overwhelming, loneliness and isolation envelop him, as well as a sense of confusion. He begins to think that she is still alive, that she will return to him. In the final paragraphs, however, when he comprehends the extent of his delusion, he decides to go to her. On a cold autumn night, he opens the window of his apartment and steps out "and down to the pavement a hundred feet below." [18]

The story has a haunting, believable aura to it, reminiscent of Kate Chopin's tales published thirty years earlier. The restricted point of view and especially the passages of interior monologue attain an obsessional conviction, once the man realizes that he is the one who has been abandoned. Above all, "Freedom" is densely compacted — fewer than two thousand words and filled with ironic surprises and reversals ("The Wrong Man" is longer by four hundred words).

Both of these early stories tell us that marriage is often a precarious balancing act, especially when spouses have not been honest with each other and have concealed aspects of their former lives. Although I hesitate to carry this too far, they suggest that the strife within the Larsen-Imes marriage, which would end in divorce in another half-dozen years, had already reached a difficult phase. Furthermore, the titles themselves must have been warning signs thrown up between the two of them, clear to Elmer if he read between the lines.

"The Wrong Man" and "Freedom" are free of any racial context, though Ralph Tyler of the former is jokingly referred to as an Indian, his "face yellowed and hardened as if by years in the tropics." [19] Larsen's decision to ignore race – the substance of her two published novels – was no doubt prompted in part by her market. *Young's Magazine* was devoted entirely to fiction, publishing a dozen or so short stories each month. Most of the stories included in the magazine would be called pulp fiction; the writers of these stories have become as forgotten as the magazine itself.

Why did Nella Larsen publish these stories under the pseudonym Allen Semi? The question takes on particular significance because in her published work – the two Danish children's pieces in *The Brownies' Book*, the two short stories in *Young's Magazine*, a third short story that would appear in 1930, and the two published novels – she employed three different names: Nella Larsen Imes, Allen Semi, and Nella Larsen. The first of these is the easiest to understand. Newly married and undoubtedly contemplating a change of careers, she used her legal name, though she included Larsen because of the Scandinavian identity. Letters that she wrote to her friends at this time were always signed Nella Imes. By the time *Quicksand*, *Passing*, and her third story were published, the marriage had become one in name only. To use Imes would have been a sham, so she retreated into the authenticity of her former identity as Nella Larsen.

Yet there is still the question about Allen Semi. In part, I suspect, she devised the name because of where the stories appeared: a slick magazine. Although the stories are interesting because of the way they prefigure her later work, they are in no way equal to the quality of her novels. There is also the avoidance of the racial context – certainly a deliberate choice, because as an informed reader and critic (a librarian) she would have known what the market would bear. At the beginning of 1926, so-called Negro writing was still not entirely acceptable to many readers. Then, too, there must have been a certain satisfaction knowing that she was playing a little game by using the anagram of her name.

Still, there were others in the know — friends who were aware that she was working hard as a writer, trying to break into print. Dorothy Peterson, a teacher and a talented actor and one of Nella's closest friends throughout the decade, knew about the stories, which she read (along with others) in manuscript form. Carl Van Vechten knew about them, and so did Walter White. There may have been others, though it is in connection with Walter White that the name Allen Semi takes on the greatest significance.

The correspondence between Larsen and Walter White which has survived (less than a dozen letters) begins in 1926 and lasts until the early 1930s. Some of it covers purely social matters, such as the Imeses being invited to the Whites' for dinner. Yet it also includes references to Nella's unpublished fiction — White was reading both her stories and what eventually became *Quicksand* — and responses to Nella's idea in 1926 to open a bookstore in Harlem that would specialize in black writers.

White, the assistant secretary of the NAACP, was also a novelist. In 1924, Knopf had published his first novel, *The Fire in the Flint*, a book that was primarily of interest to readers because of its author. Nevertheless, White thought of himself as a creative person and he used his position as NAACP spokesman to encourage artistry in others. In appearance a white person (and frequently mistaken for one), he had made the decision years earlier to work hard for his race, to invigorate it with pride and vitality. What he said was listened to; what he did set an example for others.

When White's second novel, *Flight*, was published in the summer of 1926, it met with generally sympathetic reviews. The novel received its most negative criticism from Frank Horne in the July issue of *Opportunity*: "It is in the failure of [the] central character to diffuse anything of glowing life and reality that the novel suffers its death blow."[20] White was irate. Why would a black critic in a black publication treat his novel in this manner? He must have wondered, also, why Charles S. Johnson, *Opportunity's* editor and supposedly his friend, chose to run such a harsh review.

In an attempt to assuage White's pain, Johnson solicited a rebuttal to Horne's review from Nella Larsen, which he published in the September issue of *Opportunity*. Larsen's emotional response, signed Nella Imes, is filled with praise for White's novel and attacks on Horne's critical abilities: "I do not like this review. . . . I read this review with mingled feelings – surprise, anger, pity. . . . the reviewer . . . so entirely missed the chief idea of the book. . . . It may be that your reviewer read the book hastily, superficially, and so missed both its meaning and its charm."[21] Horne responded to Larsen's letter in the October issue of *Opportunity* by saying, "Your correspondent's answer is most brilliantly illogical."[22] For the final word, White himself jumped into the fray with his own rebuttal in the December issue: "It is beginning to become apparent that hereafter I must write two versions of any book I want understood – one of them designed for readers of normal intelligence or better; the other supplied with maps, charts, graphs and pictures and written in words of not more than two syllables."[23]

Our interest here is with Larsen's role in the dispute. In a letter from Johnson to White, telling of his intention to publish a rebuttal to Horne's review, Johnson describes Nella as a person "who writes well and has a most extraordinary wide acquaintance with past and current literature."[24] White already knew that, though Johnson may not have known the extent of the White-Larsen friendship. I assume that this is so because in the NAACP files there is a carbon copy of Nella's *Opportunity* letter, following a note from her to White on August 12, 1926. This copy (a draft of the published response) has "Albert L. Semi" typed at the bottom. Nella obviously wanted White to read her rebuttal before it would appear in print, though she didn't want anyone else who happened to come across her draft to realize that she had sent a copy to him. There is the possibility, also, that she wanted to publish her response under the pseudonym and Johnson talked her out of it.

When Johnson solicited the response to Horne's review, Nella no doubt welcomed the opportunity to ingratiate herself to her important friend. White had numerous contacts who could aid her in her own incipient writing career. It was a matter of one writer patting another on the back, of services rendered that would likely be returned. Nella didn't have to wait very long. By October 1, White had read Nella's own novel-in-progress, *Quicksand*, and had sent her a short critique of it. When the work was completed later in the year, he arranged for his secretary to type the manuscript. To be fair to Larsen, there was another less calculated reason for her sympathetic response to White's novel. Like *Quicksand*, *Flight* centered upon a black woman who, after living in the white world, decides to return to her own people. Since both of Nella's novels are variations on this theme, she must have felt a strong emotional and artistic affinity for White's work and perhaps with White himself. To her credit, both of her novels treat this theme more imaginatively and convincingly.

Throughout much of the summer and the fall of 1926, while the pages of *Opportunity* bristled with the Horne-Larsen-White shouting match, Nella worked hard at her writing. In addition to Walter White, she had another enthusiastic reader and friend who encouraged her to keep at her fiction: Carl Van Vechten, whose *Nigger Heaven* had stirred up even more of a storm during those months. The Imeses were close friends of the Van Vechtens. It was, in fact, Elmer who had first read Van Vechten's novels (*Peter Wiffle*, *The Blind Bow-Boy*, and *Firecrackers*), though there was hardly a "New Negro" around who wasn't on a first-name basis with the successful writer-critic. Nella's many letters to Van Vechten literally gush in their effusiveness for his work. They are also sprinkled with frank comments about her own writing and her conflicts with the issue of race.

Van Vechten sent her a copy of *Nigger Heaven* as soon as it was published. Nella responded within minutes of its arrival on August 6, 1926:

> I'm terribly excited. Too, almost inclined to forgo [sic] the ritual which the reading of particular books always demand [sic] from me, a Houbigant scented bath, the donning of my best green crepe de Chine pyjamas, fresh flowers on the bed side table, piles of freshly covered pillows and my nicest bed cover, – and set right down to it. But no, impatient as I am, I shall make it a ceremony. Not to do so would be blasphemous.
>
> Therefore, this is a mere note to record its safe arrival. Thanks and other things will follow after the pleasure. Just now, everything waits but that pleasure.[25]

On Wednesday of the following week, she sent Van Vechten her four-page response, after having read the novel three times (Elmer had read it once also during those five days). "It is a fine tale, this story of the deterioration and subsequent ruin of a weakling who blames all his troubles on that old scapegoat, the race problem,"[26] she began. She praised Van Vechten's "dispassionate way of simply proceeding with the tale,"[27] telling him how forceful the story was. What impressed her most was his use of Negro material: "it's too close, too true, as if you had undressed the lot of us and turned on a strong light. Too, I feel a kind of despair. Why, oh why, couldn't we have done something as big as this for ourselves?"[28] She continues by saying how anxious she is to see the reviews, particularly those by black critics. Her letter concludes, "you have caught the spirit inherent in us, the urge, the sweet craving for happiness – and the bitter knowledge of unfulfillment, and our blindness to the reason. And the mixedness of things, the savagery under the sophistication."[29]

In a letter written two months later on October 6, Nella commented about several of the reviews which had appeared in the interim, referring to *Nigger Heaven* as "the most reviewed book of the season."[30] She also made two references to her own project: "Oh, I do understand that the bookshop is only a vision. But it's an exciting one."[31] About *Quicksand* she wrote, "I have gone back to my novel. Celebrated the return by destroying a good half of what was completed. It *was* awful."[32] Still, by late fall, she had finished all of her revisions. By December Van Vechten had read the manuscript and taken it to his publisher, Alfred A. Knopf. Thus, within the year, Larsen had seen two of her stories in print and finished a soon-to-be-accepted novel. If she had had any qualms about giving up nursing and changing professions, they must have disappeared. Soon she would be living proof, along with Jessie Fauset, that the Harlem Renaissance would not be dominated by the talents of men alone.

With the successes of 1926 behind her, the next year was a bit of a letdown. Knopf accepted *Quicksand* sometime around the beginning of the new year, but then everything seemed to slow down. In a letter that Elmer Imes wrote to Carl Van Vechten on March 18, he informed him that Knopf was getting *Quicksand* ready for the printer, yet the book did not appear until the following spring. The time required for a publisher to bring out a book during the 1920s was much shorter than it is today. Nella must have found the delays unsettling, though it is impossible to know what caused them. Knopf's records concerning her two novels – including the information regarding printing and sales figures – have been lost.

Other literary activities kept her busy. Early in the year, Nella served as a reader for the yearly *Opportunity* short story contest. The work, as well as her earlier work at the 135th Street Library, increased her desire to live in Harlem. In a letter to Van Vechten dated March 14, she informed him of their intended move. Three weeks later the Imeses were settled in a walk-up apartment at 236 West 135th Street. Among other things, the move from New Jersey made it easier to participate in cultural and social events.

Larsen's summer correspondence describes numerous parties and dinners. The names she frequently mentions include the Van Vechtens, Blanch Knopf, Muriel Draper, James Weldon Johnson, the Walter Whites, Ethel Waters, and Edward Wasserman, the "millionaire banker"[33] who, like Van Vechten, was fascinated by black culture. Elmer and she gave a tea for Ethel Waters in June, but the guest of honor never showed up. In a letter she sent to Dorothy Peterson (who was in Europe), Nella mentioned attending the opening of Water's new musical, *Africana*, which she described as very good.

At the beginning of June, a burn from hot grease on her face and neck incapacitated her for a time. Still, she kept at her writing, and by the end of the month she had submitted a six-thousand-word story to *Harper's*. As for so many other things Nella wrote later in her life, there is no record of what happened to the story, though it did not appear in *Harper's*. By July, both the heat of the summer — "hot as hell here . . . I haven't had on clothes for days"[34] — and the tensions of trying to earn a living by writing had made her particularly anxious. In one of her letters to Dorothy Peterson she mentions earning $5 for reading a manuscript for Knopf. In another she states her need for money and remarks, "I have to work like a nigger"; something else — which may have been tension with Elmer — was bothering her: "I'm still looking for a place to move. . . . It's really rather ridiculous I suppose but –."[35]

Her letters to Dorothy Peterson also suggest an undercurrent of racial ambivalence, as if she had second thoughts about her blackness now that she and Elmer were finally ensconced in Harlem. Dorothy's niece, Carla Peterson, told me that both women had a tendency to look down at darker-skinned blacks (such as Zora Neale Hurston) and to take pride in their own lightness. Nella's letters are often full of gossipy, condescending comments about her contemporaries, such as her dismissive remark about Countee Cullen's new book of poems, *Copper Sun*, which was published during the summer: "It's fair. Just that."[36] The strongest comment about her situation appears at the end of the letter, when she mentions looking for another place to live: "Right now when I look out into the Harlem streets I feel just like Helga Crane in my novel. Furious at being connected with all these niggers."[37]

Throughout the winter of 1927–1928, she was working furiously on a new novel while suffering from repeated bouts of colds and flu. In letters to Van Vechten, who she said was the best friend she'd ever had, she related her difficulties with writing, as well as her constant financial concerns. In a letter written in March, for example, she said, "I'm having the most hellish time with my novel. I've torn it all up and now face the prospect of starting all over again – if at all."[38] In the same letter she told Van Vechten, "Dr. DuBois is about to celebrate his sixtieth birthday. Some committee is sending around letters asking people to subscribe $50 and $100 towards a purse of $2500 as a gift. Some nerve I say. I'm about to celebrate a birthday too and I feel like writing and telling them that I could use $2500 myself."[39]

Some of her anxiety was created by the long wait for the publication of Quicksand, though other factors were involved. One of these was another move, which took place early in May, to the 2588 Seventh Avenue top apartment, which she referred to as "Uncle Tom's Cabin."[40] Still, it wasn't all anxiety and depression. The active social life continued. In a letter she wrote to Edward Wasserman in April, before the move, she asked if he could come to cocktails on the ninth, before the Countee Cullen-Yolande DuBois wedding. A follow-up letter written on the sixteenth informed him that Elmer and she never made it to the ceremony because people kept arriving for cocktails until the time of the wedding had passed.

In the same letter to Wasserman and in a subsequent one dated April 23, she refers to a review that he wrote of Quicksand, which apparently never saw print (unless anonymously). The novel had been published a month earlier on March 30, and Wasserman gave a party for her, after sending out engraved invitations, on April 25. Then reviews began to appear. The Amsterdam News reviewed the book May 16 and featured an article about Nella a week later.

The Amsterdam News piece, under the heading "New Author Unearthed Right Here in Harlem," provides information about Nella available nowhere else. It was written after the singular occasion in her career when Nella permitted someone, Thelma E. Berlack, to interview her. Besides her height (five foot two inches) and weight (122 pounds), the article reveals that for the previous three years she had had problems with her health. Her writing,

Nella Larsen, circa 1928. Courtesy of Harmon Collection, Library of Congress.

it is implied, began because of these complications, though *Quicksand*, the interviewer states, was written during a period of only six weeks after germinating in her head for five months.

> Described as a modern woman, Nella smokes, wears her dresses short, does not believe in religion, churches and the like, and feels that people of the artistic type have a definite chance to help solve the race problem.
> Her hobbies are doing her own housework, and there is much to do to keep a five-room apartment so clean (and from the smell from the kitchen door she must be an excellent cook), sewing and playing bridge.[41]

After a paragraph devoted to Elmer, the interview concludes, "The only relatives she has in this country are her mother, who is white, and a half sister. They live in California. Her father, a Danish West Indian, died before she was old enough to know much about him."[42]

Quicksand is the story of an educated black woman's inability to find her niche in the world. The scope of her search is international (America and Europe) and exacerbated by the fact that Helga Crane is a product not only of the middle class but of a biracial marriage – a so-called mulatto. What separates Larsen's novel from earlier works concerned with the plight of the tragic mulatto (Frances Harper's *Iola Leroy*, 1893, or Charles Chesnutt's *The House Behind the Cedars*, 1900, for example) is the depth of her characterization, as well as her superior narrative technique. Helga Crane, dare I say, is the most fully realized and convincing black woman depicted in American fiction to that date. Above all, hers is a portrait of loneliness and pain, despair and sorrow – qualities which bind her to the heroines in any number of later works by black women writers, such as Toni Morrison, Gayl Jones, Alice Walker, Toni Cade Bambara, and Marita Golden.

Like Toomer's *Cane*, *Quicksand* has a geographical symmetry to it: the story begins in the South, in a town called Naxos, where Helga teaches English at an all-black school; from there it moves to the North to Chicago and New York, though the extensive episodes set in Harlem are the most important; next it shifts to Denmark, where Helga confronts the question of her Scandinavian blood; then it returns to Harlem for a kind of symbolic resolution vis-à-vis the urbanized black middle class; and, finally, it concludes in the South, where Helga finds her place among the folk. At each one of these geographical points, Helga's quest for happiness and for that ever more elusive niche in the world is thwarted by the tragedy of her childhood, by the men she confronts, and by her own sense of superiority, which inhibits her relationships with both the women and the men she encounters.

Helga's childhood is never treated directly but always through brief flashbacks or indirect references to her family, beginning with the epigraph from Langston Hughes at the opening of the novel:

> My old man died in a fine big house.
> My ma died in a shack.
> I wonder where I'm gonna die,
> Being neither white nor black.

Helga is neither white nor black but a "despised mulatto"[43] who suffers from the stigma of that designation all her life. Though she thinks of herself as attractive, "with skin like yellow satin,"[44] other people, she believes, do not. Conditioned by years of regarding herself as neither black nor white, she projects her hatred upon all those around her – particularly upon blacks.

As a child, like Pecola Breedlove in Toni Morrison's *The Bluest Eye*, Helga was taught to regard her color with hatred and self-loathing. Her mother was white; her father was a black gambler who deserted her mother – "It is even uncertain that they were married."[45] Helga dreaded the stigma of illegitimacy from their liaison because of her own subsequent desires for acceptance within the middle class. What might have been a tolerable situation became intolerable once her mother married "a man of her own race"[46] and Helga's role became one of self-effacement: "Memory, flown back to those years following the marriage, dealt her torturing stabs . . . the savage unkindness of her stepbrothers and -sisters, and the jealous, malicious hatred of her mother's husband."[47]

Helga was the dark child – psychologically if not physically abused – hidden away as the family secret until age fifteen when her mother died. At that time, she was rescued by her Uncle Peter, who sent her to a school for Negroes, "where for the first time she could breathe freely, where she discovered that because one was dark one was not necessarily loathsome, and could, therefore, consider oneself without repulsion."[48] Her happiness, however, was short-lived. Other girls at the school had families they spoke about and visited during vacations. Helga had no one. At the school, "She had been happier [than at home], but still horribly lonely." [49] Once established, the reality of her mixed heritage and painful loneliness follow her all of her life, creating a situation which disallows happiness in all of her adult encounters. Psychologically, she has been conditioned to regard herself as a cultural half-caste, trapped between the races, "neither white nor black." [50]

Larsen uses variations of the word *lonely* to describe virtually every episode in Helga's adult life. Her loneliness feeds upon itself, intensifying her withdrawal from the world around her. At the school where she teaches in Naxos (modeled after Tuskegee), Helga tells Dr. Anderson, the principal, "I don't seem to fit here." [51] In the opening paragraph of the novel, she is sitting alone in the darkness of her room, isolated and reclusive – a fitting image of her place in the world, especially the way *she* perceives her place. One of Helga's colleagues tells her, "You never tell anybody anything about yourself," [52] but it is already too late. She has decided that she cannot stand the hypocrisy around her, that she hates the South.

When she flees to Chicago, where she spent her childhood, she is alone again and recognizes that the windy city is not her "home," that "she had not even any friends" [53] there. Even Harlem, which initially nourishes her, becomes a dreaded monster similar to Naxos. She realizes that she is, in fact, caught between two worlds, at home in neither.

> Like thousands of other Harlem dwellers, she patronized its shops, its theatres, its art galleries, and its restaurants, and read its papers, without considering herself a part of the monster. And she was satisfied, unenvious. For her this Harlem was enough. Of that white world, so distant, so near, she asked only indifference. No, not at all did she crave, from those pale and powerful people, awareness. Sinister folk, she considered them, who had stolen her birthright. Their past contribution to her life, which had been but shame and grief, she had hidden away from brown folk in a locked closet, "never," she told herself, "to be reopened." [54]

The delicate balancing act of life in Harlem, almost as a refugee, is only temporary. Larsen begins one of the chapters in this section of the novel by writing, "But it didn't last, this happiness of Helga Crane's." [55] Harlem becomes just as loathsome as everywhere else she has ever lived: "More and more she made lonely excursions to places outside of Harlem." [56] She begins to dislike her friends, including Anne, who has become closest to her. Black people become for her objects of hate and scorn: "There were days when the mere sight of the serene tan and brown faces about her stung her like a personal insult. . . . Life became for her only a hateful place where one lived in intimacy with people one would not have chosen had one been given choice." [57] Helga asks herself, "Why . . . should she be yoked to these despised black folk?" [58] She finally concludes, "She didn't, in spite of her racial markings, belong to these dark segregated people." [59]

These are strong, painful statements about the psychological aspects of miscegenation – the result of years of social conditioning. Yet in one sense they represent a completely logical response to racism in the United States, given the time when *Quicksand* was written. Black may have been beautiful for the artists of the Harlem Renaissance, but the characters they wrote about in their novels and stories had yet to discover this. Helga knows that black people will always be mistreated. She has seen the evidence all of her life. Why should she be a part of this mistreatment when an escape route lies directly in front of her? Was this not the same question that Jean Toomer asked of his own personal situation? Why live as a black person when life as a white person can be so much better? Instead of criticism, Helga's situation demands understanding and sympathy.

After two years in Harlem, Helga flees to Copenhagen, living with an aunt and uncle "where there were no Negroes, no problems, no prejudice." [60] For the most part, this turns out to be true, though in time she feels that she is a kind of rarity, like a pet dog being exhibited: "A decoration. A curio. A peacock." [61] Although Larsen never states that Helga is lonely in Denmark, in time she has her heroine experience loneliness in the form of absence. When Anne invites Helga to her wedding to Dr. Anderson, Helga wonders why she should "go back to America, where they hated Negroes . . . where Negroes were not people." [62]

Then, quite by coincidence, absence in the form of nothingness engulfs her. At a circus she sees two black entertainers, "two black men, American Negroes undoubtedly," [63] and the old sense of loathing returns: "she was filled with a fierce hatred for the cavorting Negroes on the stage. She felt shamed, betrayed, as if these pale pink and white people among whom she lived had suddenly been invited to look upon something in her which she had hidden away and wanted to forget." [64] Nevertheless, the black entertainers open up the Pandora's box within her and make her aware of something that can never be hidden away. Her old unhappiness returns: "she returned again and again to the Circus . . . gazing intently and solemnly at the gesticulating black figures, an ironical and silently speculative spectator. For she knew that into her plan for life had thrust itself a suspensive conflict in which were fused doubts, rebellion, expediency, and urgent longings."[65] Helga becomes "homesick, not for America, but for Negroes."[66]

Back in Harlem, she experiences the duality of her heritage, "the division of her life into two parts in two lands,"[67] the old conflicting emotions. She believes that she has returned to "her people,"[68] though only for a six-week stay. It isn't long before she experiences "a slightly pitying superiority over those Negroes who were apparently so satisfied"[69] with their lot.

The resolution of her problem, the denouement of the novel, comes quickly. Isolated by despair, in the depths of mental torment (in part because of conflicting feelings about sexuality), Helga lets herself go. Intellect, particularly pride and her sense of superiority, gives way to emotion. During a rainstorm, she seeks refuge in a Harlem storefront church, weeping "soothing tears"[70] that almost threaten to drown her. She sinks down and down, and the cathartic moment unites her with the folk, with the blackness she had scorned all of her life.

Hereafter Larsen's thinking becomes somewhat murky. Helga marries the Rev. Mr. Pleasant Green, a "rattish yellow man,"[71] and goes with him to his parish in a small Alabama town. Larsen says that "she did not at that time reason about anything."[72] Emotion has won over intellect, religion becomes a "protective coloring,"[73] physical passion is a release. Within eighteen months, three children are born, twin boys and a girl. In spite of the discovery of her physical side, Helga develops an "unconquerable aversion"[74] for her husband, whom she hates. After another pregnancy and the death of the child, she admits to herself that "she [has] ruined her life"[75] and renounces religion. Though she contemplates suicide, soon she is pregnant again, and as the novel concludes, she is expecting her fifth child.

The grim ending implies that educated black women – sophisticated and cultured black women, middle-class black women – are trapped in life with no satisfactory alternatives. Sexuality must be repressed, yet intellect is a dangerous commodity, because thinking leads to unhappiness and misery. Since intelligence and passion cannot operate simultaneously with any degree of relative happiness, the only possible escape is into emotion – abandonment of the mind.

The men in Helga's life do not particularly help her understand her situation, though in no way can they be considered her major problem. (Nor are they presented as negatively as black male characters in a number of more recent novels by African American women writers.) The problem is Helga herself: her restlessness, her feelings of superiority, her deeply rooted sense of insecurity about her blackness, all the seemingly contradictory aspects of her personality. Self-hatred can manifest itself in many ways, and certainly one of the most common is to disdain everyone else.

Helga's feelings about James Vayle, her fiancé while at Naxos, are shaped in large part by his family: "They had never liked the engagement, had never liked Helga Crane. Her own lack of family disconcerted them. No family. That was the crux of the whole matter." [76] One cannot help concluding that these remarks were based upon the cool reception that Nella had received from Elmer's family at the time of their marriage. She was a little too much of a bohemian for them, in spite of the fact that Elmer was the errant child of the family. In Quicksand, James Vayle is depicted as one of the Naxos community; Helga is not. He fits in; she does not. The most fitting comment regarding their relationship is Helga's realization that "Negro society . . . was as complicated and as rigid in its ramifications as the highest strata of white society." [77] Middle-class blacks, she implies, have become as bourgeois as middle-class whites – perhaps even worse.

For Axel Olsen, Helga is more of an exotic beauty than anything else, a dark and mysterious rarity it was better for him to paint than to court. Ironically, Olsen thinks that Helga is too conventional, too proper – the same way that Helga regards James Vayle and Dr. Anderson. Helga rightly fears that a relationship with Olsen might replicate the situation she knew as a child: "We can't tell, you know; if we were married, you might come to be ashamed of me, to hate me, to hate all dark people. My mother did that." [78]

Robert Anderson is the most likely candidate of the three. Part of Helga's initial attraction to him is that he appears to be more open-minded than James Vayle. As it turns out, however, he is not nearly as liberal as she. The pass he makes at her, after his marriage to Anne, catches her off guard and makes her briefly think that he has the vitality and life (and eroticism) which she has been seeking. But he turns and runs, once he realizes that

Helga has taken his kiss seriously. Part of the troubling denouement is Helga's precipitous response to the ironically named Rev. Mr. Pleasant Green.

The fact is that Helga is unhappy with all of the men in her life, though they are not dissatisfied with her. Marriages have been made (and have lasted) between people with fewer affinities than Helga and her potential life mates share. The problem redounds upon Helga herself, the unresolved questions of her heritage, and perhaps even a certain dishonesty with herself.

Helga dislikes conformity and conventionality and, above all, middle-class blacks who have accepted the values of their white counterparts. She has permitted herself, however, to be swamped by materialism, choked by objects and possessions. Repeatedly, Larsen describes her protagonist in all her finery, beginning with the second sentence of the novel:

> Only a single reading lamp, dimmed by a great black and red shade, made a pool of light on the blue Chinese carpet, on the bright covers of the books which she had taken down from their long shelves, on the white pages of the opened one selected, on the shining brass bowl crowded with many-colored nasturtiums beside her on the low table, and on the oriental silk which covered the stool at her slim feet.[79]

Helga loves clothing. "All her life Helga Crane had loved and longed for nice things,"[80] Larsen states of her; and this "craving, this urge for beauty, . . . had helped to bring her into disfavor in Naxos – 'pride' and 'vanity' her detractors called it."[81] On the verge of starvation in Chicago, she spends her dwindling savings on frivolous purchases. Her initial attraction for Anne appears to be because of the woman's extraordinary number of possessions, her happiness in Copenhagen because gifts are dumped upon her as if she were a princess – "Always she had wanted, not money, but the things which money could give, leisure, attention, beautiful surroundings. Things. Things. Things."[82] Unfortunately, the things that Helga demands can only come from money. She wants to have her cake and eat it, too.

That last statement fittingly describes Helga's problem with color also. Of Anne and Robert Anderson she asks, why "didn't they find something else to talk of? Why must the race problem always creep in?"[83] Yet her own concern with race has become obsessional. So many of her actions are designed to escape blackness and flee into white obscurity. Her claustrophobia has in fact become a self-fulfilling prophecy; it is not just at the end of the novel that Helga finds herself sinking into quicksand.

These feelings of suffocation, of claustrophobia, of confinement and entrapment accompany her wherever she goes, beginning with "the cage which Naxos had been to her."[84] In Harlem she quickly feels "shut in, trapped,"[85] "in a locked closet,"[86] even "boxed up, with hundreds of her race . . . yoked to these despised black folk."[87] In Copenhagen, in the scene in the theater, she thinks of that "something . . . she had hidden away and wanted to forget."[88] In Alabama, married to the Rev. Mr. Pleasant Green, "she had felt only an astonished anger at the quagmire in which she had engulfed herself."[89] She feels trapped in a bog; "Her suffocation and shrinking loathing were too great. Not to be borne. Again. For she had to admit that it wasn't new, this feeling of dissatisfaction, of asphyxiation."[90] Yet if her realization that she has hidden her true identity, her true self away from others is to be meaningful, why does Larsen describe her final situation with such negative imagery?

To a large extent, there is no other exit. There is no escape from racism, and even a return to one's roots may offer only temporary solace for a woman like Helga Crane. The ending of *Quicksand* is utterly different from that of Zora Neale Hurston's *Their Eyes Were Watching God*. In that novel, Janie finds her self, her identity, and her happiness with the folk, her people. For Nella Larsen, as for Jean Toomer, the return to one's heritage was no easy journey, at best an ambivalent adventure. The educated mulatto was indeed of two contradictory worlds. The artist could articulate the pain but never fully alleviate it.

The critical response to Nella Larsen's novel was generally enthusiastic — particularly by black reviewers, who were relieved that *Quicksand* was not another novel about the seamy side of Negro life. W. E. B. DuBois, who was a bit of a prude, reviewed the novel in the *Crisis* along with *Home to Harlem*, noting of McKay's novel: "*Home to Harlem* . . . for the most part nauseates me, and after the dirtier parts of its filth I felt distinctly like taking a bath."[91] Of *Quicksand*, he said, "Nella Larsen . . . has done a fine, thoughtful and courageous piece of work in her novel. It is, on the whole, the best piece of fiction that Negro America has produced since the heyday of [Charles W.] Chesnutt."[92] Ruth L. Yates, in the *Pittsburgh Courier*, sounded a similar chord:

"*Quicksand* . . . permits one to elevate his mind above the mire of lasciviousness that has been the general theme of late with books dealing with the Negro. This is Miss Larsen's first attempt at writing a novel and she is to be commended on bringing us something different."[93]

The reviewer in the *Amsterdam News* expressed the same idea by commenting about the liaison between Helga's parents:

> This is original and enlightening. It is original because in a mulatto's parentage the father is generally white and the mother colored. It is enlightening because an American publisher has dared to issue a book in which a Nordic white woman voluntarily has a child by a Negro. And the unhappy result of this union is due not to the miscegenation but to the personal character of the man. If Helga's mother had married a decent colored man she would have been happy.[94]

The idea is reiterated in an interesting comment at the end of the review: "One feels that a much stronger story could have been written around Helga's Danish mother and the Negro gambler who was Helga's father."[95]

The *Amsterdam News* critic wondered, as did Ruth L. Yates, if Helga could ever be satisfied with any group of people and regarded the novel's ending as disappointing. Roark Bradford made similar remarks in the *New York Herald Tribune*. Yet Larsen is praised for her style, "Especially in the first chapters. It is fresh, clear and limpid; in its easy, natural crystal grace there is no striving for effect. If the plot were as good as the style it would raise the story considerably."[96]

Larsen's style was praised even more lavishly by Margery Latimer in her review in *New York World*: "The style, in its elegance and some of its mannerisms suggests Mr. Hergesheimer."[97] Latimer – who would marry Jean Toomer in 1932 but had yet to meet him – began her review with the following enthusiastic statement:

> This book makes you want to read everything that Nella Larsen will ever write. It is neither distinguished nor excellent and it is not "a modern masterpiece" but it wakes you up, it makes you aware that there are other races besides the white race. You see the great space between black and whites, the elaborate mental barrier, and in the same moment you are conscious of the reason for it and the inhumanity of it.[98]

The most negative critique appeared in the *Saturday Review of Literature*. The anonymous writer claimed that *Quicksand* was "put together to a large extent from autobiographical materials"[99] – a particularly interesting comment because the book jacket stated nothing about the author. By contrast, most reviewers praised Larsen for her objectivity. Roark Bradford, for example, concluded: "Miss Larsen seems to know much about the problems that confront the upper stratum of Negroes, and happily, she does not get oratorical about what she knows. She is quite sensitive to Negro life, but she isn't hysterical about it. There is a saneness about her writing that, in these hysterical literary times, more than compensates for her faults."[100] The unnamed reviewer in the *New York Times Book Review* largely agreed: "This is an articulate, sympathetic first novel, which tells its story and projects its heroine in a lucid, unexaggerated manner. In places, perhaps, it is a little lacking in fire. In vitality one finds it more convincing than moving. But it has a dignity which few first novels have and a wider outlook upon life than most negro ones."[101]

Few writers probably enjoy reading reviews of their books (unless they are masochists), but Nella must have been pleased with the ones garnered for *Quicksand*. She made one comment to Van Vechten in her letter of March 19 about the "hellish time" she was having with *Passing*, yet by September 3, the novel was finished, and Knopf had accepted it by the middle of October. The reviews of *Quicksand* must have given her the final spurt of energy to complete the manuscript.

They gave her the confidence, also, to apply for a William E. Harmon Award for distinguished achievement among Negroes at the end of the summer. She sent the completed application to the Harmon Foundation, which was administered by the Commission on the Church and Race Relations of the Federal Council of the Churches of Christ in America, August 10. When the announcements were made at the end of the year, Nella learned that she had been voted the Bronze Award for Literature, which consisted of a medal and a $100 honorarium. She was probably disappointed, because the first prize, a gold medal and $400, was not awarded that year, in spite of nearly thirty contenders. Although there was no way that she could have known about the internal negotiations for the award, she could have guessed that Claude McKay's *Home to Harlem*, Jessie Fauset's *Plum Bun*, and W. E. B. DuBois's *Dark Princess*, published the same year, were strong contenders.

The documentation for the award has survived in the files of the Harmon Foundation, and it provides information about Nella Larsen that is available nowhere else, as well as some revealing comments about her work by her friends. She was nominated by Mrs. E. R. Alexander, identified as a housewife, who was married to a rather famous black physician and living at 234 West 139th Street. The three referees listed on the application are James Weldon Johnson, Jerome Peterson (Dorothy's father, and a leading journalist), and Edward Wasserman. Johnson's response was nonjudgmental, composed of clipped statements that are mostly factual in content. Peterson's remarks were much more detailed, stressing that Larsen's achievement in Quicksand is the psychological insight into feminine character. He praised her style and complimented her for avoiding the formula of a happy ending. Wasserman's praise was the strongest, referring to Quicksand as a "brilliant novel of great racial interest,"[102] elevating the image of black people from the bars and brothels of the works of her contemporaries.

The five judges for literature were William Stanley Braithwaite, John C. Farrar, W. D. Howe, Dorothy Scarborough, and J. Melvin Lee. The summary of their decision, made by George E. Haynes, secretary for the commission, was as follows:

> Claude McKay has the majority vote [three votes for the Gold Award] but we wish a more decisive opinion because one judge only gives him honorable mention; one judge does not mention him at all.
>
> It seems that Nella Larsen Imes is the choice for the Bronze Award as she has 2 votes for the Gold Award and two other judges enter her name, which places her far in the lead of any other candidate except McKay.[103]

The Harmon files also include a fact sheet on Nella Larsen. It was unsigned, probably written by someone on the staff, and apparently intended to serve as background on the subject to help the judges make their decision. One piece of information on the sheet says as much about Helga Crane as it does about Larsen, though in a rather curious way:

> [Larsen] entered a training school for nurses in New York City and after graduating accepted a position as Head Nurse of the hospital at Tuskeegee Institute, – the school founded by Booker T. Washington –, but her dislike of conditions there and the school authorities [sic] dislike of her ap-

pearance and manner were both so intense that after a year they parted with mutual disgust and relief.[104]

The fact is that Nella Larsen was a rather outspoken person, as all of her letters attest. Clever, sarcastic, sophisticated, and abrasive, she held strong opinions which were likely to offend even her closest friends. Her deepest friendships often came to abrupt endings. The few photographs of her that have survived confirm the statement in the Harmon files that she dressed in colorful clothing and rather elaborate hats. She may have worn the patience of her friends and husband at times, though in many ways she was simply a typical artist, given to erratic shifts of mood and temperament.

The year that had come to a close with the announcement of the Harmon Awards had been filled with alternating currents. It had begun with the expectation of fame from the publication of Quicksand, followed by the laudatory reviews, and yet there had been the difficulties with the completion of Passing. Still, that novel was finished and quickly accepted by her publisher. In the autumn, while Larsen waited for the announcement of the Harmon Awards, Elmer Imes was ill. Nella probably realized that their marriage, because of his womanizing, had reached a dangerous state. It would be the last year that they lived together for any significant period of time. Undoubtedly, she was worried about the future.

In a letter written during the fall, she stated the need for employment. She wondered if she should return to library work. Quicksand had not brought her fortune, though, ironically, McKay's Home to Harlem had been a best-seller. Perhaps she thought about DuBois's concluding remark in his review of her novel: "White folk will not like this book. It is not near nasty enough for New York columnists. It is too sincere for the South and the middle West. Therefore, buy it and make Mrs. Imes write many more novels."[105] Her writing would not be sufficient to support her, should it be necessary for her to go it alone.

The ceremony for the Harmon Awards was held February 12, 1929, and the month after that Nella began working again as a general assistant in the New York Public Library. This work lasted only a few months, until July 1, during which time she continued to face economic problems. In a letter to Van Vechten, dated July 28, 1929, she wrote that she feared the public had lost its interest in Negro books, and — with one eye on money, apropos of her discovery that Forum paid $200 to $250 for stories — she said, "I can't write short stories." [106]

The appearance of Passing, on April 19, had apparently not offered much solace, given the problems in her life. The day before, Blanch Knopf had given a tea in honor of the book's publication, yet increasingly the correspondence that has survived for this period of Larsen's life centers on two unresolved issues: marriage and economic stability. Not surprisingly, these are also the themes of her second novel.

Passing has frequently been misconstrued as Clare Kendry's story, beginning with her chance encounter with her childhood friend, Irene Redfield. When the two of them meet in the restaurant atop the Drayton Hotel in Chicago in the heat of August, Irene learns what had been rumored for years: Clare has passed for white and married a white man. The story that follows, set in New York, relates Clare's precarious life of concealment during a period of two years, since her husband, John Bellew, does not know about her Negro blood and is, in fact, a rabid racist. Racial ties are so all-pervasive that Clare is unable to escape her blackness. She is pulled back into the vortex of Negro life. Her story concludes at the tragic moment when Bellew discovers that she is not white.

Superficially, Passing shares a number of similarities with Quicksand. Both novels are the stories of fair-skinned women, psychological explorations of mulatto life, sociological examinations of the often tragic results of miscegenation. At the time when the novel appeared, black consciousness as we think of it today was still in an incipient form: white cultural values were all too often accepted as the ideal. Why shouldn't light-skinned blacks step over the color line and pass for white?

Passing is a major theme in black American fiction, beginning with the first novel published by an African American writer: Clotel, or The President's Daughter (1853), by William Wells Brown. That novel, loosely based on the life of one of Thomas Jefferson's mulatto children, also introduces the most common theme of early black fiction — the tragic mulatto, caught between races. The tragic mulatto, usually light enough so that passing is a viable option, is a central figure in most early black American novels, including Frank J. Webb's The Garries and Their Friends (1857), Frances E. Harper's Iola

Leroy (1893), and Charles W. Chesnutt's *The House Behind the Cedars* (1900). It was not until W. E. B. DuBois published *The Quest of the Silver Fleece* in 1911 that a strong black heroine appeared in any novel by a black American writer. Passing as a theme, though as a less desirable option, continued in the writings by blacks until the end of the Harlem Renaissance, as shown in the fiction of James Weldon Johnson, Jessie Fauset, Walter White, Jean Toomer, and Nella Larsen.

Larsen's account of passing is consistent with those of other earlier writers: people are driven to such drastic measures because of American racism and the need for economic survival. No passing novel can be regarded as anything other than a strong indictment of American life. Larsen brings to the theme, however, her superior craft as a novelist as well as her usual depth of psychological probing. When Irene first muses over Clare's boldness, Larsen states, "She wished to find out about this hazardous business of 'passing,' this breaking away from all that was familiar and friendly to take one's chance in another environment, not entirely strange, perhaps, but certainly not entirely friendly. What, for example, one did about background, how one accounted for oneself. And how one felt when one came into contact with other Negroes." [107] Here, in this first discussion of the subject in the novel, passing is described as hazardous, risky, and potentially dangerous to one's health. Clare, who is always viewed externally from Irene's perspective, comments rather glibly about passing, by saying, "It's such a frightfully easy thing to do. If one's the type, all that's needed is a little nerve." [108] Yet Clare is consistently described as "stepping . . . on the edge of danger," [109] while Irene is someone who sits back and watches, usually remaining uninvolved.

As Larsen's narrative makes clear, one of the worst aspects of passing is loneliness, since the ties to one's former friends by necessity have been severed. Clare remarks of her pregnancy, "I nearly died of terror the whole nine months before Margery was born for fear that she might be dark. Thank goodness, she turned out all right. But I'll never risk it again. Never! The strain is simply too — too hellish." [110] Clare is a sympathetic figure because she is so utterly alone. Living on the parameters of two racial groups, but within neither one, she has no one with whom she can communicate – not even her husband. It is that loneliness which precipitates her decision to seek out her former friend. (Irene's husband remarks about people who pass, "They always come back. I've seen it happen time and time again."[111]) Passing, Larsen observes, is not something that attracts only those daring enough to attempt it; it also fascinates those who do not, as if there is some kind of vicarious involvement impossible to ignore. Irene remarks to her husband, "It's funny about 'passing.' We disapprove of it and at the same time condone it. It excites our contempt and yet we rather admire it. We shy away from it with an odd kind of revulsion, but we protect it."[112]

It is, in fact, Irene Redfield's almost morbid fascination with Clare Kendry's fate that is at the core of Larsen's novel, for *Passing* is not Clare's story. She is not the central character. Nor is the racial theme the most important in the novel, though it is used as the starting point for bringing Irene and Clare together, as a kind of springboard for the more important theme — security. Expressed another way, the racial question is the framework for Larsen's second novel, the context she used to develop her major theme of marital stability. *Passing* describes Irene Redfield's attempts to keep her marriage intact in the face of her husband's possible adultery with Clare Kendry. In many ways, the story is an old-fashioned one of jealousy, infidelity, and marital disintegration, issues which have led some readers to dismiss the book as "women's fiction."

Irene's problem is that she cannot leave things alone. Her passivity has a fatal aspect to it. In her attempts to remain uninvolved, she becomes a kind of voyeur, attracted, one might say, to other people's danger. She lives vicariously through them; it is this fascination — to know what passing is really like — that draws her initially to Clare, even though she repeatedly tells herself that she is going to end the relationship. But she cannot stop looking. Clare has for her "a fascination, strange and compelling."[113] Irene cannot keep her eyes off her, and that almost morbid sense of curiosity becomes her downfall, since Irene is the one who brings Clare into her household and introduces her to her husband, Brian.

Temperamentally, the two women could not be more unlike. Clare seeks out Irene because she has learned that she cannot obliterate her past, that she cannot live outside of black life. Irene permits the relationship to continue because she can do nothing else: she wants to see what will happen. She wants to see if Clare's husband will discover the truth about her life. It is as if Irene is standing on a corner hoping to see an accident. She is the kind of person drawn to burning buildings because she knows that people will be harmed by the fire and she wants to observe their misery.

Clare also delights in danger, but she is not afraid to participate and accept the consequences of her actions. Though her marriage has brought her economic security, she has learned that money is meaningless without freedom, something that Irene will never learn. Clare lives for the moment, in the present and in the past memories of her lost heritage. Irene lives trapped in the future – "the old fear . . . fear for the future" [114] – constantly worried about money and security. When Clare asks Irene about her life, Irene responds, "I've everything I want. Except, perhaps, a little more money." [115] Irene's husband, who is a doctor, has been able to provide her with all the upper middle class advantages – servants, beautiful clothing for charity balls, summer camps for the children, endless parties and dances – yet she's unhappy, afraid that they will all be taken away from her.

Placed side by side, Clare literally sparkles because of all her boldness and assurance, while Irene, by contrast, is unimaginative and conventional. She wants to keep things as they are ("Irene didn't like changes" [116]), to keep the status quo. Nothing appears to upset her more than Brian's dream to take the family to Brazil and thereby escape American racism. As an overprotective mother, she also tries to isolate her sons from the realities of racism. A large part of Nella Larsen's achievement in the novel was her decision to take the less-appealing character and assign the central role to her. As readers, we sympathize with Clare, who has turned her back against her people, and feel ambivalent about Irene.

Passing is composed of three sections, each of which contains four chapters. A quotation from Countee Cullen's "Heritage" – ending with "What is Africa to me?" – introduces the theme of identity: what is blackness for someone light enough to pass? In the opening scene, Irene Redfield glances at a letter she knows is from Clare Kendry, afraid to open it. All the rest of the first section, "Encounter," is a lengthy flashback describing the women's meeting two years earlier in Chicago, the subsequent encounters that followed, and Irene's mixed feelings about Clare's presence in her life.

Ironically, during the encounter in the restaurant two years earlier, Irene was also passing. She had gone to the segregated restaurant in order to escape the heat of the Chicago street, and when Clare first glanced at her, Irene believed that a white woman had caught her in her deceptive act. The incident is similar to the "Bona and Paul" section of Toomer's *Cane*, in which Paul fears that his Negro identity has been discovered. Once they identify themselves, Clare believes that her old friend has also crossed over the line and passed for white.

In the major scene that follows, Irene meets Clare's husband, whose racism is not only rabid but who dares to call his wife "Nig" in her friend's presence. As Irene sits there trembling, Bellew explains the reason for the nickname: "When we were first married, she was as white as – as – well as white as a lily. But I declare she's gettin' darker and darker. I tell her if she don't look out, she'll wake up one of these days and find she's turned into a nigger." [117] Though not exactly a redneck, Bellew is nevertheless the crudest character in the story, lacking the education and the refinement, as well as the tolerance, of the middle-class blacks around whom the narrative revolves.

If Clare is the main interest of the first part of the novel, the second ("Re-Encounter") and third ("Finale") sections tilt the focus to Irene. At the beginning of "Re-Encounter," the time returns to the opening incident of the novel, the arrival of Clare's letter, and Irene's conflict over whether or not she should let Clare back into her life. This conflict is the beginning of her mental agony, depicted by Larsen in brief passages of stream-of-consciousness internal monologues. Eventually Irene gives in to Clare's request to renew their friendship, though she has already concluded that "she had toward Clare Kendry a duty. She was bound to her by those very ties of race, which, for all her repudiation of them, Clare had been unable to completely sever." [118] This is perhaps the only unselfish moment Larsen assigns to Clare in the story, for soon she turns to jealousy and treachery.

The third section of *Passing* describes Irene's growing suspicion that Brian is having an affair with Clare. The first chapter in this section – describing the preparations for a tea party, as well as the actual event – resonates with Virginia Woolf's *Mrs. Dalloway* and contains some of Larsen's finest writing. During the course of the party, Irene realizes her fear of losing Brian: "in the short space of half an hour all of life had changed. . . . Yet, life went on precisely as before. It was only that she had changed. Knowing, stumbling on this thing, had changed her. It was as if in a house long dim, a match had been struck, showing ghastly shapes where had been only blurred shadows." [119]

The epiphanic realization results in Irene's desire to be rid of Clare in her and Brian's life and brings out an ugly, calculating side of her character. First, she wishes that something would happen that would make Bellew aware of his wife's identity – something to "put Clare out of her life!" [120] That hope, however, gives her second thoughts about her heritage: "She was caught between two allegiances, different, yet the same. Herself. Her race. Race! The thing that bound and suffocated her." [121] For the first time in her life, she even wishes she were not a Negro. The language that Larsen uses to describe her feelings is similar to that she used at the end of *Quicksand*, for Irene is similarly trapped in a kind of quagmire.

Soon Irene realizes, however, that if John Bellew learns of his wife's racial heritage, he will divorce her and she will be free to marry Brian. In her torment, Irene goes so far as to wish that Clare were dead. Then, after a fair bit of coincidence in the plot, her wish is fulfilled. While out shopping with a black friend, Irene encounters Bellew, who clearly realizes that Irene is black. The rest of the story is predictable except for the ironies of the final scene. Bellew follows Irene, Brian, and Clare to a party at Mrs. Freeland's on the seventeenth floor of a high-rise apartment. As he barges in, he snarls at his wife, "So you're a nigger, a damned dirty nigger!" [122] The next thing everyone knows, Clare has fallen out of an open casement window.

Clare's death is deliberately ambiguous and somewhat melodramatic, but it is not suicide, as Hugh M. Gloster and others have suggested: "Trapped by her husband and embarrassed before friends, Clare falls from a . . . window to her death." [123] Such an implication is inconsistent with Clare's character. She has come to the place in her life where she does not care if her husband learns of her heritage. One might say that she even desires it, because she is tired of living a life of deception. She is not the suicidal type, nor is she embarrassed before her friends, nor does she faint and accidentally fall out of the open window.

One of the guests suggests that John Bellew pushed his wife, but that is not what happened either. She was pushed, instead, by Irene, who again feared that if Clare were divorced, she would be free to marry Brian. The evidence for this interpretation is cryptic because it is dispersed over the final pages of the novel. After Bellew's arrival, Irene thinks, "She couldn't have

Clare Kendry cast aside by Bellew. She couldn't have her free." [124] Two paragraphs later, Larsen comments, "What happened next, Irene Redfield never afterwards allowed herself to remember. Never clearly." [125] She is described as not being sorry: "What would the others think? That Clare had fallen? That she had deliberately leaned backward? Certainly one or the other. Not —" [126]

The entire scene is told from Irene's point of view, from her emotionally charged perspective: "If only she could . . . put from her memory the vision of her hand on Clare's arm! . . . There had been her hand reaching out towards Clare. What about that?" [127] She thinks of the death as "that sudden moment of action," [128] *her* action, yet she fears for a moment that Clare might still be alive. Finally, Irene faints and is lifted up by strong arms, belonging to someone other than her husband. [129]

Murder. That is what Larsen shows us. That is what she tells us a woman can be driven to when she fears the breakup of her marriage, the loss of her future: "to her, security was the most important and desired thing in life. Not for any of the others, or for all of them, would she exchange it. She wanted only to be tranquil. Only, unmolested, to be allowed to direct for their own best good the lives of her sons and her husband." [130] Whether Irene has retained that security, however, is not clear, because of Brian's absence from the final scene. More likely, it seems to me, she has lost both her husband and her old friend.

Though the melodramatic ending weakens the impact of the novel, it is consistent with the focus upon Irene Redfield and her attempts to keep her marriage intact. It is also consistent, I believe, with the autobiographical material Nella Larsen drew upon for much of her fiction. On one level, *Passing* is an account of Nella's marriage to Elmer Imes and her fear of its eventual disintegration. Elmer, who was described by one of his students as "a ladies' man," had apparently engaged in a string of affairs, which Nella tolerated for some time — presumably because she felt that being married to an adulterer was better than not being married at all. Writing *Passing*, she was able to work out the tensions of her own life and even disguise them to a certain extent as a novel about race instead of infidelity.

If *Passing* is a lesser novel than *Quicksand*, its rank as second in Larsen's canon is only the matter of a slight degree. Readers have been misled by its supposed sensational theme and failed to realize the author's true intent. In part this was a result of the way the novel was promoted. The description of the novel on the original book jacket read as follows:

> The heroine of this novel is a beautiful colored girl who crosses the color line into the white world. Her life as a white woman brings her superior advantages of almost every kind, and yet after a time there comes an inexplicable longing to go back to her own people. A chance meeting with a Negro school-mate – and she renews her old racial contacts, although she is aware of the accompanying danger and senses the tragedy that will undoubtedly overtake the double life she attempts to lead.[131]

A quotation from Carl Van Vechten added as a wraparound to the cover further confused the issue: "A strangely provocative story, superbly told. The sensational implications of PASSING should make this book one of the most widely discussed on the Spring list."[132]

There is much to admire and ponder in Larsen's second novel, beginning with her portrait of an unlikable woman driven to recklessness and murder. Intentionally, I believe, Larsen has used the "tar baby" story to develop the basic situation between her two main characters. It is Irene who cannot control her curiosity and thrusts her hand into the tar baby (Clare) and thereafter finds herself trapped in a situation she never intended. The resolution of that situation is achieved in the final scene of the novel, which juxtaposes the themes of race and marital security by disposing of the first and enhancing the second. If passing is a metaphor for slavery – a denial of one's heritage and one's self – then Clare is freed by death, escaping from the world the way slaves did when they jumped or were pushed overboard during the middle passage. Irene is freed from Clare's annoying presence, but she can never be freed from the realization of what she has done.

The reviews of Nella Larsen's second novel were, again, generally enthusiastic. W. E. B. DuBois's praise was even stronger than it had been for *Quicksand*. He described *Passing* as "one of the finest novels of the year, . . . done with studied and singularly successful art, . . . consummate art."[133] He surmised, however, that the success of the novel would be limited because the passing theme would be threatening to white readers: "so many white people in America either know or fear that they have Negro blood."[134] In time, he hoped, the instances of passing would decrease: "It [passing] is all a petty, silly, matter of no real importance which another generation will comprehend with great difficulty." [135] He concluded his review, which he knew would be read mostly by black readers, by saying, "If the American Negro renaissance gives us many more books like this, with its sincerity, its simplicity and charm, we can soon with equanimity drop the word 'Negro.' Meantime, your job is clear. Buy the book." [136]

W. B. Seabrook, in the *Saturday Review of Literature*, agreed with DuBois about Larsen's talent. He began his review,

> Negro writers seldom possess a sense of form comparable to that of Miss Nella Larsen. Her new novel, "Passing," is classically pure in outline, single in theme and in impression, and for these reasons – if for no others – powerful in its catastrophe. The whole tragedy is prepared and consummated in less than fifty thousand words, without the clutter of incident and talk which impede the progress of most novels, and without a single descent, so far as this reviewer could perceive, into sentimentality. [137]

Seabrook had reservations about Larsen's use of language, but he attributed these elaborations to the problem of the double audience. Clearly sympathetic to the black writer's dilemma, he stated that "a large proportion of her readers must be white people, which is to say, either uncomprehending or hostile." He ended his review by saying, "She has produced a work so fine, sensitive, and distinguished that it rises above race categories and becomes that rare object, a good novel." [138]

The unnamed reviewer in the *New York Times Book Review* was not as understanding. Although the review began with an attempt at praise, it was actually a left-handed compliment: "Nella Larsen is among the better negro novelists." [139] There were two major criticisms: the sudden ending, and Clare Kendry, who "seems a little too beautiful to be true." [140] Thereafter, the review digressed into plot summary and vague comments which refer to passing as a "vexatious problem." [141]

As with *Quicksand*, there are no reports in the publisher's files about *Passing*'s success in the marketplace. Copies that say "Third Printing" do, however, exist. The novel was reprinted in 1935 by Greenberg Publishers in New York City. Then it went out of print, and when the copyrights on both novels were about to expire in the mid-fifties, Larsen failed to renew them. Both books were brought back into print (in hardback and paperback editions, though not by Knopf) in the 1970s during what is now referred to as the Second Black Renaissance.

Planning for her future both as a writer and as a woman separated or divorced from her husband, Nella Larsen applied for a Harmon Award and a Guggenheim Fellowship in the second half of 1929. The nomination to the Harmon Foundation was once again made by Lillian Alexander, with Carl Van Vechten, Dorothy Peterson, and W. E. B. DuBois listed as the persons who would write letters of support. In the foundation's files, there is no letter from DuBois; it may have gotten lost, or it may have been an oversight on his part. When the winners were announced in December, Nella was again disappointed, if not confused. Her name was not on the list; Walter White was given the Bronze Award for *Rope and Faggot*, his study of lynching.

What Nella could not have known was how close she had come to winning one of the awards. Once again, the jurors – Alain Locke, Joel E. Spingarn, Dorothy Scarborough, Lewis Mumford, and John C. Farrar – were in disagreement. Only Locke voted for Nella for first place, though three others gave her the second position. White had two votes for first place as well as a qualified first by Mumford, who noted, "It would be fairer to those who have reached a high standard before to give a second prize rather than a first one this year." [142] His statement apparently convinced George E. Haynes, the secretary, who wrote in his letter to the judges, "Our understanding is that your votes give Walter White the Bronze Award. As two judges do not favor giving a Gold Award this year and Mrs. Imes is not eligible for the Bronze Award a second time, we conclude you will give only one award." [143]

Still, Larsen could set her hopes on the Guggenheim. Since Walter White had already been awarded the fellowship and would write one of the letters of support, she probably assumed that his voice would carry particular weight. White had, in fact, been looking out for her interests for some time. The year before, he had written a letter to Samuel Craig, who was president of the Book League, recommending that Nella become a part of their staff. After praising her writing, White had written,

Aside from the general experiences and ability I feel that it would be a very real advantage to the Book League of America to have a young colored person of ability attached to its staff. There is a large and constantly growing number of book reading and book buying Negroes in the United States and Mrs. Imes is very well known among them. Her connection with the Book League would I am sure commend the Book League instantly and favorably to those persons.[144]

Although Nella was interviewed by David Roderick of the Book League, nothing came of it. No job materialized.

White, however, continued his encouragement and support. During the last part of 1929, he made two attempts to find free-lance work for Larsen. In November, he wrote a letter to Mrs. Samuel Marks, suggesting that Nella be considered as a writer for a publication she edited called *Intimate Talks on the Theatre Arts and Letters*. In December, he asked Nella to write an article, originally requested of him, on Negro children and their parents. Obviously, since she had no children, White misunderstood Nella's qualifications, though he thought of her as enough of a professional to write the piece. I am unable to find evidence that either of these potential assignments resulted in any work.

So Nella counted on the Guggenheim. In her application in November, she listed her field as creative writing and described her project, another novel, as follows:

The scene will be laid partly in the United States and partly in Europe. The theme will be the difference in intellectual and physical freedom for the Negro – and the effect on him – between Europe, especially the Latin countries, France and Spain. I have never been in these countries and therefore feel that I am not prepared without visiting them to judge attitudes and reactions of my hero in a foreign and favorable or more unfavorable environment. My plan is, travel and residence in Europe, principally the South of France and Spain, while completing the novel.[145]

For present occupation, she wrote, "Hack writing. Housework. Sewing."[146] On the section for language proficiency, she listed Danish ("Speaking – fairly fluent. Reading – good. Writing – fair") and French ("Reading – fair").[147] Under the education category, she listed the University of Copenhagen (as an auditor, 1910–1912), the library school of the New York Public Library (1922–1923), and the Lincoln Hospital Training

School for Nurses (1912–1915). For publications, she listed two stories in *Young's Magazine* and her two novels, though none of these is identified by title. Of her most recent work, for 1929, she wrote, "Writing short stories, reviews. Working on third novel when time is available."[148] Her references for letters of support were Carl Van Vechten, Walter F. White, Muriel Draper, Mrs. Alfred Knopf, and James Weldon Johnson.

During the year that was about to end, Elmer had frequently been away in Canada, Ann Arbor, and Nashville, and Nella had spent her time writing, though apparently with limited success. There are references to her novel-in-progress in her correspondence, and sometime late in 1929, *Forum* accepted a short story called "Sanctuary." As it turned out, this story – which appeared in the January 1930 issue – would be the last piece of fiction she would publish during her lifetime. It wasn't for lack of trying that her literary career was about to come to an abrupt halt. Her life, and the life of the nation as a whole, simply had too many unknowns.

Endgame

You don't know, you can't realize how I want to see Negroes,
to be with them again, to talk with them, to hear them laugh.
– Clare Kendry in Nella Larsen, *Passing*, 1929

. . . he had drawn a distorted, inky black skyscraper, modeled after
Nigerrati Manor, and on which were focused an array of blindingly
white beams of light. The foundation of this building was composed
of crumbling stone. At first glance it could be ascertained that the
skyscraper would soon crumple and fall, leaving the dominating
white lights in full possession of the sky.
– Wallace Thurman, *The Infants of Spring*, 1932

Nigerrati Manor was the setting for much of the activity of
Wallace Thurman's 1932 novel, *The Infants of Spring*, which satirizes the Harlem Renaissance. Many artists of the renaissance, including several of its most articulate representatives, were easily recognizable as characters, though by the time the work was published, they may have thought there wasn't much to laugh about. The Harlem Renaissance was largely a thing of the past, especially for the writers, who had already discovered that so-called Negro writing was no longer in vogue.

True, some of the writers still published important works at the beginning of the new decade, but these publications became fewer and fewer as the depths of the Depression became widespread. Late in 1930, James Weldon Johnson, ensconced in a teaching position at Fisk University, published *Black Manhattan*, still regarded as one of the major sociological studies about

Harlem. Langston Hughes's only novel, *Not without Laughter*, was published the same year and won the Harmon Gold Medal. Besides Thurman's *The Infants of Spring*, there were George Schuyler's *Black No More* (1931) and Countee Cullen's *One Way to Heaven* (1932), two other satirical novels that offered more oblique glimpses of the era just ended. Other writers – Jessie Fauset, Claude McKay, and Rudolph Fisher – published their final novels, but the bite was missing from most of this writing.

The problem was largely one of economics – the old bugaboo for the black writer. Books had become luxuries, not just for black people but for white people also. Historians of American literature refer to the decade as one of decline. The writers of the Harlem Renaissance knew that their days were numbered and sought other means of employment. Countee Cullen, Arna Bontemps, and Jessie Fauset followed James Weldon Johnson and accepted teaching positions. Rudolph Fisher and Wallace Thurman both died in 1934. Only Langston Hughes sustained his career as a full-time writer, though, as his biographers have shown, these were extremely difficult years for him.

And the images of black life and Harlem itself? They were changing too. Marc Connelly's *Green Pastures*, his folk play based on Roark Bradford's short stories, was a Broadway success in 1930. Dorothy Peterson, Nella Larsen's close friend, had an important part in the production. Serious drama by black playwrights, however, was still in the future, later in the decade. And Harlem itself was beginning to look a little frayed at the seams.

Though the statistics vary from historian to historian, Stephen H. Bronz's statement is typical: "Harlem in the 1930's was an unlikely place for a respectable, middle-class literary set; sixty percent of the population was on relief and another twenty percent was supported by WPA jobs." [1]

Larsen

Viewed in connection with the careers of these other writers, Nella Larsen's appears fairly typical. "Sanctuary" appeared in *Forum* in January 1930, but then, even before she learned that she had been awarded a Guggenheim in March, her career suffered a serious setback.

The story – one of her strongest statements about race – centers on Jim Hammer, "a big, black man with pale brown eyes in which there was an odd mixture of fear and amazement."[1] In the opening scene, Jim enters Annie Poole's house, seeking refuge from his pursuers. He tells Annie that he has shot and killed a man, probably a white man, and knows if he is caught he will be lynched. Jim has sought refuge in Annie's house because she is the mother of Obadiah, his closest friend.

After Annie hides him, covering him with blankets in her bed, the story shifts to Jim's point of view, as he listens for the approach of his pursuers. Yet when they arrive, it is not to inquire of Jim's whereabouts but to deliver the body of Obadiah to his mother, for it was Obadiah whom Jim Hammer accidentally shot, not a white man as he had thought. Realizing his tragic error, Jim becomes paralyzed, certain that Annie will turn him over to the men. Soon, however, he hears them leave the house and Annie Poole enter the room where he has been hiding. Her final words to him are "Get outen mah feather baid, Jim Hammer, an' outen mah house, an' don' nevah stop thankin' yo' Jesus he done gib you dat black face."[2]

The power of the story is undeniable. Race is the strongest tie that binds people together. Even though Jim killed her son, Annie will protect him because he is black. Nowhere else in her published work had Nella Larsen made such an emphatic statement about blackness. The story is terse, direct, totally convincing in its use of character and motivation as well as in its successful employment of dialect. It is the sole piece of dialect fiction that Larsen published during her career. Followers of her work coming upon "Sanctuary" must have been surprised. Did the story herald a shift in her attentions – away from middle class blacks to that of the folk?

We will probably never know the answer to this question, for scarcely had the story appeared in *Forum* than there was talk behind her back of plagiarism. Harold Jackman, writing to Countee Cullen (his sometime companion who was in Europe at the time, recovering from his marriage to Yolande DuBois), described the incident as follows:

Literary dirt: Nella Imes had a story in the *Forum* for this month called *Sanctuary*. It has been found out – at least Sidney Peterson was the first to my knowledge to discover this – that it is an exact blue print of a story by Sheila Kaye-Smith called *Mrs. Adis* which is in a book called *Joanna Godden*

Married and Other Stories. The only difference is that Nella has made a racial story out of hers, but the procedure is the same as Kaye-Smith's, and Anne and Sidney have found that the dialogue in some places is almost identical. If you can get ahold of the *Forum* and the Smith book do so and compare them. But isn't that a terrible thing. It remains to be seen whether the *Forum* people will find this out.[3]

Jackman's letters to Cullen during the next few months contain a running commentary about the affair and not only demonstrate his rather spiteful character but the literary backbiting and jealousy that apparently had been part and parcel of the movement itself. On February 10, he wrote, "No one who has heard about Nella Larsen's steal has quite gotten over it." To Cullen's inquiry about Larsen's visibility, he added, "No, 'dear' Nella is still in New York."[4] February 28, Jackman described an encounter with Nella at a party at Dorothy Peterson's, after the opening of *Green Pastures*: "you should have heard painful Nella Imes tell about a cocktail party on Park Avenue and a luncheon date here; she thinks she is so much hell – I could have strangled her that night . . . I have been so broke I haven't been going anywhere."[5]

In his letter of March 13, he continued his attack:

Hon, "don't be too hasty in your judgment against poor Nell." Poor Nell is right; it is poor, sad Nell. Boy, that gal has used some of the identical words Miss Smith uses . . . and as for the dialogue, little Nell, I'll call her this time, has just changed it to make it colored. The technique and the method is identical – description, dialogue, denouement – are incontestably congruent. . . . All literary Harlem knows about it, and I hear that the *Forum* has gotten wind of it – and has written Nella about it. Nella's benefactor, Carl Van Vechten, is trying to justify his protegee but his arguments are so weak and in this case so stupid.[6]

The *Forum* had, indeed, gotten wind of it. In the April issue, the editors state that the magazine had received several letters about the affair – one, by Marion Boyd, which they published. Admitting to the "striking resemblance"[7] between the two stories, the editors wrote Nella and asked for an explanation. Nella sent them her four drafts which they examined and concluded were adequate proof that it was simply an extraordinary coincidence.

Then – implying that literary and scientific inspiration are the same – they cited other "authenticated cases of similar coincidence in history":[8] Thomas Edison and an Englishman simultaneously inventing the incandescent lamp, Charles Darwin and A. R. Wallace similarly working out theories of natural selection.

Nella's explanation, published after the editors' remarks, states that she based "Sanctuary" on a story she had heard during her nursing days from "an old Negro woman":

> Her oft-repeated convictions were that if the Negro race would only stick together, we might get somewhere some day, and that what the white folks didn't know about us wouldn't hurt us.
>
> All this used to amuse me until she told some of us about the death of her husband, who, she said, had been killed by a young Negro, and the killer had come to her for hiding without knowing whom he had killed. When the officers of the law arrived and she learned about the man, she still shielded the slayer, because, she told us, she intended to deal with him herself afterwards without any interference from "white folks."[9]

At the end of her statement, Larsen said that for fifteen years she believed that the old woman's story was true, but more recently she had realized that there were so many other variations of the story that it was "almost folk-lore."[10] She originally thought of setting her version in Harlem, "But that little old Negro countrywoman was so vivid before me that I wanted to get her down just as I remembered her."[11]

Whatever the truth behind the matter, Nella's career and her credibility among her so-called friends were seriously jeopardized. As Harold Jackman had detailed in his letters to Countee Cullen, the two stories are remarkably similar in incident, in detail, and even (in some cases) in dialogue. "Mrs. Adis" is set in Sussex and has an ending which is somewhat different from that of Larsen's story, yet there are still too many similarities between the two to be explained as coincidence. Although Nella begins her Forum response by stating that she hasn't yet read "Mrs. Adis" – and "that anyone who intended to lift a story would have avoided doing it as obviously as this appears to have been done"[12] – it seems more plausible that she had read Sheila Kaye-Smith's story and, then, forgotten it.

Larsen was an accomplished artist. As a librarian and as a professional writer, she fully understood the consequences of plagiarism. If she had wanted to borrow from someone else's work, why would she have done it so visibly? ("Mrs. Adis" had not only been included in Kaye-Smith's collection of short stories but had been published, originally, in the January 1922 issue of *Century* magazine.) It seems more likely that Nella possessed something akin to a photographic memory, and for that reason "Sanctuary" contains all those embarrassing similarities to "Mrs. Adis." Perhaps, also, it was written out of a need to prove to herself that she could survive as a writer, support herself between novels. When she submitted the story to *Forum*, it was still months before she would learn the results of her application for a Guggenheim.

The "Sanctuary" controversy had caused tongues to wag, but the announcements of the Guggenheim Fellows in March must have been even more unsettling to some of Nella's erstwhile friends. She was the first woman of her race to receive such an honor, a grant that amounted to $2,500. It could not have come at a more significant time in her life, given the ongoing problems with her marriage. Elmer's latest infidelity had created a minor scandal at Fisk, where he had settled in as a one-man Department of Physics.

Her European plans had been in the back of her mind ever since she had applied for the Guggenheim. The extended period abroad – besides permitting her the freedom to write without interruption or constraint – would permit her to test her independence from Elmer. Nevertheless, she must have wondered if there was some way to patch up the marriage. On May 12, she went to Nashville, intending to stay two weeks. In her letter to Van Vechten the day before, she described herself as "a dutiful wife going down to visit her husband." [13]

How long Nella remained in Nashville is unclear, since very few letters have survived for this period of her life. On May 22, she sent the Van Vechtens a letter tinted with local color, as if she were some kind of stranger in an antique land:

Carl would adore the Negro streets. They look just like stage settings. And the Negroes themselves! I've never seen anything quite so true to what's expected. Mostly black and good humoured and apparently quite shift-less, frightfully clean and decked out in the most appalling colors, but some how just right. Terribly poor.[14]

In a letter she sent Van Vechten August 16, she says that she returned from Nashville the day before, yet this must have been from a second visit with Elmer. Her passport was issued by the State Department July 28. She had taken the oath of allegiance three days earlier on the twenty-fifth in New York City. On her passport she had listed an August 9 sailing date from New York on the *Rochambeau*. My assumption is that after Nella booked passage on the ship, there was some kind of temporary rapprochement with Elmer be-cause he, also, applied for a passport at the same time. (In a letter to Van Vechten only a month before, she had stated her intention to stay in Europe for two years.)

However conflicting her feelings about Elmer may have been during the summer of 1930, by the time of her actual departure, September 19, they had flip-flopped again. In another letter to Van Vechten, who was in Europe, Nella mentioned having to alter her plans because the Guggenheim Foun-dation required a September beginning, and she concluded by saying that "it has been a rotten summer – from my point of view."[15] The extent of the rot can only be surmised, though a letter from Elmer to Van Vechten, dated the day before his wife's departure, candidly describes the situation:

Early in the year and quite by accident Nella became possessed of in-formation which pointed decidedly to the fact that I was at the time very much interested in another girl. Like the sweet little sport she is she de-cided to keep along and not say anything about it, feeling that no matter what happened nothing could change our relationship. Of course this created a situation beyond even her ability to carry off. . . .

About three weeks ago she decided that she must talk it over and has taken the attitude that she is to eliminate herself – that it is best all the way around. I had no means got that far – just what might have happened I do not know, but I do know that there was never any question of desert-ing her or of shirking any responsibility toward her. I am sure that no matter what new thing may have come into my life, Nella has her own place and if it had ever seemed advisable – as it doubtless would have

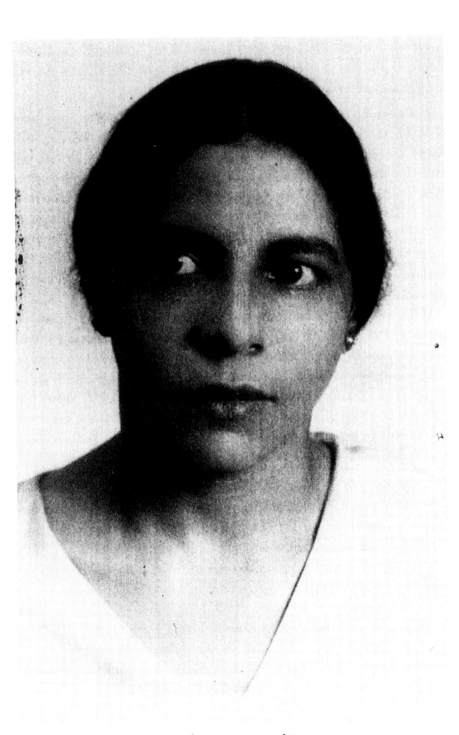

Nella Larsen, circa 1930. Courtesy of U.S. Department of State.

Elmer S. Imes, circa 1930. Courtesy of U.S. Department of State.

seemed – to talk to her about it, this would have been as to a friend asking what we should do under the circumstances.

What I want you to know is the stage setting – the fact that she knew and I did not know that she knew and that therefore she has made herself unduly miserable and has perhaps come to the wrong conclusions as to what is immediately necessary to do. It is not necessary for her to feel that there is any question of her "going it alone" or being under necessity of taking steps of any sort to guarantee support. I want to do all for her that I can and be everything to her that she will let me be. I am not denying that I am very much in love with the other girl – very much indeed, but she does not expect or wish me to forget to love Nella. A quite involved situation – but possible if we can be clear headed.

If I am to work and do the things I must do for myself there can be no publicity – my job would be done in ten minutes and I wouldn't be able to do anything for anybody. I have asked Nella not to do anything or make any hard and fast decisions until I see her next summer.[16]

Elmer's letter reads as if it might have been written by Clare Kendry. In one of her more humorous moments, Nella had remarked of her, "The trouble with Clare was, not only that she wanted to have her cake and eat it too, but that she wanted to nibble at the cakes of other folk as well."[17] What could be better for Elmer than to be free of Nella during the year that she would be overseas? Much less understandable is Nella's decision to tolerate a situation that had been going on for years.

Nella sailed for Lisbon on the *Patria* September 19 and arrived in Portugal on the last day of the month. Her postcard to Van Vechten the day of her arrival indicates that the voyage had improved her spirits: "Arrived! Very amusing trip. Letter follows this. Millions of churches in this place. Also millions of men ready for – anything. Nella."[18] By the next day, she had moved into the Avenida Palace Hotel in Lisbon and had written a letter, obliquely referring to the last time she had seen the Van Vechtens: "You and Fania were sweet . . . to let me cry on you the day before I left."[19] Somewhat later she described an incident on the ship: "I met a couple on the boat who were passing. And really, I never would have suspected them if they hadn't asked me if I knew you."[20]

Soon she was busy settling into a routine – after moving on to the Reina Victoria Hotel in Mallorca – and looking for a house to rent. She found a place – Jose Villalonga 32, in "an English settlement just outside Palma" [21] – on the twelfth of November and moved in the following day. Her agreement with the owners was for five months at $55 a month, which included a servant, and an additional $30 for food. About the same time, she became quite ill with what was later diagnosed as pneumonia. A letter to Van Vechten, however, demonstrates her usual acerbic wit: "I was quite shocked at Sinclair Lewis getting the Nobel Prize. How come?" [22] The next day she wrote again: "There is a Lord Douglass staying here. He has remants [sic] of fine looks. I'm awfully curious about him, but of course one can't go up to him and say: 'Pardon me but are you the Lord Douglass who slept with Oscar Wilde?'" [23]

The letters she wrote to Henry Allen Moe, the president of the Guggenheim Foundation, during her year overseas often contradict the ones she wrote to Carl Van Vechten. Read side-by-side, they create a difficulty in charting the course of her writing during her fellowship year, though I believe the ones to Van Vechten are more accurate. In her first letter to Moe after arriving at Mallorca, Nella alludes to a "series of misadventures" [24] during the trip, though she does not describe them. She informs him that she is busy at work, enjoying the "heavenly weather," [25] and only disappointed that her Spanish is not as good as she had thought it was.

Three weeks later, she described her work to Van Vechten as follows: "I think my book, my white book[,] is really good. Perhaps being a bit lonely is doing me good, or rather doing what I'm trying to do, good." [26] Her "white" book was probably *Mirage*, which she would mail to Knopf the following summer, though for a time she appears to have changed the title to *Crowning Mercy*. Whatever, by the end of January, she told him that she was retyping it for the last time, and finding the typing difficult "because I'm learning to ride these days and after hours in the saddle its [sic] hard to sit on a chair." [27] She was also using a typewriter for the first time in her career.

Earlier in the month, when she wrote to Henry Moe, she had said that her writing was going a little slower than was typical for her and, projecting her work throughout the year, she had asked him if the Guggenheim Foundation would be able to extend her grant by three or six months. In a later letter dated March 31, after he informed her that her request could not be honored, she states of her writing: "I am something more than about half-finished, what with going over and over again and revising and casting away and adding."[28]

The five months in Mallorca, however, were not all restricted to the type-writer and horseback riding. For a time she appears to have been caught in a tailspin of social activity, not unlike the life she had known in Harlem during the height of the Harlem Renaissance. She mentions John Galsworthy, Somerset Maugham, Liam O'Flaherty, and "some rather queer French painters who, I am told, are quite famous,"[29] as well as Robert Graves and Laura Riding, whom she visited. Lady Newton, the wife of the governor of Nigeria, who was in Mallorca for the winter, had taken an interest in her. Nella also mentions two German dancers (husband and wife) as well as a woman from Richmond, Virginia named Lucky Jones, who was attracted to her because she was black. Moreover, her personal life picked up considerably:

> There is a delightful young English-Scotsman staying at one of the hotels who appeared suddenly at my house one evening offering . . . a gold and green enamel cigarette lighter which he informed me I'd forgotten in the American Bar. Well, I had been in the bar. But I'd never seen the lighter before. We both knew this. But I took it and thanked him for bothering, returning it some days later because as I told him I'd noticed he'd been using matches ever since he'd brought me the lighter. It develops that he's rather important. Terribly good-looking, filthy rich, a rather famous polo player and all that. Anyway he's been convenient for opening doors, picking up handkerchiefs – and such things. Besides, he thinks we look awfully well together because he's so tall and blonde and I'm so little and brown.[30]

Nella's interest in the unnamed Scotsman must have been serious, since as early as January 25 she altered her travel plans for that period of the year after her novel would be finished. April in Nice would be followed by Toulon and then Paris, and then June and July in Scotland, which had never been listed as part of her original itinerary. She told Van Vechten that she intended to return to Mallorca in October: "It's comfortable and I like it. It is fun you know dashing about all night from one place on the island to another with people to whom time means nothing. Besides shocking the Latinos."[31]

Nella's affair with the Scotsman, however, had ended by spring and she once again found herself in a state of depression. On March 22, she wrote to Van Vechten, "I've never been so lonely in my life."[32] Her response to Henry Moe's denial of her grant extension begins "Thanks for your letter. Your news was a disappointment. However, life is like that."[33] She continues by stating that she understands that other people are also in need of Guggenheim support. Still, in a letter written earlier in the month to Van Vechten, she had managed to show a bit of her old self. About George Schuyler's *Black No More*, which Van Vechten had sent her, she commented: "I didn't, however, think it was as well done as might be. I should love to have seen the reviews in the nigger papers. Dorothy sent me two from the ofays."[34]

The ups and downs with her writing continued, no doubt exacerbated by the recent events in her life. On April 7, she sent a letter to Van Vechten which included the following:

I have been doing over my book. I had given the manuscript to my playwriting friend to read and he gave me his candid opinion that it was rotten. And on re-reading it I came to the conclusion that he was right, though I was sure that there was good stuff in it. Since then I have sweated blood over it.[35]

All the blood and sweat, however, must have ended toward the end of the month. On April 27, she sent a postcard to Van Vechten from Monte Carlo: "Won gangs of money here today."[36] By May 3, she was in Paris, staying at the Hotel Rovaro, at 44 Rue Brunel: "I stayed in Nice with Jack Carter's mother and step-father. They are both very fair. I can't make out whether they pass or not, or simply say nothing about it."[37] By June 4, she was waiting to learn about Knopf's decision on *Mirage*.

Her departure from Spain had been difficult because of the political instability within the country. As she described the situation to Henry Moe,

The fact is that everything is at a standstill, no taxis, buses, trains, and few boats are running. For the past week we have been living on what we had in the house or what we could get from the peasants round about, since all or most of the shops are closed. The populace seem to think that republic means an eternal holiday.[38]

To Van Vechten, in a letter written after she was in Paris, she remarked, "I didn't tell you about my experiences in Spain at the time of the revolution. . . . *Why* do the papers always say that these things are done with utmost peace and quiet. I was simply terrified. I don't care if I ever see Spain again."[39]

Nella remained in Paris longer than she had originally intended, in part because she was once again ill and confined to bed. The illness may have been caused by the trauma of fleeing from Spain, or it may have been a recurrence of her earlier respiratory problems. She mentions visiting Bricktop's place, but "she was not there and the whole thing was pretty dull."[40] And Man Ray, she wrote, "is going to do some pictures of me."[41] Her other activities in Paris can be only a matter of speculation, but by June 4, Dorothy Peterson had arrived and the two of them were together for the next few months.

By the end of the summer, Elmer had come to Europe also, though he traveled on his own, spending some time in Germany. Apparently, there was no significant change in the Larsen-Imes marriage during this time. Nella had written to Van Vechten June 4, describing the situation as follows:

About Elmer; I heard from him the other day for the first time in four months. And then only to berate me for having spent as much money as I have. Before I sailed he promised to come over when school closed. Now, I do not know. It seems pretty doubtful. I have a suspicion that he will do as he did the most of last summer − that is, spend his vacation with Mrs. [Ethel] Gilbert. I don't care about that. But I do object to being left short of money.[42]

During the fall, Nella and Dorothy traveled together in Spain and North Africa. The exact itinerary is unknown, though it did include Gibraltar and Tangiers. On a postcard, Nella complained of the cold in Tangiers and the need to purchase wool clothing. On another postcard, dated November 24 and written in Spain, she told Van Vechten that she was getting ready to return to the States, though Dorothy intended to remain in Europe until early in 1932. Whatever the exact date for her return to the United States, this period of her life was once again fraught with increasing tensions. Clearly, the state of her marriage would have to be dealt with once she returned to the States. It could not be kept in a holding pattern indefinitely, as it had been throughout the year of her Guggenheim. Equally troublesome was the state of her writing career.

Throughout the summer, she had waited for a decision about *Mirage*, the novel she had sent Knopf early in June. The manuscript, however, had not reached them until August 22, presumably having been sent by surface mail. Knopf compensated for the delay, however, by having it read immediately — two readings, in fact, within the next three weeks. The first reader, C. Abbott, submitted his report to the publisher August 31. Since this is the only piece of information in the Knopf files in the New York City Public Library relating to Nella Larsen, and the only description of *Mirage* that exists anywhere, it is worth quoting in its entirety. C. Abbott's critique reads as follows:

A novel about a woman whose second husband turns out to be still in love with his first wife by whom he has a child (who arrived after their divorce unknown to him). To get even with him and his sister, who has her nose into all their marital troubles she goes to the first wife to try to take her husband back. Rebuffed by the divorced wife, she has an affair with a man who turns out to be a cad. She is so baffled in her quest for love that she kills the latter by veronal in the moment of a sudden inspiration and opportunity. They [sic] she goes to his funeral.

The end of the book is very well done, but the rest of it is pretty ordinary. The woman is very impulsive, jealous and stupid, and the husband is a perfectly awful character, but drawn in an obscure way so that it is difficult to see why two women are so crazy over him.

The sister and other characters are well done, and the woman is a vivid, even if unlikable person.

The scene is laid in a New Jersey suburb.

I don't think this book approaches *Passing*. It is, after all, a conventional triangle story, except for the ending. The husband is the chief defect of the novel because of the passive and shadowy characterization — a lay figure.

The book ought to be rewritten to bring him out and perhaps to excite some sympathy for the sex-mad wife who deserves nothing but derision as she exists here.[43]

With so little information about *Mirage*, it is difficult to place the work within Larsen's canon. Abbott mentions nothing about race in his critique, and I therefore conclude that this is Nella's "white" novel, which she had considered calling *Crowning Mercy*. Several aspects of *Mirage*, however, suggest links with Larsen's earlier work, especially the theme of marital strife. Once again Larsen created a rather unsympathetic heroine, though the husband is apparently the real cad. It appears that Nella drew directly upon her own failed marriage and Elmer's affair with Ethel Gilbert. The violent ending, which Abbott says is the strongest part of the novel, is also in keeping with Nella's earlier works, especially "Freedom" and *Passing*.

Knopf's letter of rejection was sent to Nella in care of Guaranty Trust Company of New York, 4 Place de la Concorde, Paris, September 14. Assuming that it was sent by air mail, it would have reached her before September 27, the date when Nella and Dorothy left for their extended travels. It appears likely, also, that when she wrote to Henry Moe the day before, she was under extreme psychological distress. That letter begins with her thanking the Guggenheim Foundation for the year of support, but then it continues,

> I am very grateful and should have written earlier to say so, but I have been sick since the beginning of September.
>
> I have not quite finished my work, but now that things seem quieter here I mean to go back to Spain, where the weather is pleasanter and living cheaper, and get on with it.[44]

It was the last letter that the Guggenheim Foundation would receive from her. When she returned to New York later in the year, she could not help being preoccupied with the failures of her life.

Nella Larsen's life of withdrawal began in 1932, after her return from overseas. The correspondence with her friends Carl Van Vechten, Dorothy Peterson, and Walter White thins out. The addresses where she lived are often unknown. Moreover, the daily activities of her life – what she did to keep herself busy – can only be matters of speculation. So little factual information about her life in the middle and late 1930s has survived that it might be easiest to refer to this stage as the "lost years," comparable to similar periods in the lives of many talented individuals. As her biographer, I confess to a feeling of intense frustration. How is it possible for anyone in our society to disappear, to vanish so thoroughly, and leave hardly a footstep or a footnote on the track of time? I can't help thinking of Ralph Ellison's invisible man, "hurt to the point of abysmal pain, hurt to the point of invisibility,"[45] and hibernating in the basement of an abandoned building.

It is clear that Nella did not want to end her marriage to Elmer Imes, in spite of the fact that the two of them had ceased living together. On April 21, 1932, she took off for Nashville again to stay with him for a short period of time. Since no correspondence between the two of them has survived, we can only guess as to which party instigated the visit. One element, however, is known. Elmer's womanizing had become a problem for the administration at Fisk. They thought his wife should be visible – that is, living with him.

After she had been in Nashville for three weeks, Nella wrote to Van Vechten and described an amusing incident with Grace Johnson, James Weldon's wife. The two of them drove to a small town south of Nashville, passed as white, and ate at the best restaurant. Larsen commented, "I who have never tried this much discussed 'passing' stunt have waited until I reached the deep South to put it over."[46] In the same letter, she summed up the state of her relationship with Elmer:

Elmer is looking very unwell, poor dear; but I don't know what I can do about it. Dr. Jones – the president [of Fisk] – seems to feel that I ought to come here to live for at least a portion of the year and offers to build the kind of house I want, but I haven't made up my mind about it. There seems to be a lot of gossip floating about. But then, theres [sic] always gossip anywhere.[47]

By the first of June, she was back in what she referred to as her "small, depressing"[48] place in New York City. Elmer explained his own feelings about Nella's recent visit in a letter written later in the month: "I don't know how wise it is to have her here. She has the most ungodly ability to keep me in an unpleasant stew."[49] Nevertheless, the pretense continued. Nella had returned to Nashville by Thanksgiving. Ann Allen Shockley states that the Imeses' house on Morena Street – possibly still under construction at this time – was rumored to be "designed for 'two people who did not get along.' "[50]

It seems unlikely that Nella remained there until the following summer, though the surviving communication with Van Vechten and Dorothy Peterson indicates this. A telegram to Van Vechten dated May 12, 1933, included the following remark: "I DO MEAN TO WRITE BUT LIFE IS PRETTY TERRIBLE THESE DAYS HOWEVER I CAN'T SAY I WASN'T WARNED."[51] On June 27 she wrote him and described a novel, called *Adrian and Evadne*, she had written with a young man named Edward: "He did the men and I the women. It was rather fun to do."[52] Her collaborator was Edward Donahoe, an Oklahoman, whose own novelistic career would begin in 1937 with the publication of *Madness in the Heat*. A month later, in a lengthy letter to Dorothy Peterson, Nella revealed that she had also been revising *Mirage*, which she hadn't looked at since "we celebrated its departure to the U.S.A. in Paris."[53] She thought the book was appalling, so she rewrote it and changed the title to *Fall Fever*. Then – indicating a continued spurt of creativity – she mentioned a new novel in progress, tentatively called *The Wingless Hour*. Although she used Bryant and Bryant as her agent for some of these works, their records indicate that no sales were ever made.

A letter that Elmer wrote to Dr. Thomas Jones on July 22 suggests how claustrophobic the Imes-Larsen marriage had become. Elmer's mother had shared the house on Morena Street with the two of them, but the two women could not get along together. In part, Elmer wanted to get Nella out of his life in order that his mother, who was ill, could move back in with him. The letter further alludes to "certain conditions [of the divorce] which I couldn't quite meet but am trying to modify quietly and honorably."[54]

In Nella's July 29 letter to Dorothy Peterson, she too addressed the question of her marriage: "About the divorce – I've about come to the conclusion to get it here. It can be done *discreetly* in *ten* days for a hundred dollars or so. Can you imagine that?"[55] Then she listed eight grounds for divorce in Tennessee and adds,

As I see it you pays your money and you takes your choice. And that's that. Much simpler, don't you think, to get it over quickly, quickly, and cheaply, and be done with it? No waiting around to establish residence. No hanging about to have the decree made final. A session with a good lawyer, a morning in court. And then finis! [56]

A month later, August 30, the divorce was final. Nella left for Chicago, where she had grown up as a child. When she wrote to Peterson on September 6, she said,

> I divorced Elmer last Wednesday very easily quickly and quietly. He is getting married tomorrow in Wellington Ohio. The new Mrs Imes (or shall I say the second) will live in the North while he works in the South. It wont [sic] be so much different from last year. She was on [the] road a great deal and he was always away meeting her places. So much for that! [57]

Of her own situation she adds, "I haven't decided anything about my name yet. I wonder if there is much use in changing it back and then changing it again. There is nothing else to tell. Oh! Yes! Elmer expects to be a father along in February or March of next year. Isn't that swell!" [58] One wonders if Elmer hadn't been deceiving Nella in more ways than one – possibly to hasten the much-delayed divorce. He never married Ethel Gilbert, though when he died, in 1941, he left the bulk of his estate to her.

Nella remained in Chicago for several days, looking up old friends and visiting the World's Fair, which she described as "just about as boring as the Paris Colonial Exposition." [59] Then she returned to New York City and, for all practical purposes, disappeared. A letter, dated October 11, 1933, from Carl Van Vechten to James Weldon Johnson poses the question of what happened to Nella: "If you know of anything official about Nella Imes I wish you would let me know. I read a story in the *Afro-American* which said she was getting a divorce." [60] Her withdrawal may have been prompted in part by negative publicity, which appeared a month after her return. The discreetness which she had sought in a Tennessee settlement ended when the Baltimore *Afro-American* published a sensational article about the Larsen-Imes divorce.

One of the main headlines on the front page of the newspaper for

October 7 read, "NEW YORK NOVELIST DIVORCES FISK PROFESSOR."[61] The words above a photograph of Nella read "Broke Leg Now She's Divorced." If that weren't enough, the article itself begins after four bold-print headings:

FISK PROFESSOR
IS DIVORCED BY
N.Y. NOVELIST

Friends Think Love
Cooled While Wife
Wintered in Europe

RECALL "JUMP"
FROM WINDOW

Friendly Comforter's
Resignation Accepted[62]

The article, with a Nashville dateline, reads as if it were the plot outline for one of Larsen's novels.

The first two paragraphs identify the three parties involved: Nella, Elmer, and "a white member of Fisk University's administrative staff [Ethel Gilbert],"[63] with whom Elmer was frequently seen. Nella's lengthy absences from Nashville are mentioned, as well as the university's decision to provide a home for Elmer and her. Then the article continues, "Last spring the campus was startled by the story that Mrs. Imes had fallen down the steps and broken her leg. But the story that was whispered was that she had jumped or had fallen out of a window and done herself bodily harm."[64]

Elmer's white companion offered her resignation, which was accepted by university officials. Nella is identified as the author of *Quicksand* and *Passing* and the forthcoming *Fall Fever*.

Mrs. Imes is now in the East. She is colored. One of her parents was white. Several years ago she spent a winter with her white relatives in Denmark. She spent the winter of 1931 with Dorothy Peterson, New York school teacher, in LaPalma, Majorca, in the Balearic Isles. She was then said to be working on a novel which she termed "Mirage."[65]

No doubt some of the details in these articles are distorted – if not incorrect – but a number are accurate. Did Nella jump through a window trying to commit suicide? Did she jump through a window to gain sympathy from Elmer? Did she even jump through a window? The problem with this piece of information is the lack of supporting evidence from Nella's correspondence written during this time. If she had actually broken her leg, wouldn't that have affected her general mobility sufficiently that she would have mentioned it in letters to Van Vechten or Dorothy Peterson? Perhaps not. Perhaps the broken leg was the primary reason for her continued stay in Nashville – much longer than her visit or visits with Elmer the year before. I suspect, however, that details from Nella's novels have been confused with her personal life. Perhaps she twisted an ankle and walked with the aid of crutches. The mere existence of the article on the front page of the *Afro-American*, however, must have been cause for further consternation. As Nella had said in her letter to Van Vechten in the spring, there is always gossip. She had been the subject of slander before, and coupled now with still another failure, it is no surprise that she turned away from her friends. There are no letters to Van Vechten that make any references to her divorce. For all practical purposes, the letters ceased once her marriage ended. Her last communication with him was posted in Brooklyn on April 18, 1934, thanking him for a party given the night before in celebration of her birthday. Even her friendship with Dorothy Peterson – with whom she may have lived for a time after the divorce – ceased sometime later in the decade, after a falling out between the two of them. So determined was Nella to make a break with these earlier friends that she changed addresses in New York City at least once, and, on another occasion, she concocted an elaborate ruse to make her former friends believe that she was moving away from the city.[66]

So what did Nella Larsen do? How did she survive during these lost years? The question of her economic livelihood is the easiest to explain, since it can be answered by looking at the Imes divorce settlement. The court determined that

the defendant has been guilty of such cruel and inhuman conduct towards complainant as renders it unsafe and improper for her to cohabit with him and be under his dominion and control, and that he has offered such indignities to her person as to render her condition intolerable and thereby forced her to withdraw and that he has abandoned the complainant and turned her out of doors and refused and neglected to provide for her.[67]

The court decreed that Elmer would pay Nella an immediate sum of $375 before September 1, 1933 (before she left Nashville). Alimony payments for the first year after their divorce were set at $175 per month and thereafter decreased to $150 per month. There were additional terms relating to the property of both parties. Nella was to take the furniture that she chose, and Elmer was to ship it to New York at his expense. Elmer paid all the legal fees.

While Elmer was a womanizer, he was evidently also a gentleman. I believe that he faithfully paid the alimony and that Nella lived decently during the Depression on those payments. The monthly amount would have been adequate, given the times. The few letters that Elmer wrote to Van Vechten during the final years of his life suggest that he remained concerned about Nella's state. On February 24, 1940, for example, he wrote,

> Nella seems to be o.k. as evidenced by typewritten and addressless note a few days ago about money. I replied in care of her bank which was the only way I could think to reach her since her note implied that she had not received a letter addressed to 320 Second Ave in Jan. (and not returned because of non-delivery).[68]

During the summer of 1941, when Elmer was in Memorial Hospital in New York City and dying from cancer (caused, according to his niece, by radiation encountered in his professional work), he added to a note to Van Vechten, "I am taking care that Nella does not know I am here."[69] Contradictory information in a letter Dorothy Peterson wrote to Van Vechten later in the year states that "Grace [Johnson] wrote . . . that Elmer wanted to see Nella at the end. Do you know anything about this?"[70] When he died September 11, he was fifty-eight years old. Dorothy Peterson's postcard to Van Vechten, mailed early the next year states, "I saw Sally Alexander . . . and she said that Elmer had given Nella his last dollar."[71] Yet Elmer's will designated nothing for Nella. In addition to the money he left his mother and each of his brothers, he left the bulk of his estate to Ethel Gilbert, who scattered his ashes over the Fisk University campus.[72]

By 1941, Larsen had returned to her earlier nursing profession. On February 14, 1944, she was appointed chief nurse at Gouverneur Hospital in New York City. Another nurse who met her at that time said that Nella had worked for some years in a nursing home prior to taking the position at Gouverneur, though there is nothing on a later application form to substantiate this claim. Her residences from 1940 on (and possibly before then) were 320 Second Avenue and then 315 Second Avenue. For reasons that are not clear, she did not apply for Social Security until 1954. Beginning with the Manhattan telephone directory for 1955–1956, she is listed at the 315 Second Avenue address as "Imes, Nella L. Mrs." In the nursing positions which she held from 1944 on, she was known as Nella Imes.

In September of 1954, her position at Gouverneur was changed from chief nurse to night supervisor. Then in 1962, after she had been mugged, she transferred to Metropolitan Hospital as a supervisor of nurses and held that position until she retired September 12, 1963. According to her job-transfer application, she was seventy years old. On that application, she listed April 13, 1893, as her date of birth, though I have reason to believe it was two years earlier. She was found dead in her apartment the following year, March 30, 1964. The interment – at Cypress Hills Cemetery, in Brooklyn – was on April 6.

Two of Larsen's coworkers – Alice Carper and Carolyn Lane, with whom she worked at Gouverneur Hospital – attest to her reclusive personality. In conversations I had with these women, the comments that kept recurring about Nella were that she was a "lonely person," she "kept to herself," she was "not a happy person"[73] – remarks which are not very surprising. She had very few friends the last dozen or so years of her life, and even her friendship with Alice Carper came to an abrupt end some months before Nella died. There was a disagreement over something, as there had been with a number of her earlier friendships, and the ties between the two women were suddenly broken. Larsen had told Carper that she intended to leave some of her possessions to her and had even drawn up a document indicating her intention. Yet when the two women had a falling out, Carper refused to keep the document in her possession, even though Nella kept sending it back to her.

Nella's death certificate lists the cause of death as "acute congestive heart failure due to hypertensive and arteriosclerotic cardiovascular disease."[74] When Carper was called to Larsen's apartment, she discovered the place in shambles. Papers were strewn everywhere – many of them no doubt of value to the literary world – though nothing of monetary value, including books, survived. "She had nice things,"[75] Carper told me, meaning jewelry, clothing, and household possessions, but all of these were gone.

Nella claimed that she had a house in Danbury, Connecticut, where she vacationed from time to time, but I have been unable to locate anything pertaining to it. Otherwise, she did not travel or go overseas during all of the years that Carper knew her. Because there was no one else, Alice Carper made the arrangements for Nella's funeral and provided that the interment be in Carper's own crypt, where her husband had been buried some years earlier. There were no obituaries at the time of Nella's death, and that in part has contributed to the common belief that she "vanished." More than a year after her death, Edward Donahoe, the writer Nella collaborated with in 1933, asked Grace Johnson in a letter, "Do you ever see Nella Larsen?"[76]

The extent of the belief in her disappearance can be demonstrated most easily by quoting from a 1969 letter written by Jean Blackwell Hutson, the curator of the New York Public Library's Schomberg Collection. Responding to an inquiry about Larsen that year, Hutson began, "Nella Larsen is the most elusive of the authors whose biographies I have tried to trace."[77] The letter continues by listing various inaccuracies about Larsen's life and then concludes:

> In her later years she lived down in Greenwich Village and did not come to the attention of the Harlemites. Some people report that she was "passing" in the manner developed in her novel of that name. However, her complexion was not like that of a white person. Of course, in New York there are many dusky complexioned people from foreign countries that among them, perhaps, she might not have been identified as a Negro.
>
> These informants said that she was found dead in Brooklyn, N.Y., several years ago, but the *New York Times* reported that there was no card for her in their morgue.[78]

Part of the difficulty in locating details about the late part of Larsen's life stems from her use of her married name, Imes. When I began searching for information about her, I erroneously concluded that, since she had used

Larsen for her two published novels (both written when she was married), she went under the name Larsen all her life. Once I began looking for Imes, many of the pieces of the puzzle began to fall together. Yet apparently no one had considered doing that earlier. The telephone directories in New York City were certainly available to Hutson's access — no doubt back copies were in the 135th Street Library, where Nella had once worked — yet clearly she did not use them. The day I stumbled upon "Imes, Nella L. Mrs." listed in those directories, I couldn't help thinking that she must have waited the last ten years of her life for someone to rediscover her. No one did.

Carolyn Lane said that Nella Larsen was a proud woman, proud of her race. She gave copies of her novels to Lane and Carper, though both women believe that she no longer spent time writing. Rather, she put her energy into nursing and was admired by the people with whom she worked as well as by her patients. Lane said that Nella taught a young male patient from North Carolina how to read and that he in turn came to treat her as if she were his mother. Yet, in spite of these satisfactions from her profession, the image of the lonely, isolated woman persists.

There is another and perhaps deeper reason why Nella Larsen's withdrawal and her disappearance from the literary world form such an acutely painful story. It is the reason, also, why her story does not conclude with her death. She was estranged from her family — her mother and her half sister — most if not all of her adult life. Like Helga Crane in *Quicksand*, Nella had a mother who was white and a father who was black. It is from her stepfather, Peter Larsen, that Nella acquired her surname. Her half sister, Anna Elizabeth, was born June 21, 1892.

Nella's mother and her stepfather moved from Chicago to Los Angeles sometime around 1922. Her stepfather, who had worked much of his life as a streetcar operator, died in 1945. Her mother, Mary, died in 1951, when she was eighty-three years old. She had had her own source of income for many years, making dresses for a rather elite clientele in Santa Monica. There is no evidence that Nella was in contact with either of her parents during her adult life. They were separated not only by an entire continent but by the stigma of race, which had poisoned their relationship for years.

Anna Elizabeth and her husband, George Henry Gardner, whom she had married in 1913, moved to California shortly before her parents. Anna and

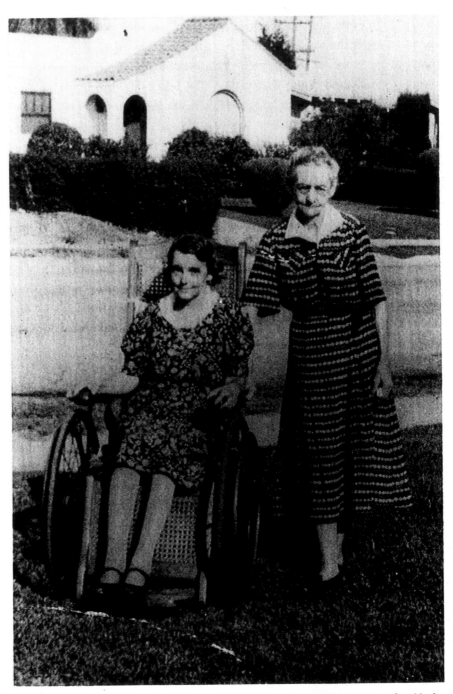

Mary Hansen Larsen (standing) and Anna Larsen Gardner, circa 1950. Courtesy of Mildred Phillips.

George's son, George, Jr., born in 1914, was largely raised by his grand-mother (Nella's mother), in part because of Anna's prolonged illnesses. The two families – the Larsens and the Gardners – for many years lived side by side in a duplex in Santa Monica, California. Sometime after her parents' deaths, Anna and George Gardner separated, though there was never a divorce.

Approximately a year and a half before Nella died in 1964, she may have attempted a reconciliation with her half sister. Alice Carper claimed that Nella went to California to see Anna but was not well received, that she returned to New York distressed – despondent because her half sister had rejected her. In Carper's words, "Nella gave up the idea of having a family." [79] About the same time, Nella's arm was broken during a mugging. This event (and perhaps the unsuccessful reconciliation, if it actually was at-tempted) was largely responsible for her decision to leave Gouverneur Hos-pital to take the less-demanding position as night supervisor at Metropoli-tan. In her depressed state, Nella began the final stage of her withdrawal, "Shutting herself out from me," [80] in Carper's words.

When Larsen died in March 1964, it was Carper who wrote to Anna in California and informed her of her half sister's death. Nella had listed Anna on her last job application at Metropolitan Hospital (in December 1961) as someone who should be notified in the event of her death. Since Nella left no will and the document she had drawn up listing Carper as her beneficiary had disappeared, Anna received the spoils of Nella's estate.

The estate was valued at $36,478.13 – all of it in cash except for $240.00 in property. After probate, on May 5, 1965, the amount remaining for Anna totaled $27,722.71. When she received the check, Anna said to a friend who had known her family for nearly fifty years, "Why, I didn't know that I had a sister." [81] By that time Anna was pretty much alone in the world, limited in mobility because of multiple sclerosis. Mildred Phillips, who took care of all of Anna's correspondence, insisted that she would have been aware of any attempt by Nella to contact Anna. Anna's husband, from whom she had been estranged for many years, was dead. Her son, George, Jr., who lived with his wife in the other half of the duplex, would die in 1967, childless. Her daughter-in-law, with whom she had never been close, would shortly disappear. And Anna Elizabeth Larsen Gardner – bedridden for years because she could no longer move her hands or feet – died April 23, 1976.

Toomer

By the time Nella Larsen's marriage to Elmer S. Imes had reached a nervous state of jeopardy, Jean Toomer's bachelor existence was similarly threatened. His quest for harmonious existence had carried him across the Atlantic to Fontainebleau and Gurdjieff's fiefdom several times. He had been a leader for the great man for half a dozen years — mostly in Chicago — pursuing not only his own separate vision quest but also a kind of genital urge, as if the balance of spirit and flesh would fuse the disparate parts of his existence into one inner whole. Yet he was not really his own man, since his work for Gurdjieff and the money he raised for him were constant reminders of his continued dependence upon the will of another. In one sense, it was time for him to move on and assert his own identity. What could be more fitting than to merge that character with the spirit of another? What could be better than to find that soul among the workers of his own fields?

Jean met his future helpmate, Margery Bodine Latimer, in Chicago in the spring of 1931. They were drawn together by their Gurdjieff connections. Margery was no novice to the movement. She had met A. R. Orage on many occasions in New York City, where she had lived sporadically for a number of years, pursuing her career as a writer. She considered Orage one of her mentors. Chicago was close to her family's home in Portage, Wisconsin, where she also spent extended periods of time. Both Jean and Margery had mutual friends in Chicago, including a journalist named Blanche Matthias. The two of them also shared a number of striking affinities.

Born February 6, 1899, Margery grew up in Portage, where she formed a close relationship with the successful novelist and playwright, Zona Gale. Gale was the first woman to receive the Pulitzer prize for drama, for *Miss Lulu Bett* in 1921. She took a special interest in Margery, even going so far as to endow a scholarship at the University of Wisconsin in 1921 so that her protégée (who had been in and out of school) could continue her studies there. The relationship between the two of them has been called mystical, though there have been numerous speculations that it also extended to the physical. It is not very difficult to regard the interdependence between the

Margery Latimer, circa 1930. Courtesy of Yale Collection of American Literature, Beinecke Rare Book and Manuscript Library, Yale University.

two of them as similar to the Jean Toomer-Waldo Frank relationship, when Toomer was also learning his craft.

The main character in Latimer's first novel, *We Are Incredible* (1928), was regarded as an indictment of Zona Gale, another instance of biting the hand that feeds one. Portraits of Zona in Margery's later fiction (especially in the novella "Guardian Angel") would be equally unsettling for the older woman, though cathartic for the young writer, who recognized the need for making the symbolic break with her mentor. In contrast to the Toomer-Frank breakup, the seduction of a spouse was out of the question, since Zona was single. That was also part of the shock for Margery, because Zona married rather suddenly for the first time in 1928, when she was fifty-four years old.

By all accounts, Margery Latimer was considered an unusual person. Her contemporaries noted her psychic abilities and her interest in the mysterious and the occult. As an adult, she suffered from continual stomach disorders, frigidity — as far as men were concerned — and repeated premonitions of her death. Her interest in Gurdjieff would have been natural, especially considering her impressionable nature. Small wonder that when Jean Toomer came along, Margery, like so many other women, felt her personality merging into his. Ironically, however, it appears that Margery herself created the situation that resulted in the collapse of her singular identity.

By the time they met, Jean was clearly looking for ways to put his psychological theories into practice. What he wanted more than anything else was to recreate Gurdjieff's Fontainebleau Institute in America, on his own turf and on his own terms. It was Margery who made that possible. In an undated letter to Blanche Matthias, Margery explained how the possibility came about:

Such a remarkable thing has happened here in Portage, outside of Portage, rather. I rented a farm house for a week and invited Jean Toomer, Yvonne Dupee, her brother Chaunce, the Groves and Lanes. Doesn't that last sound summery — the groves and lanes. It was like Eden. It was as if I hadn't *seen* Toomer for the first time, as if I had only felt him. This time he was marvelously attractive, his skin, his eyes, all of him. . . . It was like paradise. Every one working and liking to work, every one deeply fond of every one else. I wish I could describe the change that came on me but I can't seem to.[1]

The letter continues as Margery explains that living together with Toomer (and the others) in the cottage for a week liberated her from Zona's power:

Suddenly, Zona fell into her place and I realized that it wasn't important really how I felt or acted . . . whether I saw her or not. . . . I know now what I want. I mean my reason now feels in harmony with my desire because my desire seems right now and the other, the possessive, was wrong. It fed only my suffering and my egoism.[2]

In a letter to Ruth Ware, written July 5, 1931, she elaborated more fully:

I invited . . . them up for a week in the country, rented a house in a wood with some deer, a red pump, a brook, and an old barn and farmhouse – adorable – and they supplied the food. I lived with them for the week, rowed sometimes for the milk and pulled water lilies along the way, ate with them, played cards, drank wine, talked, bathed in the slough, and went riding. It was all a paradise. Everyone, male and female, was quite in love with everyone else. . . . Jean brought about such a wonderful thing in me. I got in him what I have sought in men – a rebirth, a cleansing, so that I have cut off the old person, the old life, it is an island floating somewhere off, farther and farther away from me. . . . I had thought only a knock out blow could have broken loose from my obsession, only *death*. It was like being closed in circles – sin, guilt, sin, guilt, never getting out. Now it is in the past. And I cannot make the past different. No. Only this, this new – love from Margery.[3]

Initially, Margery's feelings toward Jean had not been so positive. In an earlier letter to Matthias, she described a visit to her cousin in Chicago and an evening at the Groves, when Jean and Jeremy Lane and his wife were present. She described her love for the Lanes as "instantaneous": "as we stood together, I felt as if we were three sprouts of corn, coming from the ground, quite fresh and green and ourselves."[4] Her feelings toward Toomer, however, were much more guarded, perhaps in part because she had already suffered from a sustained though platonic involvement with another man: "Toomer I couldn't bear to look at. He sat at the head of the table and I was next to him. . . . I felt he was so tainted with his master, Gurdyieff [sic]. I felt he was consciously being G and also unconsciously being him. I'm sensitive to it, having been so dominated myself." [5]

Latimer told her friend that the evening was quite uncomfortable: "I could hardly bear it." [6] Yet in the next paragraph, she said, "There was none of that destructive feeling that usually comes with a group. It was all very harmonious and essential, so that every one, or so I believed, felt released and natural. Except Toomer." [7] As her annoyance with him continued, she explained:

> I felt him fumbling with his formulas and I longed to say, "Please stop trying things on people. Let's all be just sprouts of corn, nothing more, until we know each other." I couldn't look at those rolling eyes. Suddenly I wanted to ask him to sing some spirituals and I held back because I felt he was trying to transcend being a negro. [8]

The courtship gavotte continued. After dinner, Lane played the piano and Jean sat down in a chair next to her. Margery felt that all eyes were upon them:

> He said, "Now I'm going to hold Margery's hand if I may, Mr. Lane." I couldn't stand it for more than a second. His hand seemed moving inside and mine got perfectly static. I had to take it away and he said, "You're protecting yourself. You've heard things about me." Of course I hadn't at all, except from Georgia O'Keeffe, who thinks he is simply great, much finer than Waldo Frank. But as I sat there not saying anything something quiet seemed to rush from my head downward and I felt more quiet than before. I seemed to lose all memory, everything was washed away. I left early and suddenly as I said goodbye to those three – Lane, his wife, Toomer, I couldn't bear to go. I didn't know why but I couldn't bear it. I said goodbye over and over until they were all laughing but I couldn't laugh, I couldn't bear to go. I thought I was only pretending it all but I was almost crying. [9]

The week that Margery had provided for her friends in the country soon developed into a more extended experience guided by Toomer, who realized that the opportunity had come for him to set up his experiment in communal living. The cottage outside of Portage was engaged again, and Toomer and his friends – including Chauncey and Yvonne Dupee, Ray Klenert, Katherine Green, Margery, and their "chaperon," Mrs. Bliss – moved in together. Ostensibly, the goal was to break down artificial barriers through the sharing of work as well as play (i.e., compulsory games) and the close proximity of communal activities. As Toomer explained the following year:

> As a result of the experiment, I am satisfied that it is entirely possible to eradicate the false veneer of civilization, with its unnatural inhibitions, its selfishness, petty meanness and unnatural behavior, under proper conditions. Adults can be re-educated to become as natural as little children, before civilization stamps out their true or subconscious instincts. I am satisfied that an interior life exists in all of us, a true life which will come to the surface under proper conditions.[10]

The experiment lasted a couple of months during the late part of the summer of 1931, during which period as many as thirty-five guests visited the commune at a time – mostly, it appears, to listen to Toomer lecture. At the beginning, Zona Gale Breeze gave the cause a boost by inviting Jean to lecture to her friends in Portage. Thereafter, some of the town's most prominent citizens were participants in the meetings at the camp (after they paid the $1.25 charge). Reactions to the experiment are contradictory and difficult to evaluate, but one Portage denizen said that Toomer "talked about the false veneer of civilization which we build about us and advocated breaking that crust so that we could live a fuller life."[11]

Margery Latimer's biographer, Nancy Loughridge, has written that Margery's greatest frustration was having to share Toomer with the others:

> One evening, as the group sat around the campfire, Margery lost her temper over a seemingly trivial incident and the next morning she was gone. Jean dashed into Portage to persuade her to come back (she did) and it was probably during this interview that Jean declared his love. She, usually so adept with words, could find only one phrase to describe her feelings. Over and over she wrote to her friends, "I am miraculously happy."[12]

The idea of the commune itself – unmarried men and women living together – generated rumors from the beginning. Not everyone in Portage fell under Jean's spell. It probably didn't help that Toomer and Chauncey Dupee arrived in an ancient Pierce Arrow, or that the women were often observed smoking in the back of the car. Soon Portage was buzzing with rumors of Communism and – worse – nudity: specifically, skinny-dipping at the swimming hole and climbing trees "like a flock of loony monkeys." [13]

The wedding between Jean Toomer and Margery Latimer took place in Portage in the Episcopal Church, October 30, 1931. Defying tradition, Margery was dressed in a black velvet gown. The honeymooners left for Chicago, where they remained for a month before traveling on to New Mexico by train. They spent some time in Santa Fe and, according to Nancy Loughridge, were invited to Taos by Mabel Dodge Luhan. Both Jean and Margery were actively involved with their work, writing about their experiences at Portage. Jean's account, called *Portage Potential*, was factual; Margery's version was a novel she intended to call *The Ship*. In December, before Christmas, they decided to move on again, this time to California. They spent six weeks in San Diego and then went to Pasadena and finally Carmel, where they settled down for a lengthier period.

Although 1931 had been dominated by their courtship and marriage, it was a year during which both actively pursued their writing. Margery's *Guardian Angel and Other Stories* was accepted for publication toward the end of the year. Much earlier, on April 28, Jean had submitted a novel to Alfred A. Knopf, with the following cover letter:

> Under separate cover I am sending you the manuscript of a novel called, *The Gallonwerps*, for possible publication by your firm.
>
> For this novel, as for subsequent books in a similar vein – I have in mind a series of Gallonwerp novels – I am using an assumed name – Satran Terum.[14]

The Gallonwerps was rejected, which is no surprise given its rather quirky nature. The plot – if one wants to call it that – is one long practical joke centering on social conventions. Characters in the story have names such as Lopelab Firebutt, Lukroar Noop, Rivernice Dripstitch, Hybelia Hokus, and Greekor Suipe. In his foreword to the manuscript, Jean wrote, "There is fun in this book. But it is fun of a strange kind. Unless the reader has a sense of the ridiculous similar to mine, the probability is that he will be more irritated than entertained."[15] I hazard to say that Jean explored a new genre with The Gallonwerps – vexing satire. So caught up was he with his material that he mentioned three planned sequels: Mrs. Banty, Prince Klondike, and Little Gasstar.

Sometime late during the same year, Toomer published his second book, Essentials, after paying $614 for the printing of a thousand copies. The flier-order form, which was printed after the work had already received several reviews, described the book as "A Philosophy of Life in Three Hundred Definitions and Aphorisms."[16] The volume was self-published, and there appears to have been no exact publication date. In their critical study of Jean Toomer, Brian Benson and Mabel Dillard state that Essentials was mentioned in newspaper accounts of the Toomer-Latimer wedding. The title page says "PRIVATE EDITION, CHICAGO, 1931," though the Library of Congress did not record the book until May 26, 1932. The copyright page includes the following statement:

THIS BOOK WAS DESIGNED BY JEAN TOOMER
AND PRINTED AT THE LAKESIDE PRESS, CHICAGO
UNDER THE DIRECTION OF WILLIAM A KITTREDGE[17]

The dedication is "To My Friends in and Near Chicago," and the foreword reads as follows:

This volume is a collection of definitions and sayings bearing on the nature and forms of human existence – some three hundred crystallizations in words of observations and understandings which have arisen in me during a five year period.

For me, the lines contain the gist or heart of the matter; and this is why I call them Essentials. Not the full heart, to be sure; but, I hope, something of it.

With few exceptions I have left each line as it originally formed. I have added no fillers. I have, however, attempted to organize the book so that in addition to having independent meanings the lines might have some measure of meaning in relation to each other.

> The totality conveys accurately though not completely my world-view. To this extent it can be said to express my philosophy of life.[18]

Had *Essentials* been written by anyone else, it would no doubt be completely forgotten. It was largely ignored when it was published. The contents have not been widely reprinted in recent years, as sections of *Cane* have. Virtually all of Toomer's critics ignore the book, as they should. Gorham Munson said of it: "I don't think it's a very good book. Jean didn't have a good aphoristic style. The book is very derivative. It's a re-statement of some of Gurdjieff's ideas in a rather bare, uninteresting way. But Jean valued it a great deal."[19] Coming after *Cane* as the author's second and final volume, *Essentials* gives one the impression of the collapse of Jean Toomer's artistic talent. Brilliance had turned into drivel. The creative genius had been transformed into a two-bit philosopher, a huckster of second-rate ideas.

There are actually 320 aphorisms or sayings in the book, printed in sixty-four groups of five, i.e., five per numbered page. These clustered statements are never poetic, though the material in "Reflections," published in the *Dial* (April 1929), was incorporated into the volume. Unfortunately, the statements are not particularly profound – e.g., "Now and again something does happen."[20] Nor are they always original with Toomer: "Modern man is losing his sense of potentiality as regards himself. Hence he is losing his sense of himself and of reality."[21] Instead, they seem to indicate Toomer's eclectic affinities with other writers and thinkers: Henry David Thoreau ("We have many reformers, few transformers"[22]); Benjamin Franklin's Poor Richard ("Do now what you won't be doing an hour from now"[23]); Walt Whitman ("I am neither male nor female nor in-between. I am of sex, with male differentiations"[24]); even Dale Carnegie ("True initiative is a self-activating force which needs no sanction save that of awakened conscience"[25]).

At times, Toomer's essentials are humorous: "Occidental romance has led to Freud,"[26] and "We have two emblems, namely, the machine-gun and the contraceptive."[27] More often they are simply trite: "We learn the rope of life by untying its knots."[28] They touch on politics, business, and self-improvement, and occasionally on race: "I am of no particular race. I am of the human race, a man at large in the human world, preparing a new race." [29] Apparently, Toomer incorporated them into his lectures, which observers say were quite successful. There is, in fact, little question about his effectiveness as a lecturer.

Why did he publish the book? Partly, I suspect, because of the need for validation. A writer publishes books, and though in the minds of others he does not cease being a writer if those publications stop, in his own mind, one part of him has ceased functioning. Jean Toomer wanted to continue publishing books after *Cane*, but editors were not receptive to what he wrote. *Essentials* was a grasping, a frustrated attempt to express something within him, yet it was also, I think, an admission of failure:

LXII

Perceptions of reality are man's main food.

Each person at least once in his life rises to be a major critic of mankind.

The true critic is a critic of meanings and of values.

True ideas and true values grow strong in proportion as they are affirmed and realized by beings.

The science of life consists in deriving significance from all possibilities. [30]

When he published *Essentials*, Jean must have realized that publishing would become increasingly difficult for him. Though the records are not totally clear, few copies were sold at the asking price of $3; many were given away to friends. Jean had already had a singular moment of glory, and it was now behind him. Chances are that he had realized this for years, since he had clairvoyantly referred to *Cane* (about the time of its publication) as his swan song. All the rest would be grasping for straws. But there was the comfort, at least, of knowing that Margery's career was still before her.

Life in Carmel for the two of them during the early part of 1932 began auspiciously enough. They rented a spacious house (which Margery believed was haunted) overlooking the ocean and quickly made friends with a number of other writers, including Robinson Jeffers and Lincoln Steffans. Jean gave new lectures, and both worked on their writing. Then suddenly, the bliss and the happiness of newly married life (including the delight both shared in the fact that Margery conceived shortly after their wedding) came to an abrupt halt. The Portage Experiment began to haunt them. Nancy Loughridge says that a Hearst reporter read an interview that Jean had granted to the local Carmel newspaper, pieced some information together, and then "added some lurid details of his own to produce an outrageously malevolent story which made headlines from coast to coast."[31]

It was the old question of race, which Toomer had been unsuccessful in burying. Perhaps he even knew that there was no way he could disguise the fact that he had identified himself as a black writer when he was still working on *Cane*, that others had continued to regard him as black even if he himself no longer did. (On the marriage certificate he identified himself as white.) Some continued fear of the old question must certainly have lingered within him because he had written a brief statement concerning the fact a few days before his marriage to Margery the year before:

> There is a new race in America. I am a member of this new race. It is neither white nor black nor in-between. It is the American race, differing as much from white and black as black and white differ from each other. It is possible that there are Negro and Indian bloods in my descent along with English, Spanish, Welsh, Scotch, French, Dutch, and German. This is common in America; and it is from all these strains that the American race is being born. But the old divisions into white, black, brown, red, are outworn in this country. They have had their day. Now is the time of the birth of a new order, a new vision, a new idea of man. I proclaim this new order. My marriage to Margery Latimer is the marriage of two Americans.[32]

In one sense, the journalistic attacks on Toomer were nothing unexpected. He fully understood American racism, having observed it innumerable times throughout his life. If he, specifically, had not been the object of such virulent prejudice, he knew plenty of African Americans who had been. It is impossible to be a black person in America without always being aware of this troublesome duality: of being black and of being American, of belonging to incompatible worlds, to paraphrase W. E. B. DuBois. In periodicals across the country, the proof was repeated dozens of times: America was not for black people. Besides ignoring and exploiting them, it wanted nothing to do with them, as if this second duality was confirmation of the first. Why else had Toomer spent so much of his adulthood trying to prove that the two were not a contradiction in terms? By calling himself an American – a term that became a leitmotif in his existence – he denied his being as either black or white. Instead of being, he accepted nothingness. Worse, here was a man who was perceived of having committed the ultimate offense – marrying a white woman.

Time magazine began its racist account of the Toomer-Latimer marriage, titled "Just Americans," with the following statement: "No Negro can legally marry a white woman in any Southern State. But Wisconsin does not mind, nor California."[33] After referring to Jean's grandfather as "a mulatto carpet-bagger who became Acting Governor of Louisiana,"[34] the article described Toomer's Portage Experiment, stressing that of the eight participants "all [were] white except [Toomer] himself."[35] The article in Henry Luce's magazine was only the tip of the iceberg.

Some of the newspaper accounts of the Portage Experiment had a rabid tone to them. Although the Milwaukee Sentinel's front-page exposé was published under the headline "Elite of Portage Shocked by Tales of Toomer 'Cult,' "[36] it was not the experiment in communal living (referred to as a "love cult") that came under strongest attack but Toomer's assumed blackness. In this newspaper and in many others, Margery Latimer's heritage, which she could trace to Cotton Mather and Anne Bradstreet, was clearly perceived as being threatened, and the threat was miscegenation. One Portage denizen remarked of Toomer, "They get a picture, of course, of a big black fellow like Jack Johnson carrying off an unsuspecting little white girl. And Jean Toomer is a tall, slender man with a finely chiseled face. Looks and acts like a, well, like a Spanish cavalier or something."[37] Of the wedding itself, the Sentinel noted, "Margery, a soft spoken, beautiful young woman, was clad not in white tulle, but in coal black, softly lustrous velvet. Against it her rose-white face gleamed strangely ethereal. Beside her strode the murky, black eyed Othello."[38]

The Milwaukee Sentinel couldn't drop the story. The day after the first article, it ran a follow-up, again beginning on the front page. This time the innuendo included the Chicago phase of Jean's activities. The Portage locals were not alone in being duped by Jean Toomer, the article implied, since hundreds of Gurdjieff disciples in Chicago had been also. Yvonne Dupee is quoted as saying, "I assure you there is nothing substantial to indicate he is of mixed blood. Jean himself has told me that he doesn't know of any Negro ancestors in his family." [39] Dupee further attributes the mix-up to Waldo Frank, who was angry at Toomer for running off with his wife. She could only have learned that story from Toomer himself, whose private history must have undergone severe revision.

Toomer's denials of his blackness reached a crescendo during the time of his marriage to Margery Latimer. Early in 1932, he responded to Nancy Cunard's request for material for her forthcoming anthology *Negro* (1934) by stating, "Though I am interested in and deeply value the Negro, I am not a Negro." [40] Apparently, however, feeling the need for further clarification, he circulated a brief pamphlet called "A Fact and Some Fictions." [41] Much of what it said he had already expressed before in other places, though some of the details he revealed are worth noting. His grandfather, P. B. S. Pinchback, is described as having claimed Negro blood for reasons of political expediency. There is the usual amount of vacillation ("I have neither claimed to have or disclaimed having Negro blood" [42]) typical of his earlier racial statements. The most important passage denies any black heritage: "As for being a Negro, this of course I am not – neither biologically nor socially." [43] Nevertheless, one cannot help concluding that Toomer himself was not able to make up his mind:

> In my view, and indeed in reality, the black race is a branch of the tree of human life, as is the white race a branch of the same tree, as are the yellow, brown and red races branches of this same tree. I am not concerned with any of these branches, as branches, except to do what I can to help to overcome "branch-consciousness," to attain "tree-consciousness." I am, however, vitally concerned with all these branches, and all equally, as integral members of the One Great Tree. I would have each and all work together and come to the realization that all are primarily members of the human race. All are Human Beings. This has been my realization for some twenty-five years. All people are my people. [44]

Life became miserable for the newlyweds. In addition to the articles in the press, the Toomers received a flood of hate mail, including a curious little book called *From Negro to Caucasian*, which was addressed to Margery. The author, Louis Fremont Baldwin, inscribed the book as follows:

To Margery Latimer Toomer
Wife of Him of Childhood Memories
Is this little volume Presented
By The Author,
March 25, 1932.

Published by the Society for the Amalgamation of the Races (New York, Paris, and London), the complete title read as follows: *From Negro to Caucasian, or How the Ethiopian Is Changing His Skin*. The title page includes the following statement:

A concise presentation of the manner in which many Negroes in America who, being very fair in complexion, with hair naturally or artificially free from kink, have abandoned their one-time affiliations with Negroes, including their own relatives, and by mingling at first commercially or industrially, then socially with Caucasians, have ultimately been absorbed by the latter.[45]

How Margery reacted to the pamphlet, we do not know. The booklet, however, was saved and included in the papers sent to Fisk University in 1963.

By June 1932, the scandal had begun to subside. Margery's parents, who had left Portage temporarily at the height of the uproar, had returned home. Perhaps Margery's final word about their marriage was beginning to be heeded: "You do not protest against a person's religion. Why should you judge people by their color? I and hundreds of others have taken my husband for what he is – a brilliant man."[46] Jean and Margery returned to Portage and then continued on to Chicago to await the arrival of their child.

Then the very worst occurred. Margery died from complications of childbirth. It was believed that she had a fear of hospitals, that she refused to leave their place at 69 East Division Street. Nancy Loughridge suggests, however, that a hospital was probably avoided because of the fear of additional publicity about their marriage. The midwife engaged to assist at the delivery walked out before labor began, for reasons that are still not clear. The doctor similarly engaged arrived too late. Thus, Jean and Margery's mother assisted with the birth. Several of Margery's contemporaries believed that she placed too much confidence in her husband. Commenting on the tragedy many years later, Blanche Matthias noted, "She so believed in her husband's power, understanding, and love that she refused to have a doctor. He acted as midwife, so I was told."[47] Her death, on August 16, was attributed to septicemia caused by a lack of sterile surroundings, hemorrhaging, and complications because of a weak heart. The child survived.

It had been a short and tragic courtship and marriage, fraught with tensions at the beginning, plagued by scandal in the middle, and abruptly terminated by a miscalculation that might have been averted. Much of what we know about the marriage is one-sided, limited to Margery's ecstatic effusions of love in the letters she wrote to her friends. Toomer's part in their relationship was more reserved – perhaps even calculating. Certainly this is the conclusion that one draws from a reading of *Portage Potential*, which Jean subtitled *An Adventure in Human Development*.

The person in need of human development, of course, was Margery, whom Jean renamed Marian (also spelled Marion) Kilbourn in order to protect her privacy. In his initial sketch of her in the narrative, Jean wrote,

> Marion Kilbourn was in her early thirties. She had an [sic] fine woman's body, a sensitive fine-featured face, large blue eyes full of light, and a wealth of golden hair. She was an exceptional person. I saw, however, that something was wrong. One thing was obvious. She was wearing trowsers of duck colored blue cut somewhat like a sailor's, and a midy-blouse [sic] of reddish-orange. The colors were not right. They were too cheap for her. They made her seem heavy and reddish. She should have appeared curved and radiant. The trowser-blouse combination was not right. So to speak it destroyed her womanliness. In short, the habit failed to enhance any of her fine qualities, but, on the contrary, it tended to neutralize them and to bring out features which were false for Marion.[48]

Astute observer of clothing that he was, Toomer decided to set himself up as a godlike force and remake Marian's image as well as her world. In order to accomplish this, he states of himself,

> I threw myself vigorously into things and gave liberally of my energies. I was intolerant of inertia, intolerant of sluggish lukewarm states. When I was with the people something had to happen each minute. Things had to move. Experiences had to occur electrically. I was building a world. I was creating a form. It had to be my own.[49]

Thus he created a new Margery. *Portage Potential* might be called *The Re-education and the Wooing of Margery Latimer.* Toomer refers to Margery-Marian as someone who is

> unprotected as a child and I could see many reasons why she had painful and difficult relationships in a world of people, most of whom used buffers and wore masks. Among other things I could see that she had received much hurt, pain, and disappointment. Much of this, for some strange reason, a reason I was interested in finding, had merely clogged her, giving her the weighted, down curving posture I had noted earlier. Why was this? Somewhere in her Marian had plenty of force and sunshine. She was, indeed, an unusually forceful young woman. She had, I was sure, sufficiently good digestive and assimilative powers.[50]

At the beginning of their relationship, Jean worked at breaking down Margery's defenses, her lines of resistance. Of the Portage Experiment, Yvonne Dupee said that Margery was a "particularly difficult pupil. . . . She . . . considered herself unathletic, but Toomer forced her to play tennis, to row and do the Gurdjieff exercises. When she talked about her writing he would be rude to her."[51] That writing, Jean states, Margery-Marian used as a substitute for living: "If she could not meet and have satisfactory relations with people through the instrumentality of her immediate person, she would meet them through her books. She would write them."[52]

Slowly, Margery-Marian was reborn in Jean's image. He interested her in sports: "Before the summer was over what had been her source of torment was her source of pleasure."[53] The remolding of her personality was so complete that it prompted Jean (as the self-conscious narrator, he did not change his name in the account of the experiment) to observe: "Marian presented herself to me, and I had to take her in hand."[54]

Portage Potential — part autobiography, part novel, and part philosophical dialogue — suggests that Margery had a strong masochistic streak to her personality, which Toomer took advantage of by playing the role of the Gurdjieff bully. Still, one cannot help asking if there were other reasons motivating Toomer's eventual proposal of marriage. One critic has concluded that Toomer married Margery Latimer because she had a steady source of income — the royalties from her books. After her death, Jean spent a month editing Margery's letters, intending them for publication. Though they were not published, one might wonder if the project was undertaken out of love for his deceased wife or for commercial exploitation.

Jean and Margery's daughter, named Margery Latimer Toomer, became the ward of Toomer's Chicago friends, Max and Shirley Grove, who were childless. The decision to turn over custody of the child, nicknamed Argie, to the Groves must have been prompted by the bereaved father's fears of inadequacy in raising her, yet it resulted in a great amount of pain on both sides in later years. It may also have been a matter of economics, for Jean's total source of income during these years was derived from his Gurdjieff work. In a letter to Harrison Smith, the publisher, written two months after Margery's death, he remarked, "For the past six years my main means of support has come through lectures which I have given, sometimes as many as seven a week." [55]

During this time, his writing fell apart. He wrote, of course. After *The Gallonwerps*, there was another novel called *Caromb*, which was shortly followed by still another one called *Eight-Day World*. *Caromb* is the more interesting of the two, largely because of what it reveals about Jean's feelings concerning the attacks on his marriage in the press the year before. The characters representing the Toomers are named John and Marian Andrews. *Time* magazine is called *Ourpas*. The conflict — what little there is — centers upon the Andrews' anticipation and response to the *Ourpas* article. When it finally appears, Andrews feels that he has been "fooled, tricked, [and] betrayed" [56] by the reporter who interviewed him.

> Damn everything, he was cursing inwardly. This son-of-a-bitching magazine, it has a nation-wide circulation. It will reach where the newspapers did not. It will drop fresh bombs in all of the places where the storm raged . . . and the whole wild thing is likely to flare up again. Damn fool that I was and am to place any trust or hope in any printed sheet. Here I was believing that *Ourpas* would put a desirable period to the whole affair. [57]

Caromb suffers from the author's talky intrusiveness, a lack of objectivity, as does *Eight-Day World*, Toomer's *Ship of Fools*. Publishers were not interested in

these works or in the various autobiographies Toomer worked on during
the thirties and forties. Reading the manuscripts today, particularly the novels, one can easily understand why they were not published. At the end of
1932, Toomer published a poem called "Brown River, Smile," but once
again it was marred by Gurdjieff's teaching and his own ongoing problem
with race. The poem appeared in the December issue of a little magazine
called *Pagany*, and it probably resulted in no remuneration.

Indebted to Walt Whitman and Toomer's Chicago contemporary Carl
Sandburg, "Brown River, Smile" celebrates the raw material, the energy,
and the dynamic potential of America: "It is a new America, / To be spiri-
tualized by each new American."[58] The Mississippi, "sister of the Ganges,"[59]
is described as the "Main artery of the earth in the western world . . . /
waiting to become / In the spirit of America, a sacred river."[60]

> Whoever lifts the Mississippi
> Lifts himself and all America;
> -Whoever lifts himself
> Makes that great brown river smile,
> The blood of earth and the blood of man
> Course swifter and rejoice when we spiritualize.[61]

With a kind of rough-and-tumble expectation, Toomer states that "We
are waiting for a new God,"[62] because the "old peoples,"[63] "the great European races"[64] – who brought the first wave of nation building – have
become "congested in machinery."[65] Then, in images that are reminiscent
of part 2 of *Cane*, where he describes the lives of displaced black people in
Washington, D.C., Toomer enumerates two sources of stifled potential in
this country: African Americans and Native Americans. The former, he suggests, are now in a state of decline:

> The great African races sent a single wave
> And singing riplets to sorrow in red fields
> Sing a swan song, to break rocks
> And immortalize a hiding water boy.[66]

The poem continues with images that echo T. S. Eliot's "The Waste Land"
and implies that even though the nation is in a state of decline, the power

and the energy are still there, "waiting for a new people."[67] The seed that started the country can be found; nothing – "no clever dealer" or "machine"[68] – can undermine the potential, the people who make up this great country:

> I stand where the two directions intersect,
> At Michigan Avenue and Walton Place.
> Parallel to my countrymen,
> Right-angled to the universe.
> It is a new America,
> To be spiritualized by each new American.[69]

Bits and pieces of "Brown River, Smile" are as fine as Toomer's best poems in *Cane*. What is disappointing is the element of self-parody, though it may not have been intentional. The new America Toomer celebrates had become an obsession in his work and thinking, an idée fixe, territory that other writers had already traversed when it was still in a virginal state.

Ironically, the opposing images of decline and hopeful expectation in "Brown River, Smile" can be applied to Jean Toomer's own life during the time between Margery's death and his second marriage in 1934. There were no publications in 1933, though the year was marked by his affair with Georgia O'Keeffe.

Early in the year, O'Keeffe had been hospitalized for depression. Once she was released, she spent some time in Bermuda with her friend Marjorie Content. Afterward, in the summer, she returned to Lake George where her husband, Alfred Stieglitz, who was nearly seventy, had a studio. Toomer had known the two of them for a number of years and had visited Stieglitz at the lake on several occasions, beginning in 1925. The men respected each other's talents. Toomer would subsequently contribute an essay called "The Hill" to *America and Alfred Stieglitz: A Collective Portrait* (1934), edited by his friends Waldo Frank, Lewis Mumford, and Paul Rosenfeld. The short homage to Stieglitz, containing some of Jean's best writing since *Cane*, linked the man to his work in a manner that Toomer himself had been unable to attain: "Always I feel he is rooted in himself and to the spirit of the place. Not rooted to things; rooted to spirit."[70]

When Jean visited Lake George in December of 1933, Stieglitz was in New York City. Georgia was alone, though part of the time with a female companion. Their brief affair took place before Christmas, and then Toomer returned to Chicago. Georgia wrote him a series of letters afterward, in which she described a feeling of liberation, as if the affair had cured her of her illness. "I seem to have come to life in such a quiet surprising fashion – as tho I am not sick any more,"[71] she told him, though she described, also, her acute loneliness: "I want you – sometimes terribly."[72] Her biographer, Laurie Lisle, notes the curative aspects of their relationship but concludes, "Above all, she comprehended, though sadly and grudgingly at moments, that there was little room in her life for anything other than art – and certainly not the risk of love when she was trying to return to painting again."[73]

By the time that O'Keeffe saw Toomer again – in April 1934 – he had become emotionally involved with her friend Marjorie Content, whom he had met during the interval. Lisle states that Georgia was still interested in Toomer – that she implied in a letter to him that she wished their affair had taken place in the spring instead of the winter – but she bowed out in favor of Marjorie. The two women remained good friends and in June drove to New Mexico together. Jean followed somewhat later. When Marjorie Content and he were married in Taos on September 1, 1934, O'Keeffe was one of the witnesses.

Though the paths of their lives had crossed several times, Marjorie and Jean had not met until their mutual friend, Fred Leighton, brought Jean to her house in New York City in the spring of 1934. Marjorie was familiar with Jean's writing. Her second husband, Harold A. Loeb – made infamous as the character Cohn in Ernest Hemingway's *The Sun Also Rises* – published *Broom*, one of the earliest little magazines to print Jean's work in 1923. Loeb edited the magazine in Rome, and Lola Ridge, his American editor, had her office in the basement of Marjorie's house. When *Cane* was published the same year, Marjorie was a partner in a small bookshop called The Sunwise Turn. Years later she remembered that the copies in the store had quickly sold out.

Jean and Marjorie were both nearly forty when they married. Marjorie was the daughter of a well-known New York stockbroker, whom Gorham Munson has referred to as "a spectacular Wall Street operator. . . . He was really rich, very spectacular."[74] Like Jean's first wife, the second Marjorie was an extremely talented woman. Although an Easterner, she had spent

Marjorie Content, circa 1932. Courtesy of Susan L. Sandberg.

time in the West, working as a photographer for the Bureau of Indian Affairs during John Collier's leadership. Her photographs of Native Americans, mostly Apaches, have a stark, original quality to them reminiscent of the work of Edward S. Curtis. She also had worked as a costume designer in the New York theater, was a talented actress herself, and had been thrice married and divorced — to Michael Carmichael Carr, Harold Loeb (the father of her two teen-aged children, James and Susan), and Leon Fleischman.

On the way back East from New Mexico after their marriage, Jean and Marjorie stopped in Chicago for Toomer's daughter, Argie. As Marjorie explained in an interview in 1974,

So as not to make it too much of a shock for her we drove back East in two cars — Argie sometimes riding with us, sometimes with the Groves — trying to ease the change. They stayed here with us for a while and were very unhappy about giving Argie up. They had never said "no" to her about anything, but I couldn't live that way. So Argie was rather bitter for a while. We became quite good friends later.[75]

Jean and Marjorie would have no children of their own.

During the rest of the fall while they lived in New York City (in Marjorie's place on West 10th Street), they ran a kind of salon. The Munsons were frequent guests, as was Georgia O'Keeffe. They also entertained Udai Shandar, a famous Indian dancer, as well as many of Jean's Gurdjieff friends. For the first time in his life, Jean had enough money to live the kind of life that he wanted – plus the expectation of a great deal more at some later date. And he had friends around him, literally sitting at his feet, listening to his pontifications. But this was not quite enough. What he secretly wanted was to set up another Gurdjieff institute, not in the city but somewhere in the country.

The problem was that Marjorie had no genuine admiration for George Gurdjieff, whom she regarded "suspiciously as a fraud and a swindler."[76] She had already paid off Jean's numerous debts, incurred because of his Gurdjieff activities. Furthermore, Jean had led her to believe that he was no longer interested in such work. Then, late in 1934, Jean discovered the ideal site for his potential institute – a farm outside of Doylestown, Pennsylvania. One cannot help speculating whether the location was chosen, in part, because of Jean's desire to move to what he regarded as a race-free zone. As with his earlier marriage to Margery Latimer, the question of Jean's Negro heritage was mentioned by the press at the time of his marriage to Marjorie Content. What better place to escape such gossip than the Quaker-Amish country in Pennsylvania? Yet, as Sally Fell explained when I posed the question of Jean's acceptance by the Quaker community in Bucks County,

Certainly Bucks County – Philadelphia area – Friends were probably not yet ready for Blacks in their midst in the late 30s and 40s (though in theory, of course, we didn't admit to prejudice of any variety) so it was far easier for Jean to keep people uninformed [about his heritage] – and he must have realized that.[77]

There was also the desire to live in the country. As Marjorie Content Toomer explained in a letter to me,

[Jean] liked to think of himself as farming – His imagination saw one of the buildings (an old grist mill) as a future printing press – but the money for all his dreams came from my father – I was more down to earth – learned to make bread – churn butter when we had cows – Jean was more "mental." We had to have a farmer and his family as we were ignorant – but with the war – prices went up – inflation was with us – and we couldn't keep it up. We [later] sold the farm part (across the road) and kept our original purchase.[78]

The move to the country was gradual: "weekends – then protracted weekends,"[79] until finally they were there permanently, by the spring of 1935.

On the land, which they called Mill House, Jean hoped to find happiness, not as a farmer but as a kind of country gentleman. The buildings needed restoration, so physical labor was a necessity – enough that additional hands would be required. In interviews given after Jean's death, Marjorie listed the visitors who joined them for limited or more extended periods during the next few years to assist them: Chauncey Dupee and his wife, Margery Latimer's mother, Franklin Davenport, and an unlimited flow of weekend guests. Often there would be twelve or more people sitting around the dinner table or in a circle around Jean himself. Marjorie told John Griffin, "I think Jean was, in a vague sort of way, trying to turn the farm into a Gurdjeffian-type household, and I didn't realize what was going on."[80]

Franklin Davenport, one of the guests who came to stay, had this to say about the activities at Mill House:

There was plenty to be done. A good house to make into a place of peace, rest, beauty and a place of energy, work, creation; an old wrecked stone shell, once a water-powered grist mill, to be re-created; a semi-abandoned farm to be brought back to life. Wood and stone and metal, weather and earth, animals and people. We worked with our hands, our bodies, our minds and our hearts. We got gloriously tired and mightily energized. And for all of us what we did next, for about five years, was to build Mill House.[81]

It was a good place to be during the Depression and a good life, living off the land. Jean could have his friends with him and at the same time retain a certain anonymity, since few people in Doylestown knew about his earlier

Mill House, Doylestown, Pennsylvania. Courtesy of Susan L. Sandberg.

years as a black writer. When John Griffin asked Marjorie if Jean had been affected by the Depression, she replied, "Hardly. I acted as his secretary and I kept all the records, the checkbooks and so-on." [82]

As if to acknowledge that debt and to pay homage to its source, Jean wrote Marjorie's father, Harry Content, just before Christmas 1936, explaining the purpose of his work:

> I sometimes feel that what we really have [here], is a sort of school of a new kind, a school in which people learn how to live, not by reading textbooks with a lot of stuff in them which you soon forget, but by seeing living examples, by seeing and learning from real experience and actual life. And when I give rein to my imagination, I sometimes see this place developing through the years into a school or college of a kind never before existing in America. How do you think this sounds?

The letter continues – assuaging his father-in-law's fears of his money being wasted – by suggesting that the "school" might eventually be called the

Content College of the Art of Life; "The name of Content [should] figure prominently because it is owing to you that it is possible." [83]

What more could Jean want? He had found a life free from economic worry as well as, it would seem, a devoted wife. Marjorie gave up her photography and apparently gave her life over to him totally: "I made myself completely subservient. . . . I had no personality of my own." [84] There may be another story there, since one year Marjorie returned to the West and lived on a reservation while Jean remained at Mill House.

During the second half of the thirties, the renovations at Mill House progressed with the aid of Jean's numerous friends. The comments about Jean during this time differ greatly, depending upon the observer. Franklin Davenport described him as the center of the activity,

> a gentle man with force. He was the prime mover; from him came the ideas, principles, purposes, insights, understandings. He saw the connections, he put it all together. More than anyone I have ever known Jean knew what and where Man was, what he could become. As Jean moved we were ready to move. He opened doors we were ready to walk through, he rang bells we were ready to harmonize with. . . . He was the catalyst and primary source in a reciprocal relationship. . . .
>
> The goal was development, the development of Man, specifically the development of each man and woman. The dynamics were affirmation and denial, the basic Yea and Nay of human life. [85]

On the other hand, Gorham Munson (who did not live at Mill House but drove down from New York City for innumerable weekends) often found these visits awkward: "Jean as the host at Doylestown was often embarrassing to me. Jean imitated Gurdjieff, and these imitations were embarrassing." [86] Munson wondered what some of Jean's new friends thought about his mannerisms: "Jean would actually go into broken English too, you know, and he would tear loaves of bread apart. He would use bad, vulgar language at times. He would try to shock people by going into these seemingly rambling discourses. He was all imitative of Gurdjieff and bad, bad, bad imitation." [87] Munson implies that Marjorie at times was fed up with the whole enterprise and that Jean was often intolerable, yet she stuck it out until it was too late to change or to leave, and there was little she could do about it.

Jean's writing continued throughout these years, of course, but often the publications were in new areas and the form was altered from fiction and poetry to essays. There was a series of Mill House pamphlets: "Living Is Developing: Psychologic Series No. 1" (1936), "Work-Ideas 1: Psychologic Series No. 2" (1937), and "Roads, People, and Principles" (1939). His last major creative work — "The Blue Meridian," a long narrative poem which was published in The New American Caravan in 1936 — also appeared during this time, though he had begun it years earlier, while married to Margery Latimer.

"The Blue Meridian" can be regarded as a kind of summation of Jean Toomer's intellectual and artistic lives, a condensation of all the ideas that flowed through his work after Cane. It is, furthermore, a greatly extended version of "Brown River, Smile," lengthened nearly sevenfold from 125 lines to almost 900. All of the ideas of the earlier poem are present in "The Blue Meridian": the dynamic force of America embodied in her people's potential, the need for abandoning the old racial distinctions, the hope for a new America born from the chaos of the present time.

In this end to his creative publications, Toomer celebrates American men and women as a moving force, constantly growing and changing. Yet it is not humanity alone that will spiritualize the new America, but people working the land:

> There is land — I have worked it with my hands,
> There are materials for every known and unknown need for man
> There are houses built and more to build,
> Calling to the creator in each person,
> There are men, there are women,
> There are all the coming generations,
> There is Life.[88]

The emphasis upon becoming and upon the future — "Growth towards the universal Human Being"[89] — requires a dynamic change in attitudes toward race and religion: "An unbroken chain of ancestors, / Ourselves linked with all who ever lived, / Joined with all future generations"[90] can only emerge from a blending of the new — "Growth is by admixture from less to more, / Preserving the great granary intact"[91] — in a world in which "All belong now,"[92] a melting pot, blending all bodies to one flesh, to all humankind.

> The brotherhood of man cannot be realized
> By stunted men, nor by those dismembered,
> Closed in themselves, cut off from the mainstream
> And therefore frustrated and bent to live in hate.[93]

In the past, people living by racial distinctions were like islands, each protected by insular beliefs. The new America – haven of the "Universal Man" –

> Must outgrow clan and class, color,
> Nationalism, creed, all the fetishes
> Of the arrested and dismembered,
> And find a larger truth in larger hearts.[94]

Toomer identifies himself as a former islander, linked to those narrow perspectives of the past, and calls for an unlocking of the races: "Open this pod by outgrowing it, / Free men from this prison and this shrinkage,"[95] from prejudices and preferences. "Eliminate these – / I am, we are, simply of the human race"[96] – was this a cryptic admission that he once had thought of himself as black but now regarded himself as something else?

One new thread of the poem (and its precursor "Brown River, Smile") is the repeated stress on religion: "We are waiting for a new God, / For revelation in our day, / For growth towards faceless Deity."[97] The old religions, Toomer tells us, "tight parodies of God's intention,"[98] have withdrawn into the distance and died. Yet there is hope because

> There is a Root Religion
> And we are of it, whose force transforms,
> Whose way progressively reveals
> The shining terraces of one reality.
>
> Uncase, unpod whatever blocks, until
> Having realized pure consciousness of being,
> Knowing that we are beings
> Co-existing with others in an inhabited universe,

We will be free to use rightly with reason
Our own and other human functions –
Free men, whole men, men connected
With one another and with Deity.[99]

"The Blue Meridian," professing the need for religious values in a nonsecular way, indicates the change in Toomer's spiritual quest which would be merged with the Society of Friends, the Quaker religion, at the beginning of the following decade.

As a summation of the ideas that had been percolating in Jean Toomer's mind all of his adult life, "The Blue Meridian" is a fascinating poem, full of raw energy like the new America he celebrates within the poem itself: a praise song, glorifying America's potential, free of racial and religious distinctions and prejudices. Yet, for the reader not enamored of the writer himself, the poem at times appears tedious, pedantic, and diffuse. There is too much repetition (sometimes extending to entire stanzas), too much indebtedness to Walt Whitman, Carl Sandburg, T. S. Eliot, Hart Crane, and even Robinson Jeffers. Too often, the poem reads as a hodgepodge of borrowed ideas and images from Toomer's contemporaries (compare, for example, the stanza beginning "The eagle, you should know, America,"[100] with Jeffers's "Hurt Hawks"). Even the title image appears to be replaced by the brown river, the Mississippi, as if Toomer himself wasn't quite certain what the poem was finally to say.

Rudolph P. Byrd notes a curious oddity about "The Blue Meridian." Although Byrd describes the poem as Toomer's "most successful effort to combine the theories of the Gurdjieff system,"[101] he regards the work as a complete rejection of Toomer's vision of blackness in *Cane*. American history, in "The Blue Meridian," is described as follows:

The old peoples –
The great European races sent wave after wave
That washed the forests, the earth's rich loam,
Grew towns with the seeds of giant cities,
Made roads, laid silver rails,
Sang of their swift achievement
And perished, displaced by machines,

Smothered by a world too huge for little men
Too empty for life to breathe in.
They say that near the end
It was a chaos of crying men and hard women,
A city of goddamn and Jehovah
Baptized in finance
Without benefit of saints,
Of dear defectives
Winnowing their likenesses from synthetic rock
Sold for national organizations of undertakers.[102]

As Byrd notes, the poet wrongly attributes to "the descendants of European immigrants the full credit for the creation of the modern, industrial state."[103] The African American contribution, although briefly mentioned, is of minor significance. Worse, the poem does not acknowledge that the black man's origins in the New World are the result of slavery. Instead, the poem whitewashes American history. One cannot help wondering if "The Blue Meridian" – usually regarded as Jean Toomer's last important creative work – is still another example of the author's attempt to disavow his blackness, to obliterate any meaningful reference to race. Combined with the question of Gurdjieff's influence on his writing, this excision poses an interesting question. Did Gurdjieff's philosophy ruin Toomer's work in the same way that the Existentialists marred the later works by Richard Wright?

Still, "The Blue Meridian" tells us much about Toomer's failure as a writer of creative literature. Clearly, he had difficulty with longer works, whether poetry or prose. Short poems, short stories were his forte. The long poem and the novel appeared to be beyond his grasp, presenting some fundamental problem with structure he was never able to master. It is not difficult to understand why many readers of *Cane* fail to see the whole but regard the work as a series of images, of vignettes, of scenes only arbitrarily connected. Jean Toomer was a writer who saw beauty and terror in the close and the near, in moments rather than in months and years. Although he had reached the stage when he could no longer see the forest for the trees, he understood that no tree could be planted without starting with a seed from another.

He didn't give up – either as a writer or as a seeker. His personality, he often said, was constantly changing, reforming. His quest for the answer to life continued unabated for many more years. If publishers were uninterested in his novels, he would try another literary form. In 1938, he worked on an autobiography titled *Exile into Being*, and others would follow. Early in the same year, both Jean and Marjorie experienced a temporary period of elation after discovering that Marjorie was pregnant. Jean wrote to his father-in-law, describing the excitement: "it has brought a new joy to Marjorie, a new and deeper state of being, and it [has] joined us together as never before." [104] The child, however, was subsequently lost to a miscarriage.

By the end of the decade, there would be tensions in the marriage, no doubt exacerbated by an unarticulated sense of failure. Toomer hadn't been successful, really, in establishing a permanent commune at Mill House, though he had a coterie of devoted followers. Furthermore, there were complications with his health. He suffered from the discomfort of abdominal pains, though they, too, had been with him sporadically much of his adult life. He had problems with one eye, which at times necessitated the wearing of a patch. And he had begun drinking.

In the late thirties, as part of Jean's ongoing and incomplete spiritual quest, he shifted his interest to Eastern mysticism. Recalling the period, Marjorie said, "He thought that maybe through the [Indian] mystics he could find the answers." [105] He proposed a trip to India. Marjorie was against it; she feared the imminent outbreak of another war: "I had visions of . . . being in India, with a man who was sick, none of us knowing the language, and with a little six-year-old girl to care for. . . . But he said he'd just die if he didn't go – his last hope." [106]

Jean wrote his father-in-law, Harry Content in June 1939, explaining the reasoning behind the proposed trip:

> Were a person able to see and to understand my life from the inside as I do, he would know that I have come to a critical pass and am faced with these alternatives; either I go on and up and become virtually a new man fully able to do the work in the world for which I have been preparing all these years, or else I sink back into a condition which I do not want to imagine. . . .
>
> I can only say that I am deeply convinced that going to India is the right

thing to do, the only thing to do, and that in a years [sic] time other people will be able to realize that it was the right thing, because they will see in me and in her a new vitality, a new energy, a health, a new happiness, an enrichment, and a much greater capacity to be of real service to other human beings.

Jean was fully aware that his very existence was based upon his father-in-law's largesse. The letter alluded to this fact and then continued, "It is because of you that I am able to do the right thing now. It is because of you that other people will be able to benefit by what we do. In helping us financially and morally in believing in us, you are again helping Marjorie and myself, and . . . you are also helping all those who in one way will benefit by our lives and work." [107]

Harry Content didn't regard the trip in quite the same way. He acknowledged that Jean had written him a "beautiful letter," attempting to make his case for the trip. But he continued, "I do not understand the meaning of it all, because, I do not see where the benefits are coming in to you and your family; which, are of course, paramount in my mind." Further explaining his position, he stated that he could not ever remember "refusing Marjorie anything," [108] but, given the Depression, his financial position was not as secure as it had been. Nevertheless − probably having already given in to the request − he asked how long the trip would last. Jean responded a few days later, with a final plea, this time bringing up the matter of unrest in the world: "In India, strange as it may seem, I will obtain what I need so as to be able to successfully cope with these adverse conditions and come out on top, come out on top in practical ways as well as other ways." [109]

Jean won. Harry supplied the funds and the family left in June 1939. They visited Ceylon and then India, where Jean gave lectures at several colleges. They traveled up the eastern coast, into the mountains, and on to Darjeeling, where Jean visited a number of holy men. When asked if Jean discovered what he was looking for, Marjorie replied, "Not really. No, he didn't find anything." [110] Her response may have been colored by her own sense of frustration: "We went here, we went there. Usually I stayed in our lodgings with Argie, but sometimes, if I went, Jean would start talking with somebody inside while we were left sitting out in that God-awful heat. And he would stay as long as it pleased him. It became a very unhappy experience."[111]

The trip lasted nine months – until March 1940 – much of it spent in travel to and from India. They had stopped in England on the way, but the return was by way of the Pacific Ocean, on a Japanese ship. At one point on the return voyage, it appeared as if the ship had been ordered to turn around, and Marjorie feared they would be taken to Japan and incarcerated, but finally the voyage continued. They docked in San Francisco and were met by Franklin Davenport. After spending time in New Mexico on the way home, they returned to Doylestown, where Jean arrived "more or less the same as when he left"[112] – without the answers he had sought.

An entry in his journal of the trip, written in Bombay, reflects his growing sense of failure at the time:

> It took India to bring me to my senses. . . . What hopes I went there with! India did not destroy them; she simply did not fulfill them. She proved to me – or, more exactly, she helped me demonstrate to myself – that I had been a poor physician to myself. True, I had prescribed precisely that trip. Only in this large writing had I been right. In details, so it proved, I had been so wrong as to invite disaster. [113]

Describing himself as an idealist, he confessed that his dreams had been smashed in India. Two weeks later, he added a postscript: "It has cost five thousand dollars to complete my disillusionment."[114]

In spite of the failure, and perhaps as necessary therapy, once again Jean undertook a fictive treatment of the event, beginning a novel called The Angel Begori. The often comic narrative begins: "'Good Lord!' said Begori; and the Lord, not having praised [sic] for some time, bent down and elevated Begori to the status of an angel. This in brief is how Begori became an angel."[115] Besides Begori, there are other characters with equally strange names: Bob Gee, Mr. J. Osgood Mattermash, Miss D'Water, Mr. Foxbite, Duffel Brus. The narrative ostensibly records the preparations for a journey to India – purchasing tickets, packing bags, and so on. The narrator's explanation for the voyage includes the following statement: "I was going to see the world while there was still a world to see. . . . I said I had wanted to experience India ever since my first acquaintance with ancient religions and epic literature, and now was my chance."[116] Yet the voyage hardly begins, since the

192-page narrative abruptly concludes – after lengthy discussions about the possibility of spiritual development and the incipient threat of Nazism – as the passengers wait for the ship's departure after boarding. Such was the final spin on Jean's passage to India.

Much of the remaining portion of Toomer's life – twenty-seven additional years – can be described only as unhappy. Toomer was an intelligent man; he could no longer fool himself. He had not discovered answers to the spiritual questions he had sought after for much of his life, and he must have known that it was not very likely that he would. He was forty-five years old, and his economic viability was totally dependent upon his wife, who had lost a good bit of patience with him. Above all, it appears that he was afraid of being abandoned and thrown to the wolves. Certainly, he was aware of the patterns of Marjorie's marriages. What would happen to him if she asked for a divorce?

She didn't, as far as I know, because he found a solution to prevent the ultimate catastrophe in his life. After the trip to India, he assumed a new role, a fresh personality. He became a full-time patient, bonding his relationship to Marjorie like a sick child to a parent. As Susan Loeb Sandberg, Marjorie's daughter, responded when I asked her why her mother didn't divorce Jean, "You don't leave an ill person." [117] A mutual friend noted that there may have been another reason for Marjorie's considering, but in fact rejecting, the idea of a divorce – Jean's continued womanizing. When I asked Sally Fell (who knew Jean and Marjorie because of her activities with the Friends) about Jean's extramarital affairs during these years, she replied,

[Marjorie] didn't want to give up on the marriage. She was very conscious of her own marital failures and determined to stick with it this time around. Also, I know Jean assured her "it will never happen again," and she may have wanted to believe him. I recall her telling of the embarrassment when N.Y. newspapers headlined her marriage to a Negro. This kind of thing may have added glue to her determination to weather any – and all – storms in the marriage. Also, let's face the fact that Marjorie was living by then in a very different world than the N.Y. liberal art world she'd grown accustomed to in the earlier years. People in the Quaker circles here seldom, if ever, divorced. [118]

In June 1940, because of continued abdominal complications, Jean had a "blocked" kidney removed, though the operation did not alleviate the pain in the area. Marjorie described the situation:

[H]e became very much occupied with his health. He began to behave oddly like a patient. He was very sick. He experienced contractions around his solar plexis [sic] and as a result he couldn't sit up in a chair. He would either lie down or stand. He contributed to his poor physical condition, because he would lie in a bent-over position and remain in that position for hours. His lungs weren't diseased, but his chest – he didn't have any chest. It was deeply sunken from the bending over. Then arthritis set in.[119]

He embarked upon another solution. In August of the same year – two months after the kidney operation – Jean and Marjorie requested membership in the Religious Society of Friends, whose meetings he had attended since 1935. Cynthia Kerman and Richard Eldridge, in their biography of Jean's life, cite the letter that he wrote to the Buckingham Meeting:

For some time we have shared the fundamental faith of Friends, and now we are moved to join hands with you as members of the Society. We would also like our young daughter, Margery, to become a member. Please consider this brief note as a request for membership for the three of us.[120]

This request is illuminated by a passage from an undated essay written later in his life, titled "Why I Joined the Society of Friends": "My seeking and searching began anew after coming in contact with the Society, as my eyes opened to the Quaker treasure. The richness and meaning of the Friends' religion was not handed to me. You have to dig for it. I am still digging."[121] Marjorie, who had been brought up without any religious affiliation, was also taken by the faith, which apparently gave Jean a new hold on life. Kerman and Eldridge identify his involvement with the Friends as lasting approximately fifteen years, with the "peak concentration of his activities"[122] at about 1947.

It is difficult to regard Toomer's involvement with the Friends or his continual quest for wholeness and unity throughout the rest of his life as a "struggle toward sainthood,"[123] as Kerman and Eldridge do. My difficulty with such an interpretation lies in Jean's failure as a creative artist, after the publication of *Cane*. Rather, I consider Jean's involvement with the Friends and his subsequent attempts to resolve the problems of his illnesses as a series of moves designed to jump-start his flagging literary career. Nevertheless, many who knew him in those years, held high regard for his sincerity. Nor did it take long for him to become a leader.

Sally Fell, who was a teenager at the time, remembered Toomer as a "dynamic leader," who played a prominent role in Philadelphia Friends circles, especially in Bucks County: "[H]e was the principal Friend who spoke effectively and consistently about 'centering down' and living in the presence of God. This message was familiar to me, not only because of my Quaker upbringing, but also because my own father was heavily into that same thinking. Dad was influenced by Rufus Jones and Thomas Kelly – each of these well-known Friends and authors[–]and Jean's articulation of these same themes made a major impression." [124]

With other teenagers from the George School, Sally Fell spent weekends at the Toomer home, or at retreats elsewhere, in order to hear what Jean "had to say and to discuss these subjects." Jean "would not have been sought out as a 'speaker' on so many occasions" [125] were he not similarly regarded by others. The titles of his lectures during the early part of the decade disclose the extent of his commitment to his faith: "Man's Part, and God's," "The Importance of Belief," "What Is Religion?" and "Creative Understanding, an Essential of Inward Reconstruction."

A printed postcard announcement which has survived from the era (with no year or cancellation) delineates the scope of Jean's service for the Doylestown Friends:

THE PERSISTENT CHALLENGE

THE DOYLESTOWN FRIENDS MEETING (East Oakland Avenue near Pine) is privileged to present the following lecture series by N. Jean Toomer, well known poet and lecturer:

May 15	"Good and Evil in the Individual"
May 22	"When Two or More Are Together"
May 29	"Can Suffering Be Creative?"
June 5	"Is There a Limit to Man's Growth?"

As a lecturer, he became much in demand among the Quakers, seemingly having found the perfect venue for his genuine talents as a speaker. Perhaps even more important, his faith gave him a new focus for his writing. Beginning with "The Other Invasion," published in the *Friends Intelligencer* in July 1944, all of the rest of the publications in his lifetime would be related to the Religious Society of Friends. They included more than a dozen essays with titles like "The Presence of Love," "Today May We Do It," and "Love and Worship," and they culminated in 1949 when Jean delivered the prestigious William Penn lecture at Philadelphia – probably the most important honor the Friends could bestow upon him. His title for his lecture: "The Flavor of Man."

The published text for "The Flavor of Man" is twenty-nine pages long. Jean's delivery lasted two hours, a bit much for some of his listeners. Still, in many ways, the lecture is at the center, at the core, of Jean's relationship with the Friends. The flavor of man, he said, "the primary ingredient of man's substance is love, love of God, love of man, and through love, a sense of unity with all creation." [126] The problem in the world is that many people are without this flavor. Our work is often without love or creativity; "most of us live in spiritual scarcity." [127] Yet "Man is renewable," [128] and even wasted lives can be restored. Just as the portly Negress in the "Box Seat" section of *Cane* had strong roots that spread all the way to the South, "A man's roots must go down into what is deeper than himself. . . . Then he will be connected with the great heart and power of life." [129]

Toomer continues by speaking of the links between God and man: "Evil is evil only because it separates our consciousness from God." [130] Then, after using the example of George Fox, he turns directly to his listeners, the Young Friends, as the hope for the future, in spite of troubled times in the world. Transformation is possible because of God's design that we rise higher and because of enabling experiences, which begin as little gifts but expand to greater ones. As for individuals and their relationship with others, "We can be men only if we help each other. God alone can lift man into His order, and impart the substance of the divine." [131]

Lawrence Miller, Jr., recalled the William Penn lecture, mentioning particularly the affection that the Young Friends had for Jean. The speakers for the William Penn lectures were always chosen by Young Friends themselves. Miller remembered Jean, also, as a person of "insight and inspiration." Jean and Marjorie quickly welcomed the Millers into their circle of friends when they moved to Doylestown in 1948; yet — as is true of many people who knew Toomer during his Quaker years — Miller did not remember Jean as having any particular influence on his own thinking. Rather, Jean was "an explorer" of ideas, perhaps because of his own personal needs. His searching was typical of many "convinced" Friends.[132]

One curious incident about Jean's affiliation with the Friends related directly to the question of his race. In the 1940s, the Quakers did not extend their friendship to black people. Argie's schoolmates taunted her with the statement that her father was a Negro. The school she attended was restricted to whites. An inquiry was held, and Jean apparently convinced the membership that there were no grounds for identifying him as a black person. Frank K. Bjornsgaard remembered the racial issue in a slightly different context. When he and his wife moved to Bucks County, his uncle, who already lived there, "told us, with a straight face, that Mrs. Toomer was married to an East Indian. When I protested, my uncle told me, 'The farmers around here are very narrow. If they thought Mrs. Toomer, white, was married to a Negro, they would make life miserable for both of them. An East Indian they can live with so, remember, Jean Toomer is East Indian.'"[133]

I have talked to people who heard Toomer lecture for the Friends during the 1940s — he spoke at times on university campuses — and they were surprised to learn he was known as a black writer. That he was respected by the Friends is abundantly clear. That he had discovered some way to mesh the faith with Gurdjieff — of that there is little doubt. That he was a man still searching for answers to the questions of life — of that, too, there is no question. Whatever the case may be, the admiration from the Friends has continued. It prompted George Edward Otto to write of Jean several years after his death,

He was not a man of great physical strength or lively pursuits but one whose fundamental approach to life was essentially mystical. Hence he often spoke profoundly to the condition of contemporary man drawing upon springs of wisdom whose sources lie beyond the restrictions of this three dimensional world. Exploring deeply in this realm of the soul from which all truth derives, he was frequently able to point us toward the universal harmony where lies that Peace which passes understanding.[134]

The slowness of his speech, one of his acquaintances told me, contributed to the impression of the profundity of his statements. One wonders whether, for the Friends, Jean was less an original thinker than a compelling speaker.

There may have been other reasons for Jean's increasing solidarity with the Friends during the forties besides the failure of his kidney operation. His father-in-law, Harry Content, died in 1941, and – in Gorham Munson's opinion – Toomer's dreams for setting up "an institute of which he would be the master,"[135] à la Gurdjieff, collapsed. The old man had remarried shortly before his death, and the expected estate didn't fall to Marjorie and Jean but to his new wife.

> Jean and Marjorie . . . received comparatively little. I don't mean to say that they were cut off, because they had this place at Doylestown, and had a very comfortable income. They had some bequests that were useless to them. Jean told me, for example, the old man had left them a Rolls Royce, and they had no use for a Rolls Royce. In general, he did cut them off, cut them down, and so it was now clear that Jean would never have the resources, the considerable resources, needed to set up an institute. That was a gone dream.[136]

Then, too, there was Edgar Cayce's failure to alleviate Jean's continued abdominal pains. In his letter to Cayce's Association for Research and Enlightenment, dated April 19, 1943, Jean described the failure of the kidney operation, his difficulty with physical work that would not tire a boy, and his continued insomnia. "I feel that there is some kind of irregularity in the condition or the functioning of the vital organs in or around the small intestines."[137] He requested that Edgar Cayce help him in resolving the matter.

Cayce, of course, agreed. Why wouldn't he? Jean traveled to Virginia Beach for a psychic reading, given by the celebrated man on June 22, 1943. Cayce recommended a purification of the patient's alimentary canal, to be accomplished by California syrup of figs, followed by violet ray treatments along both sides of the spinal column, as well as an altered diet and vitamins. When Toomer wrote of his progress early in September, he thought he was much improved. The complications, however, returned the following year.

His misery – real or imaginary – continued throughout the remainder of the decade and well into the 1950s. Munson said that because of his "terrible insomnia,"[138] Jean indulged in a great amount of drinking: "He used to keep a bottle of Scotch beside his bed, drink to relax, fall asleep, but it didn't work too well."[139] He began to rely on sleeping pills. His arthritis became worse. At the end of this period, there were suicide attempts. Increasingly, he became bedridden. He became almost impossible to live with. When John Griffin asked Marjorie if Jean was a kind and considerate person, she answered, "No."[140] Eventually, he even turned away from the Quakers. "After a while, Jean refused to go," Marjorie said. "He quit that too. He said he couldn't sit up."[141]

He became a shadow of his former self. This man, who in his late teens and early twenties had been so proud of his athletic abilities, watched in horror as his body slowly turned against him, apparently unaware of the relationship between mental and physical discomfort. In pictures of him taken during the last decade of his life, he looks like a cadaver, an emaciated beanpole. Susan Sandberg described his appearance at this time: "He became very stooped over, looked about 90 years old, because, I think, of his internal difficulties. He never fastened the top of his fly because it was too uncomfortable for him."[142] His talkative streak also disappeared. Frank Bjornsgaard described visits to the Toomer household ten years before Jean's death: "When we visited Marjorie, if Jean was in evidence, it was as a silent figure lying on a chaise in a corner of the living room. Beyond a polite greeting when we arrived and a word when we left, Jean ignored us and our conversation."[143] For a man who had lived by words, the silence can only have been a bitter muzzling.

There were further complications. Again, in the words of Susan Sandberg: "He had an eye that would get blood red for no reason that anyone could figure out, usually just when he really wanted to get to work writing. It seemed to be a symptom of the internal disorders but did not clear up. . . . Then as he went down hill he mixed alcohol with the many medications he was taking."[144] Finally, "he just didn't eat anything."[145] There were times when he had trouble walking, and he feared that he might fall and hurt himself. Still, until his stays in the nursing home became more permanent, about 1955, he continued to ponder the questions of life, as well as the questions of his immediate discomfort – final attempts to control his fate.

In 1949, Toomer had decided to undergo Jungian psychoanalysis, the result of reading and studying the works of Carl Jung for several years. In a letter to me, Marjorie commented, "He used to make fun of psychoanalysis so that I was much surprised when he went to one for a short time (a Jungian)."[146] Jean's analyst, Paula Elkisch, was located in nearby Germantown. With the beginning of his analysis, June 10, Jean began recording his dreams, a process he continued rather faithfully, until August 21, 1950.

The dozens and dozens of dreams that Toomer recorded during that fourteen-month period present a fascinating mosaic of his hidden life, especially as they illuminate unresolved problems, some of them going back to his childhood. Sex, authority, and race are prevalent issues, with a fair amount of overlapping among these three primary areas. There are repeated images of Jean standing and waiting on platforms and on streets in strange towns, as well as discovering himself in unfamiliar rooms, where empty space appears to be the predominant configuration. Trains, ships, and streetcars appear in many of the sequences, as well as repeated references to water and to swimming or standing near bodies of water. A significant number of the dreams embody journeys of one kind or another. There are also a number of incidents in which Jean is standing and lecturing in front of groups of unidentifiable people in theaters. In one such incident, he noted, "it was not clear that I was [the] speaker."[147]

The dreams skip back and forth, between the present and the past. Jean's Uncle Bismark appears, as does Gurdjieff, predominantly, along with Marjorie and many other figures from his life: a boyhood friend, several early girlfriends and subsequent lovers, men and women who worked with him in various Gurdjieff groups. Still early in the process of attempting to decode their meaning, Jean wrote to his friend Douglas Steere and remarked about their significance as "some unresolved matters in the unconscious that have been there since my early boyhood."[148]

In the matter of sexuality, it is no doubt significant that the first dream Jean recorded (June 10, 1949) fell into this category: "I am in a place – not a room, no scenery – with four or five attractive, smiling young ladies, age about 20. It is quite pleasant for me to be with them, and they seem quite happy about it too." Shortly, he discovers that he is prostrate, lying on his back with one of the women straddling him, her back toward his face. They are naked; the other women have disappeared. He continues, "Gathered around her hips and vital organ is a covering. There is no contact between my organ and hers, and in me no active desire for such, nor in her. Yet she is sitting right across my organ." The dream concludes with a statement: "I just lay [sic] there, in a pleasant mood." [149]

Related dreams, often describing interrupted sexual activities, imply a voyeuristic or nonactive participation on Toomer's part. In one dream, which occurs in a public place, Toomer is naked and undergoing a medical examination given by a physician who is a female. [150] In another, Jean writes, "I have become somewhat involved with a woman on the fat side. She has a thick, stout body. I occasionally place my hand on her back in a way to suggest that I may be getting into a sex relationship that I would just as soon keep out of." [151] Several dreams also suggest veiled homosexual tendencies or at least fascination with observing homosexual acts. In one instance, Jean describes himself as a naval officer, urinating with another officer in the officers' toilet. Looking at himself and the other man, he discovers that instead of a penis, each has a slit, a vagina between his legs. Yet the dream concludes with one further glance at himself: "I now see a penis there. It is a boy's penis." [152]

Jean's sexuality, if ambivalent, can only be described as voracious. Besides his famous lovers, with whom he had numerous liaisons, there were dozens of other women with whom he had brief, casual encounters. These incidents did not cease with his marriage to Marjorie Content but continued throughout the rest of his life. Even during the years when he was a patient in the nursing home, the dalliances persisted. Before that, there were innumerable humiliating incidents for Marjorie. One affair persisted because of its convenience: the woman was married and lived around the corner from the Toomers. On at least one occasion, Marjorie had to pick Jean up at another woman's house in the middle of the night, after the woman called her and said, "Come and get him." One of Jean's acolytes in the Young Friends recalls his attempt to seduce her when she was fifteen years old. Fortunately, the setting — a public beach with others around — prohibited the completion of the act. Even Jean's stepdaughter feared that she might become a victim of his persistent sexual prowling.

The question of authority in Jean's dreams is most explicitly described within the framework of his ambiguous relationship with Gurdjieff. Yet other issues of his own authority and expertise are also questioned. For example, in one incident recorded in the dream journal, an unknown assailant accuses Jean of borrowing his ideas, his intellectual thoughts, from others —

and not being the original thinker he considered himself to be.[153] To be sure, the doubting of his originality is tied up with Jean's ambiguous relationship with Gurdjieff. In one of the earliest reported dreams (July 8, 1949), Jean discovers himself in a room, dancing in front of a group of men, while making "feminine gestures." Abruptly, he finds himself stretched out on a bed. A "strong man" stands to his left, who shortly calls to another, whom Jean recognizes as "Mr. G[urdjieff], the most powerful man I have ever known." The first man speaks to Gurdjieff: "Do you know what Toomer has been doing? He danced a dance for some men, an effeminate dance." Both men come closer and then pin him down. Suddenly, "Mr. G. is astride me, upon me. I struggle to break free. Their grip is too powerful." Gurdjieff holds a sharp instrument resembling an arrowhead. Just as Toomer fears his ear may be cut, he wakes up, "still struggling."[154] At least on some level, Jean's sexuality was tethered to the relationship he had with Gurdjieff (the menacing father who wants to castrate him?)

There are intervening dreams where Gurdjieff appears less threatening, less powerful. Then on November 17 — shortly after Jean learned that Gurdjieff had died — he recorded a more significant change vis-à-vis his mentor's assumed authority. In this sequence, Jean and another man are seated close to one another when Gurdjieff comes over to them and tells the other man to leave. The man does as he is asked, and then Gurdjieff similarly orders Toomer to leave. Jean writes, "I say I will not. I intend to stay just where I am and not to take orders from Gurdjieff. I want to show him, and perhaps myself too, now that I am put to the test, that I am no longer under his influence."[155] In the altercation that results, the two of them physically struggle. Jean finally wins the battle by socking Gurdjieff on the jaw, just as the dream concludes.

Half a year later, Jean appeared to lay the conflict with his mentor to rest. The dream describes Gurdjieff on his deathbed, lying on his back with many people surrounding him. Gurdjieff suddenly stands up. Then, "I go up to him. I feel sorrow. I put my head on his broad chest and I begin a deep sobbing. I had thought I was going to express sorrow for him. Once I begin sobbing I realize that the sorrow is for myself."[156] The dream concludes as Jean shakes Gurdjieff's hand and congratulates him on the publication of *Beelzebub's Tales to His Grandson.*

Toomer's dreams reveal that of all the problems confronting him during his lifetime, the question of his racial origins was the most troublesome, an irritant he could not wish away. He could call himself an American and thus refuse to become embroiled in racial labeling. He could think of himself as a white man and live as a white person, but others often thought of him as something else, and this he certainly must have known most of his life. It is impossible to analyze the implications of the two dreams he recorded on September 11, 1949, without concluding that Jean Toomer knew he was passing.

The first of these racially significant dreams (described in eight pages, the longest of any of those recorded) begins familiarly as a journey. Jean is traveling through the South on a train, aware of the Jim Crow section and the area reserved for whites. Standing in the segregated section, he looks around the compartment and realizes that before he entered the train, he decided to travel in the Negro section. But now that he is in the car, he hesitates, feeling that he does not belong in the Jim Crow section: "I do not feel I belong in it. I would be out of place. Among black people my relative whiteness and other different qualities would make me as conspicuous as would my relative darkness and different qualities among white people." Thus, he implies that he does not fit, does not belong anywhere – perhaps the saddest commentary of anyone who renounces his or her heritage.

The dream continues with the fear that if the people in the white section knew his true identity, they would definitely think he does not belong with them. If he sits in the white section, he commits himself to being white; if he sits in the black section, he commits himself to being black. Again, he repeats the statement that he belongs in neither. As the train begins to move, he walks through the cars searching for the conductor, since he is unable to make a commitment to either racial group. When he locates him, it is clear by the way he is treated that the conductor considers him white; Other people on the train also treat him as white: "This having happened, I can't turn around and be colored." The decision has been made for him. "I am committed to white," he says, "I [will] travel the trip as white, accepting it, but partly uneasy about it."

The next thing he recalls is being on the street of a Southern city. He has "the same mixed feelings about being neither outright white nor outright Negro, about being both white and colored, belonging in the white world, yet not belonging in it, belonging in the colored world, yet not belonging in it," in short, the classic fears of the person who is passing of being found out. His discomfort continues as he dines in a white restaurant; yet upon finishing the meal (bread), he slips out the back door instead of the front one, in order not to be conspicuous.

Outside, in a courtyard surrounded by tall buildings, he feels trapped, yet subsequently finds an exit through someone's yard. When a dog suddenly lunges at him, his fear dramatically increases. A white man appears, looks at him, and instructs the dog to be calm. The dog continues to lunge at him, without actually biting him, but prompting Toomer to question whether the dog "has been trained to know Negroes and go after them. He knows something about me that the white man does not know." You can fool a white man easily, but never a dog. The dog changes, becoming more friendly. Then "the man and I take up with each other," becoming friends. They go along together as white men, "meeting people, going places. And again in this southern city, as on the train, I find myself committed to being white, one thing leading to another."

Toomer asks the white man when they will "have some more of that good bread," symbolically bringing up the question of his final acceptance. The white man responds it will be in a day or so. Yet that breaking of bread together is not the final scene in his dream; something much more ominous is: "Seated on a bench directly in front of me there is a solid row of white sailors, rough-necks." They do not see him or acknowledge his existence — in part because they are looking straight ahead, as if in a theater, implying again his perceived isolation from the white world. The description concludes, "Though they are neither my friends nor even my casual companions, I have a feeling that I have gotten myself into the company of, or into the same gathering as, a bunch of pretty crude fellows." [157] This conclusion would appear to suggest regret on Toomer's side, that his life in the white world has been a continual struggle for acceptance among people he isn't even certain are worthy of his presence.

This conclusion can also be drawn from the second dream, recorded the same day, in which he describes himself as "a weakly inferior colored boy, who feels sick and hurt by my problem, but accepts it without outward protest or fight. When someone looks down on me I sort of fade away, cringe, shrink, and smile at him like a sick calf." Furthermore, "That colored boy has never changed much or grown up," implying always a child's status in an adult world (or a black person's status in the white world).

He is much as he was at the age of ten or eleven. Another boy has grown up. He has pushed the colored boy into the background, so as to get him out of sight, get him out of life. But there are certain outward circumstances that bring the colored boy to the fore. Sometimes he cannot be kept back. Then the discrepancy between the two becomes marked, the conflict active, acute.[158]

Whether Toomer was able to confront the unresolved questions of his life after a year of analysis is open to dispute. The next move toward discovering his true identity, however, would suggest that he was not, for by early the following year, in 1951, he was off on still another search, a final cure for his problems. This time he turned to Dianetics and subsequently took a course at the L. Ron Hubbard Foundation. When he wrote to Parker Morgan at the Hubbard Foundation describing his interest in the movement, however, his letter placed the request into another context – that of understanding his much earlier out-of-body experience:

I became *another being*, which was, strangely, my being, my self. I became my inner being, and the inner being and the other person were united as one whole being. One of the things I want to find out is whether or not what I have experienced is the same reality referred to by those in dianetics as basic personality. If so, you will find me making a place for dianetics in the thoughts and lives of those whose orientation is chiefly religious. For dianetics, then, will be seen as an *effective* means of removing the curtain between the inner being and the outer person, and uniting the two as one whole being – which is precisely one of the large things that religion ought to be doing, but often doesn't do.

There were other relevant reasons for the move, including the desire to train himself to be an auditor and thus derive monetary rewards from his efforts. His disciples, he suggested, would be his "Young Friends or Quakers – people mostly between 20 and 30 years of age, who are open, keen, searching."[159]

Gorham Munson was disappointed by Jean's latest move: "Jean was too knowing a man, too far advanced in self-understanding and in the Gurdjieff works to turn aside and study dianoetics [sic]." [160] Speculating on his friend's motivations, he concluded that Jean had reached the end of his tether. Almost everything around him had fallen apart:

> My only explanation is that Jean was just nowhere. The Gurdjieff groups had died away, such groups as he had. He had been with the Society of Friends, and somehow or other that career was closing out or didn't offer advancement to him. He had no means of income. He was married to a rich woman, but he wasn't earning a cent himself in any way. Dianoetics, apparently, offered a chance for him to set up as a practitioner of psychological counseling and to be paid for it, and perhaps almost in desperation to turn to dianoetics as a profession . . . which he would follow. [161]

Given this observation by his friend, Jean's attempted suicides in the mid-fifties are not difficult to understand. What was there to live for? He was a broken man, increasingly in and out of nursing homes, obsessed with the problems of his physical breakdown. Whether these problems were organic or imaginary no longer mattered. Marjorie said that after about 1955, "He really did *almost* nothing," [162] and he had no purpose in life. The same year, she placed him in a nursing home in Doylestown, assuming that this would be where he would remain. The strain of his presence at home had become too great. As is true of patients in various kinds of institutions, Jean created a new world for himself at the Garden Court Nursing Home. He knew all the other patients and made his life there. Except for brief visits to Mill House, the nursing home became his final domicile.

Jean Toomer died March 30, 1967, after spending almost all of the final years of his life at Garden Court. In an interview for the Fisk Oral History Collection in 1970, Marjorie Toomer stated that Jean "was definitely unhappy for many years before he died." [163] She added, "He was happy to get out of life, I'm sure." [164] In the words of his stepdaughter, Susan Sandberg, "I don't think he was ever really happy." [165] Despite the many years and the numerous paths of his quest, Jean hadn't found what he was searching for. Like those arcs in *Cane* – which when superimposed upon each other fail to make a complete circle – his life was fragmented and incomplete.

Childhood

I was an American, neither white nor black, rejecting these divisions, accepting all people as people. Having intimately known splendid and worthless of both groups, I could say and know, "Human beings are human beings." I liked or disliked them, associated or kept away from them, valued or scorned them, not on racial or color grounds, but on an individual person-to-person basis. If others had race prejudice, that was their affair as long as it did not manifest itself against me.
— Jean Toomer, "Outline of an Autobiography," n.d.

Night fell, while Helga Crane in the rushing swiftness of a roaring elevated train sat numb. It was as if all the bogies and goblins that had beset her unloved, unloving, and unhappy childhood had come to life with tenfold power to hurt and frighten. For the wound was deeper in that her long freedom from their presence had rendered her the more vulnerable. Worst of all was the fact that under the stinging hurt she understood and sympathized with Mrs. Nilssen's point of view, as always she had been able to understand her mother's, her stepfather's, and his children's points of view. She saw herself for an obscene sore in all their lives, at all costs to be hidden. She understood, even while she resented. It would have been easier if she had not.
— Nella Larsen, *Quicksand*, 1929

Childhood. Adolescence. Families. Parents and children and the relationship between the two. Role models. Awareness of one's environment, of one's similarities and differences from others. All the usual clichés.

And yet still the inescapable years of formation. Adults are what children were, what they observed and understood — what they misunderstood, hated, and loathed. What they endured.

For Jean Toomer, the details are known: a lonely, isolated childhood in his grandparents' household, fatherless and almost motherless, a household slowly falling into decay — perfect fodder, one would assume, for the later novelist. For Nella Larsen, the details are a matter of speculation: the darker child, rejected, if not abandoned; a lifetime of separation — childhood lesions so deep they never heal.

The writer, of course, overcomes these obstacles. From chaos, order emerges. The artist is born at the moment his work liberates him from his past — or so we like to believe. She becomes a better person and in the process of continuous creation liberates others — her readers — from their own tortured pasts. Art survives and makes life bearable, or so we believe from a theoretical perspective.

So much for theory.

Toomer

Colorful images of dashing men dominate the early pages of Jean Toomer's autobiographical re-creations of his youth. When he was a child playing one day in Rock Creek Park, Theodore Roosevelt picked him up and took him for a ride on his horse. Of his grandfather, Pinckney Benton Stuart Pinchback, Jean remarked, "I saw him as a dashing commanding figure, the center of an unknown but exciting world. He created an atmosphere which thrilled me." [1] Of his own father, Nathan Toomer, he wrote, "People looked up. They felt his strange power and attractiveness." [2]

Rock Creek Park, where Toomer played as a child, was not so far from the brick house his grandfather had built at 1422 Bacon Street. As he first remembered the street (later renamed Harvard), it was "little more than a short dirt road made regular by curbstones." [3] When it rained, the road became a path of liquified mud. The families in the nearby households were middle or upper class white people. Toomer was especially fond of the trees in the neighborhood: "When spring came, and blossom time, these trees released into the waiting world a riot of color and fragrance. The children of Bacon Street knew beauty."[4]

P. B. S. Pinchback had moved to Washington, D.C., in 1890, after a flamboyant political career that had begun in earnest in 1862. In that year during the Civil War, Pinchback – to the surprise of many of his acquaintances – had declared himself a Negro and thereby been able to qualify for a commission "as commanding officer of Company A, Second Regiment, Louisiana Native Guards (Corps d'Afrique)."[5] It was an opportunistic move, to be sure, yet it determined most of Pinchback's subsequent political life. After the war was over, according to his grandson,

> His rise was rapid. He became Collector of the Port of New Orleans. He became state senator. He edited a newspaper and wrote for it. He became known as a sure-fire stump speaker and political orator. A state commission sent him on an official trip to Paris. He attended national conventions of the Republican party. He became governor of Louisiana – the key-man of Louisiana politics. He was sent to the Senate at Washington, but his seat was contested, and, after a long and hard battle, he lost it.[6]

An anecdote from Toomer's autobiography about the railroad race with Governor Warmouth demonstrates his grandfather's adventurous life:

> Pinchback was lieutenant-governor. Both of them were in New York at a banquet. Pinchback had an act he wished to put over; and he could do this if he could return to Louisiana before and without Warmouth, for then he would be acting-governor. When the banquet was at its height, Pinchback slipped out and boarded a train for New Orleans. At some little town down south this side of Louisiana he was called from the train to receive a telegraph message in the station. Once he was in the room the door was shut and bolted – and there he was kept prisoner until Warmouth's special arrived. Warmouth, missing him, and suspecting his design, had telegraphed ahead to have him detained. Having arrived on the spot he had Pinchback released and told him that he was glad they had caught him just there. Otherwise, Pinchback would not have been among the living. Warmouth had sent orders that he was not to enter Louisiana alive.[7]

One wonders why his grandson never used him as a subject for his fiction. Pinchback's career reads as if it were the creation of a writer like William Faulkner. His governorship of Louisiana lasted a mere forty-three days during 1872. Besides his probable fraudulent political activities (he was considered to be fabulously wealthy), he once attempted to murder his brother. In 1888, he embarked on a legal career, shortly before moving to Washington. In his book, *Black Reconstruction in America*, W. E. B. DuBois wrote of Pinchback's appearance, "To all intents and purposes, he was an educated, well-to-do, congenial white man, with but a few drops of Negro blood, which he did not stoop to deny, as so many of his fellow whites did."[8] He lived as a white man and used his blackness – if that is what it really was – for political maneuvering. By the time of his grandson's birth, when his political days were over, Pinchback was frequently mistaken for Andrew Carnegie – a misunderstanding he was known to accommodate.

In Washington, where he had taken his fortune and his family, Pinchback lived a gentlemanly life of leisure, hanging out with his political cronies and playing the horses. His marriage to Nina Emily Hethorn, of New Orleans, in 1860 had resulted in four children: Pinckney, Jr., Bismark, Walter, and Nina. The adult lives of these children, Jean tells us, were troubled. Only Pinckney, Jr., was comfortably established, as a pharmacist in Philadelphia. In spite of his medical degree, Bismark failed in the profession and spent much of his time at the Bacon Street house. Walter also appeared slated to mediocrity in spite of, or possibly because of, his government job. And then there was Nina, Jean's mother.

The problem was that P. B. S. found it difficult to let go, to relinquish his hold over his children. This was true of his relationship with his sons but even more painfully true of the one with his daughter, born in 1868. Jean described his mother as

Neither beautiful nor pretty, there was something about her that made people sit up and take notice. Her motions were quick and lithe and she was very much her gay sparkling self at a ball. She had an olive complexion and lovely dark eyes that could be haughty, were sometimes pensive, but most often were twinkling with fun. In later life a hurt expression, an injured, baffled, somewhat hardened and defensive look took the place of the laughing loveliness.[9]

Toomer delineates his mother's many talents: "she wrote occasional poetry, played the piano, sang, danced marvelously." [10] Innumerable suitors
had failed to gain Pinchback's approval, which was always unquestionably
required. When no suitable husbands were forthcoming during Nina's mar-
riageable years, P. B. S. responded to the disappointment by continuing to
treat her as a little girl, as a child. Finally, when she was twenty-six, Nathan
Toomer came along. He was twice her age. Jean wrote of him many years
later:

> A flare for living invested his substantial physique with a romantic
> glamour. There was dignity in the man, a certain richness and largeness,
> and charm. He had, in fact, quite a presence. And he had a way with
> people.
>
> His clothes, worn carelessly, were carefully selected, in good taste, and
> of the finest materials. He liked silks. His bearing was a mixture of slouch
> and poise. His manner was by turns off-hand and lordly, suggesting that
> he was accustomed to giving commands and having his own way. He
> lived well when things went well. At such times he was a pretty fair
> person to be with. [11]

In time Nathan Toomer would be referred to as a man of mystery, but in
1894, his appearance and his general demeanor were enough to make Nina
hope that her single days were finally at an end. The courtship was brief.
Pinchback objected in part because there were aspects of Toomer's life
which didn't seem to jell. Was he really the gentleman planter he professed
to be? Could he adequately provide for Nina? The child of their union says
that "the force of life over-ruled." [12] Nina argued with her father that he
never released his hold on his children, that he never let them go. Her ar-
gument was forceful enough that Pinchback gave in, and the two were married at the Fifteenth Street Presbyterian Church, March 29, 1894. The
groom had been twice previously married.

Nathan bought Nina a house on 12th Street, paid cash for it, and made
the deed in her name, yet by the time their only child was born
(December 26), he had vanished back into the South from where he had
come: "To all appearances, Toomer had disappeared from the face of the
earth." [13] Somewhat later, when Nina was unable to make ends meet, she
moved with her child back to her father's house on Bacon Street. As he grew

up, Jean quickly learned that his father's name was never to be mentioned in his grandfather's household. The interpretation that continued as a part of family lore was that Nathan Toomer had married Nina Pinchback expecting to benefit from her father's wealth. When that money failed to materialize, he abandoned her. Thus, Nina returned to her role as the dutiful child, though by then with a child of her own. Although Jean would grow up believing that he saw his father once in his life – when he was still a child and his mother was visiting a friend – his grandfather quickly became his father. It was the surrogate who had the major influence upon the child; from his biological father, Jean received only his name, Nathan Eugene Toomer, Jr.

Jean confessed that as a child he was fascinated by his grandfather, by the man himself and the world around him. He delighted in going downtown with the old man and having lunch with P. B. S.'s political cronies. A special relationship developed between them, though it was also complicated by the way P. B. S. acted toward Jean's mother: "He treated her as if she were still a girl in her teens."[14] It was as if her marriage to Jean's father had never occurred: "She was still his only daughter and he kept an eagle eye on her."[15] When suitors returned to Nina's life, Pinchback determined who was suitable and who was not. After all, hadn't he warned her once and been proven correct in his analysis of human character? Jean's conflicting emotions often led him to side with his grandfather instead of his mother, yet his jealousy of her suitors was only natural.

As an adult reflecting upon the strange state of affairs in Pinchback's household, Toomer realized that his mother had had an extremely difficult time. Pinchback was very hard on her, and "she resented his tyranny."[16] Though she concealed many of her problems from her young son, not everything could be hidden away. There were times when she was ill, when "grandmother and the whole house seemed nervous."[17] The child worried about the doctors coming to and going from the house. The abdominal pains from which she suffered were, apparently, considered to be psychosomatic. In the midst of Nina's illnesses, young Toomer, then a child in public school, discovered an affinity with his Uncle Bismark, who suffered his own problems with the patriarch.

Exact years and dates in Toomer's autobiographies are often vague, though his relationship with Bismark reached fruition sometime after Jean himself became interested in books. Initially, Bismark read to him "myths and fables, folk tales, romances and adventures. . . . He had a decided bent for story telling, and . . . now and again wrote short stories."[18] Bismark in time became for Jean another of the several surrogate father-teacher figures that so influenced his life. (In the classroom Jean was mostly interested in cutting up, in having fun.) Their relationship was mutually satisfying. His early years Jean described as divided between "school on the one side and Bismark on the other."[19]

There were also childhood friends and companions, suggesting that the early confusions of Jean's life were limited to the confines of the Pinchback household. When he was a little older, Toomer grew accustomed to spending increasing periods of time by himself: "the conditions in my household favored my being let alone."[20] For the earlier years, however, he had both his mother and his Uncle Bismark. The description that he gives of his youthful days tells us that he was physically active. He says he was a good fighter. He liked to roller skate, ride a bicycle, and play baseball. He sounds like the typical American boy. Reflecting upon the early years of his life — the period until he was about ten – he states,

I grew up in a comparatively free and open world, subject to but few of the rigid conventions and fixed ideas which contract the human psyche and commit people to narrow lives ruled by narrow preferences and prejudices. Neither by my family nor by Bacon Street was I deliberately conditioned to hold family, class, political, racial, regional, or religious preconceptions and antagonisms.[21]

During his tenth summer, in 1905, his situation was suddenly threatened. Both his grandparents and his mother went away, and Jean was left with his Uncle Walter, since Bismark had recently married. During the day when Walter was at work, Jean stayed with neighbors. At night, Walter and Jean returned to the empty Bacon Street house. Jean felt he had been abandoned by his mother, as he had similarly felt earlier about his father. Worse, when summer was over and the household was expected to return to normal, his mother seemed remarkably changed. She was no longer intimidated by her father.

In the fall, when Jean was in the fourth grade, his mother asked him if he would like to have a new father: "I made a face and tried to forget it."[22] He liked things as they were. What could he do to perpetuate the status quo? Suddenly, he became ill. A bad cold developed into fever, and he was forced to stay home from school. As his condition worsened, the physical manifestations of the assumed threat to his relationship with his mother centered in his abdomen, his stomach — the same site as Nina's earlier illnesses. His condition deteriorated so badly before Christmas that it was feared he would die.

After two doctors were unsuccessful, a German doctor nursed him back to good health. In his autobiography, Toomer states that he owed his life to the man. From the vantage point of adulthood, he astutely recognized the situation as "basically psychological" . . . "a protest against what I sensed she [mother] was about to do":[23]

> My illness had been the climax of the long train of my experiences with mother, experiences which started in that very first year when I was bathed in the pain and struggle and suffering caused by father's going away and the divorce and her return to the Bacon Street house, which continued and increased as I grew up and loved her and resisted her loving anyone else. The wonder is, I suppose, that the psychic pain had not made me sick more often.[24]

When the inevitable came about — his mother's remarriage — his reaction was much more contained: "My illness had been a means of securing through sickness what I unconsciously feared I would not be able to secure in any other way; namely, the complete concerned attention of my mother."[25] He appears to have undergone a personality change. He was no longer active physically with his streetmates but withdrawn and reflective, "thrown on my own and alone."[26] When his mother said she was going away again, the news did not upset him. He became closer to his grandmother. (The same year of Nina's remarriage, 1906, Nathan Toomer died in Augusta, Georgia.)

Little is known about Nina Pinchback Toomer's marriage to her second husband, a man named Combes, except that it was short-lived. The house on Bacon Street was sold, and Nina took her parents and her son along with her to New York. Pinchback's fortunes had taken a rather abrupt turn for the worse, apparently because of his playing the ponies. Ironically, P. B. S. was now dependent upon his children. The years from 1906 to 1909 were spent in Brooklyn and New Rochelle, with Nina's second husband, a man Jean despised. By the time his mother died after an appendectomy, June 9, 1909, Jean had become thoroughly embittered about her as well. He had never accepted the altered situation. Years later, Toomer analyzed the conflict between his mother and stepfather: "Mother and stepfather were not a match. They were not matched. They did not correspond. . . . Mother was tall and slender; stepfather was short and pudgy. She ascended. He spread out. She glided. He waddled. Never can a glide and a waddle correspond or be harmonized."[27]

With his grandparents, Jean returned to Washington, D.C. They moved in with Bismark and his wife, who lived on Florida Avenue. There was one marked change. It was the first time in Jean's life that he lived in a predominantly black neighborhood: "an aristocracy – such as never existed before and perhaps never will exist again in America – midway between the white and Negro worlds."[28] Though the information is contradictory, he appears to have attended a Negro school while associating primarily with his earlier white friends.

The schooling, however, he regarded positively. Almost immediately, he became more active socially. In eighth grade, he had a leading role in The Merchant of Venice. He did so well in his academic subjects that he graduated from the middle school with honors. Then M Street High School: new friends, parties, dances, girls. P. B. S. took a job, a political appointment, in New York, though his wife, who was increasingly infirm, remained with Bismark. In tenth grade, Jean became interested in physics. In eleventh, after moving in with Walter, Jean had the responsibility of taking care of his grandmother. After school, he sold copies of the Saturday Evening Post and earned enough money to purchase a motorcycle. Fearing that he was being engulfed in sexual fantasies and guilty about masturbation, he sought release in physical exercises: muscle building, wrestling, and weight lifting.

During Jean's senior year in high school (1913–1914), several crises occurred. His grandfather returned to Washington and rented an apartment on U Street, a place that Jean considered his "home for the next several years."²⁹ The move is referred to in his autobiography as "the decline into almost poverty of our family."³⁰ Jean sustained an injury in athletics which kept him at home with his grandparents for a month in the last part of his school year. For a time, he worked at the Howard Theatre. Throughout the year, he became increasingly concerned with the question of his racial identity. How was he going to live the rest of his life – as white or as black?

The question had been of repressed concern since 1909, when his mother died and Toomer had returned to Washington and begun living among black people. Until that time, he was aware that his grandfather moved freely in both the black and the white worlds, yet the question was subsequently left in abeyance. In *Outline of an Autobiography*, Toomer describes the 1909 incident when he asked his grandfather about his ancestry:

> During the only talk I ever had with my grandfather about his ancestry and early life, at one point he left the room and returned with a photograph. I took it from him and looked at it intensely. I knew it was a picture of his mother (Eliza Stewart). I had reached the point where I had to know, as far as anyone did know, exactly what bloods were in me. Quite a bit hinged, it seemed, on the bloods in this mother of my grandfather.
>
> "What do you say?" he said finally. "Your guess is as good as anyone's. It was rumored that she had some Negro and Indian bloods. She believed she did, but she did not know. . . . If she had known them sometime in her early life she had forgotten who her mother and father were. Whatever admixture of bloods there was, it had first taken place two or more generations before her time."³¹

The legitimacy of Jean Toomer's blackness thus begins with his great-grandmother, Eliza Stewart. John Griffin describes her as "a fifteen-year-old slave girl"³² in William Pinchback's possession. When he was forty-two, William Pinchback, who had a white wife (possibly no longer living), began a liaison with Eliza, resulting in the birth of his son, P. B. S. Eliza was white in appearance, but, because of the laws at the time, classified as a slave. In "On Being an American," Jean wrote of her,

> Pinchback's mother possibly had some dark blood. I have seen a photograph of her but from it I could not say precisely what dark blood. It might have been Negro or Indian or Spanish or Moorish or some other.

The photograph shows a woman of olive complexion with straight black hair and high cheek bones, with a general cast of features that would not be particularly noticed one way or the other unless you were looking for something.[33]

The question of appearance is central here. Eliza's son, P. B. S., also did not appear to be dark, but white. In 1860, when he married Nina Emily Hethorne, who was of French and English descent, the dark blood was further thinned. Mulling over the racial issue as an adult (and writing about it in *Outline of an Autobiography*), Toomer argues – lamely, it seems to me – that his grandfather was a voluntary Negro because he enjoyed doing things with a certain dash and flair. He was a contrarian, who claimed to be a Negro out of a "passion for the dramatic."[34] Thus, "by his own desire he became known and, publically at any rate, accepted as a Negro. Even when his political career was over he continued to state contrary to fact that he was of African descent."[35]

It is difficult to believe that anyone living during P. B. S.'s time would voluntarily subject himself to the stigma that race always designated. Politics, however, might be defined as the art of opportunism. Perhaps even stranger is Toomer's suggestion that his grandfather claimed to be a Negro out of "the desire to improve the lot of the Negro in America."[36] There is the obvious contradiction with his appearance and public acceptance. When Jean Toomer was a child, living in his grandfather's house on Bacon Street, P. B. S. did not live as a Negro. Nor did he live among black people until 1909, when economic necessity so dictated.

For P. B. S.'s grandson, the same situation obviously applies. By the time he had reached his senior year in high school and was attempting to decide what to do with his life, he could say of his earlier life, "Fourteen years of my life I had lived in the white group, four years I had lived in the colored group."[37] Numerous contradictions about his blackness exist, befuddling both Toomer and his critics. A passage from the "Incredible Journey" mentions his mother's "olive complexion."[38] In still another autobiographical reference to her, he states, "My mother was dark."[39] On her marriage certificate to Nathan Toomer, Nina is listed as "colored" (as is Nathan). Yet Jean negated all of these facts. However we choose to interpret these contradictions, the crisis during Jean Toomer's senior year in high school was quickly resolved by his decision to escape the colored world within which he had most recently moved for the safety of another environment.

He concluded that Washington, D.C., was no longer satisfactory for him and decided to attend the University of Wisconsin and study agriculture.

> And it was then, for the first time, that I formed and formulated my views as to my racial composition and position. Going to Wisconsin, I would again be entering a white world; and, though I personally had experienced no prejudice or exclusion either from the whites or the colored people, I had seen enough to know that America viewed life as if it were divided into white and black. Having lived with colored people for the past five years, at Wisconsin the question might come up. What was I?[40]

The question did not come up, at least in the way he anticipated. That is not to say, however, that Toomer did not fear much of the time during his Wisconsin stay that he would be found out. In an odd way, he lived his life as if he were passing. The "adjustment, for the first week or two, was the most difficult one I had to make. Part of the difficulty was directly due to my anticipation of what could happen if I was called upon to put my racial position to the test."[41] But that never quite happened. If one of his professors thought he was a Hindu and a student thought he was a Native American, most people assumed he was white. After *Cane* was published nearly a decade later, one of his roommates at Wisconsin was quite surprised to discover that the author was identified as "Negro."

In his autobiographical reports of the period, Toomer claims to have arrived at Madison in June 1914 in time for the summer session. The Office of the Registrar, however, asserts that he began his studies in the spring 1914 semester. Whichever one it was, he quickly entered into the spirit of college life, giving himself fully to social rather than academic concerns. He ran for class president and lost. Although a professor in the English department interested him in writing, Jean noted of the period, "I was interested less in literature than in having a good time, talking, athletics, drinking beer and raising hell in the tradition of American college life."[42]

By Christmas, the University of Wisconsin no longer interested him. This may have been due in part to Phyllis Terrell, with whom he claimed to have fallen in love during the vacation. More likely, however, it was some fundamental aspect of his personality. All his subsequent life, until he married Marjorie Content in 1934, he would flit from place to place, from idea to idea. He was, in fact, more of a starter than a completer. During the next few years, particularly, he would move from school to school, change his degree plans almost as many times, and never complete his baccalaureate.

Toomer states that after Christmas he returned to Madison in order to take his midyear exams – no doubt to please his grandfather, who was paying the bills. Soon, however, he returned to Washington, where he spent much of the spring and summer with Phyllis Terrell. He states that he "loved her very much,"[43] and also expresses his attitude toward women in general: "In fine, though I may love many [women], one after another, I am usually faithful to the one at the time."[44] The "Avey" section of *Cane* contains a description of the girl he says he was in love with while a student at Madison, noting "her downright laziness. Sloppy indolence. There was no excuse for a healthy girl taking life so easy. Hell! she was no better than a cow. I was certain that she was a cow when I felt an udder in a Wisconsin stock-judging class. Among those energetic Swedes, or whatever they are, I decided to forget her."[45] The remark is perhaps more revealing of his attitude toward a phase of his life than toward any specific woman.

He wandered. In the fall of the same year, he made a second attempt at studying agriculture, this time at the Massachusetts College of Agriculture at Amherst. Red-tape problems with his Wisconsin transcript, however, quickly terminated his studies. He went to New York, where he stayed until his money ran out and he was forced to return to Washington. Thus began a pattern of activity that would last for several years: school, disappointment or changed expectations, return to his grandparents' apartment (and money). The tension with his grandfather became particularly acute. Toomer was forced to rely upon Pinchback's beneficence at a time when the family fortunes were in shambles. P. B. S., who had high expectations for the grandson he loved, was repeatedly disappointed by Jean's educational failures.

Early in 1916, Toomer made a third attempt at higher education – this time at the American College of Physical Training in Chicago, where he says that he developed into a respectable gymnast:

I was having quite a marvelous time. I had become good friends with Harry Karstens. Sometimes I'd spend week-ends at his home in Wheaton. He and I were the only "acceptable" men at the college. Most of the other fellows knew little or nothing about the graces of life. The place was full of girls. We had our pick. Every Saturday and many times during the week we'd go dancing in cabarets.[46]

The "Bona and Paul" section of *Cane* grew out of his Chicago experiences. It is not only one of the most autobiographical passages in the novel but also a microcosmic distillation of Toomer's clear decision to repudiate Eliza Stewart's dark blood. Bona is attracted to Paul because of his darkness, for that aspect of his life he has already renounced. As she thinks, "He is a nigger. . . . But dont all the dorm girls say so? And dont you, when you are sane, say so. That's why I love [him]."[47] Ironically, Toomer suggests that Paul has atavistic thoughts he cannot repress. When he looks out of the window in his room, he envisions

a pine-matted hillock in Georgia. He sees the slanting roofs of gray un-painted cabins tinted lavender. A Negress chants a lullaby beneath the mate-eyes of a southern planter. Her breasts are ample for the suckling of a song. She weans it, and sends it, curiously weaving, among lush melodies of cane and corn.[48]

If Paul vacillates at all about accepting his blackness, that hesitation is limited to a few brief moments at the segregated cabaret. Though he feels "apart from the people around him"[49] (presumably including Bona, as well as Art and his date), he quickly remembers "the pain which they [white people] had unconsciously caused. Suddenly he knew that people saw, not attractiveness in his dark skin, but difference."[50] Why should Paul-Toomer identify with a race of people who have known so much pain? In the eyes of white people, dark skin was not beauty but antithesis. Paul denies his blackness and loses Bona. Just as P. B. S. Pinchback identified with black people for opportunistic reasons, Paul-Toomer decides to sever that identification for similar reasons. One man's opportunity is another man's failure.

After the semester at the American College of Physical Training, followed by the summer at Harry Karstens's home in Wheaton, Illinois, Jean decided to broaden his education. He enrolled for classes at the University of Chicago, though he continued at the American College. At the University of Chicago he discovered socialism: "this was the first time I'd ever seriously thought about society at all."[51] More important, perhaps, was his feeling that the interest in socialism made him begin thinking, for the first time in his life. There was a mini-crisis with religion (he had been christened a Catholic when still a child). And then, in the fashion of so many people who lose their faith, Jean became a proselytizer of his newly discovered ideas, not only socialism, but evolution, society, and women. He began delivering lectures at the American College, talking, as he says, "on everything under the sun."[52]

His lecture "The Intelligence of Women" got him into trouble. His ideas, he says, were borrowed from Herbert Spencer. He reports, "I offended the women. The Dean of Women got mad at me. The attendance dwindled and before long I stopped."[53] At the same time, he had become quite involved with a young woman named Eleanor Davis. There was little to do but return to Washington. Yet another pattern had clearly begun, prompted in part, one can assume, by his recent reading. Women – during much of his subsequent life he treated them as if they were disposable objects.

It was back to Washington again, though not for very long. In the summer of 1917, he went to New York City and enrolled in courses in sociology and history at New York University and at City College. He moved into the Psi U house. Again his interests appeared to be more social than academic:

> I played tennis, and danced. To the fellows I was a marvel. They could not understand how I could be so excellent in my studies, carry on courses at two places, and still have time and energy for all the other things. In truth, I was a dynamo that summer. My strength and zest seemed to be inexhaustible.[54]

The summer, however, was marred by an incident involving Eleanor Davis. Her guardian tried to convince her that Toomer had Negro blood. Toomer comments that this was the first time in his life that race was used against him as "a deliberate weapon."[55] Still, he appears to have forgotten her rather quickly and moved on to someone else.

He continued at City College in the fall, developing an interest in psychology while living with his Uncle Walter. Then the question of his involvement in the war began to trouble him. For months, "It [had] seemed unrelated to my life." [56] There had already been arguments with his grandfather over patriotism. When his feelings shifted, however, Jean appears to have been somewhat surprised: "My soldiering inclinations arose and started a strong contest with my aims and values." [57] He decided to enlist, but after taking the physical in Washington, he was rejected "because of bad eyes and a hernia gotten in a basketball game. This was a great weight off my chest." [58] The incident is revealing because thereafter, for the rest of his life, Toomer was generally distanced from historical patterns and movements. He appears to have lived much of his life in isolation, removed from contemporary events, though his interests in socialism and race continued sporadically.

He drifted. In Chicago he stayed for a time in Harry Karstens's fraternity house while selling cars. During the cold winter, he considered going to Mexico or South America as a salesman, but he could find no business which would send him. During his free time, he had begun writing short stories, though his intent to become a full-time writer was still in the future. Early in 1918, he accepted a temporary job in Milwaukee as a substitute physical education teacher. The work lasted for only one month, during which time he began reading George Bernard Shaw. After the money he had earned ran out, again he relied upon his grandfather: "He sent me just barely enough for my train fare to Washington, saying that that was the last money he'd send me. He was completely disappointed in me. I had failed him and I had failed myself." [59]

He did not remain in Washington long. There was the matter of fending off his grandfather, who believed that Jean had completed his degree and was perplexed that no permanent job had come along. With money borrowed from P. B. S., Jean returned to New York and began work in another sales position for Acker Merrall and Condit Company. When he had attended City College, he had worked at one of their stores on Saturdays selling groceries. He states that he was still a socialist in his thinking. In part, the interest had continued because of his reading George Bernard Shaw. During the summer, Acker Merrall sent him to Ossining—Mt. Kisco, New York, where he spent much of his time jotting down his "thoughts and ponderings." [60]

While in Mt. Kisco, he began courting a girl who was a pianist. His interest in music became sufficiently developed that he rented a piano after he returned to New York City at the end of the summer. Though he continued to record his thoughts, he wondered if he might become a musician. Then he saw an advertisement for a physical education director for a settlement on the East Side and accepted that job, in addition to the one for Acker Merrall. For the first time – and perhaps the only time in his life – he appears to have been self-supporting on a salaried income.

> What a program I had! Breakfast early. Piano exercises. Study of harmony and composition. Readings in literature – particularly Shaw and Ibsen. My own attempts at writing. Lunch. Then to Acker Merrall. I had maneuvered to work with them half-time. Three afternoons I had piano lessons. Then back to the Settlement, dinner, and gym classes till eleven at night. This pace was kept up for six months.[61]

After holding down both jobs for several months, he broke from strain and overwork. For a day or two, he was in a semicoma. After fasting for several days and seeing a doctor, he decided to leave New York City. In the dead of winter, he fled to Ellenville, New York, in the mountains, where he wrote day and night. The period marks his true birth as a writer. He was serious enough about his "thoughts and ponderings" that he mimeographed copies of what he wrote and sent them to his friends for criticism. He says that even his grandfather began to take him more seriously after he read what Jean had sent him.

There was another return to Washington once his funds ran out. For part of the summer of 1919, however, he lived in New York City with Walt Palmer, one of his friends from the American College of Physical Training, presumably to escape his grandfather's reproaches. When he returned at the end of summer, he argued with Pinchback and told him that he had no intention of going into business: "I had seen too much of business conditions in New York. . . . If you didn't have pull, or if you didn't get a fortunate break, you just stayed down there where the majority of the workmen of the world were."[62]

Open warfare finally broke out between the two of them: "If I wanted to stay home, I could only do so by opposing him and, as it were, forcing him to let me occupy my room. In the apartment there was still a room with my things in it. It was still called my room. This was because of my grandmother's wish. But, as I say, it was mine only after I fought for it."[63]

The alternative was obvious. If he wanted to live his life on his own terms, and become a writer or a musician, he would have to make a complete break with his family. He wasn't exactly an adolescent any longer. He had had his years of self-indulgence as a student. He was twenty-five years old. It was the fall of 1919. Why not try New York City once again, where jobs had always been plentiful? What better place to unleash the artist within him?

Larsen

Nella Larsen's childhood is much more mysterious than Jean Toomer's because so little is known about it. The scanty facts that can be validated (and they are only a handful) are like a series of lights interspersed along a dark, underground tunnel. They burn brightly as we approach them, convincing us that farther down the pathway they will be more evenly dispersed. Yet the glow is misleading, often no more than a pinpoint in the unending darkness. We stumble in the night, leaving one lamp and searching for the next.

How can a person have lived in the United States so recently and yet left so little information about her existence? This is the problem that has plagued biographers of numerous other American writers – Emily Dickinson, to use an obvious example. Yet comparing the two is like contrasting night and day: Emily Dickinson stands in broad daylight (even dressed in white), while Nella Larsen is always cloaked in darkness. It is the problem of the shadow existence of African American life in America: undocumented history, unrecorded lives, unsung heroines and heroes – the story of the darker sister, removed from visibility, excised from being.

Something happened. Something awful happened in her childhood. Something painful enough that caused her as an adult to contribute to the concealment of that event. Why else does a person, early in her adulthood, begin rewriting the events of her childhood? As her biographer, I confess to an early but false assuredness about the details of her childhood. I was certain that those facts would be easy to document. My worry was about the later years of her life, after the Harlem Renaissance, when she seemed to vanish into thin air. The opposite has proven to be true. About her childhood I am much less confident than I was twenty-five or thirty years ago, when her books began to haunt me and I began to speculate about her life.

Problem one: the dearth of primary information, originating with Nella herself. Only one of her two published novels, Passing, appeared with biographical information about the writer printed on the book jacket. She gave only one interview during her lifetime (in the Amsterdam News, after Quicksand was published). All of the remaining personal information appears on job-related documents she filled in late in her life and on the applications to the Harmon and the Guggenheim Foundations during the 1920s. Problem two: determining the distortions – if not outright lies – in this information itself, since she rewrote her early life as if it were one of her novels. The childhood and adolescence she manufactured have been repeated ad nauseam, adopted by almost all of her critics, and so thoroughly entrenched as her authentic biography that until the past few years, almost every piece of scholarship related to her replicated the same distortions.

The front flap of the dust jacket for Passing begins as follows:

Nella Larsen's mother was Danish, her father a Negro from the Virgin Islands, formerly the Danish West Indies. When she was two years old her father died and shortly afterwards her mother married a man of her own race and nationality. At eight she and her half-sister attended a small private school whose pupils were mostly the children of German or Scandinavian parents. When she was sixteen she went to Denmark to visit relatives of her mother and remained there for three years.[1]

A second paragraph on the jacket describes her careers as a nurse and a librarian and concludes with a reference to the Harmon Award for Quicksand.

Later documents expand on this information. They list Chicago as her place of birth, with the date always listed as April 13, 1893. (This is also true of her application for Social Security, for which she did not apply until January 5, 1954.) Her mother's maiden name is recorded as Marian Hansen, her father's as Peter Larsen. The most detailed account of her education (which appears on her application for night supervisor of nurses at Metropolitan Hospital, dated December 2, 1961) looks like this:

- Mosely Grammar School, Chicago, Ill. 1898–1906.
- Wendel Phillips High School, Chicago. 1906–1910.
- University of Copenhagen, Denmark. 1910–1912. Number of
  Credits: 32. Major: Liberal Arts.
- Lincoln Hospital & Home, Bronx, NYC. 1912–1915. Diploma.
- Library School (N.Y.P.L.) Columbia University, 1922–1923. Diploma.
  16 credits.
- New School of Social Research, NYC. 1931. Major: Social Literature.[2]

I am unable to locate a birth certificate for Nella Larsen, though that in itself does not present a problem in establishing the correct date (there is no certificate for Jean Toomer either). The year of Nella's birth cannot be 1893, although the month and day, April 13, are correct. As early as 1928, on her Harmon application, she listed 1893 as the year. Thereafter, the month and day are always consistent. There is the possibility that she did not know the exact year; I believe, however, that she fudged on her birth date the way many people do. By 1928, she was approaching forty, and she may have thought that shaving off a couple of years would be to her advantage. Late in life, it may simply have been a matter of hoping to work a couple of extra years before retirement.

The correct year of her birth is 1891, not 1893. I draw this conclusion for several reasons. The earlier date appears on several documents pertaining to her education, beginning with the Chicago school records which have survived for her. I assume that 1891 would have been the year provided by her mother, at a time in Nella's life when there certainly was no reason to alter the date. Furthermore, on the legal documents pertaining to Anna Larsen Gardener's claim on Nella's estate – on a genealogy chart of the family – 1891 is listed as the year of her birth. The most obvious reason for concluding that 1891 is the actual year, however, is supported by Anna's birth on June 21, 1892, for which an authenticated birth certificate does exist. On that certificate, Anna is listed as her mother's second child, born at 1901 South Clark Street in Chicago. Although both parents are listed as Swedish and the spelling of their names conform to that nationality (Peteralina Mary

Hanson Larson and Peter Larson), this information correlates with other legal documents pertaining to Anna's life.

The place of Nella's birth is much more problematic. On documents that she herself completed, such as her passport application, she listed Chicago. Since little is known about her mother's early years in the United States, some critics have speculated that Marian/Marion/Mary/Marie Hansen/ Hanson, as she was variously known, may have emigrated to the West Indies and there become impregnated by a black man of Danish descent. Birth records for the West Indies do not go back far enough to be able to prove or disprove this theory. Mildred Phillips, a close friend of the Larsen family during both their Chicago and California years told me, however, that Mary Larsen on several occasions said that Nella was born in New York and that her father was a black American who was the chauffeur of the family for whom she worked. Unfortunately, no birth certificate can be located in New York.

The question of Nella's biological father remains a mystery. I doubt very much if she herself knew his real identity. Although he may have been West Indian, I suspect that Nella fabricated the story for romantic purposes. It is much more likely that he was African American. Whoever he was, he was not married to Nella's mother, since her name when she married Peter Larsen was Hansen. According to the certificate for their marriage, Marie Hansen was betrothed to Peter Larsen February 7, 1894, more than a year and a half after the birth of their child, Anna. Thus, both of Mary Hansen's daughters were born out of wedlock.

Both Nella and Anna took Peter Larsen's name as their own. Almost nothing is known about his early life. On the wedding certificate, however, Peter's age is listed as thirty-two and Mary's as twenty-seven. Furthermore, he is identified as having come from Harlan, Iowa. Mary's residence is identified as Chicago, where they were married. It is impossible to ascertain where the two of them met. Did Peter Larsen live in Harlan until the time of their marriage? Did Mary live in Chicago with her two children? It is possible that the four of them lived in Harlan after Mary and Peter's wedding, since Peter's name does not show up in Chicago city directories until after the turn of the century.

On his death certificate, Peter Larsen's date of birth is cited as February 5,

1867. He was born in Copenhagen. When he died in California on January 24, 1945, he was almost seventy-eight. He had lived in the United States for fifty-seven years, since 1888. Mary's date of birth, as listed on her death certificate, is September 24, 1867. Her parents are identified as Marten Hanson and Karen Mandensen, both of Denmark. The certificate does not mention the number of years she lived in the United States. When she died, September 17, 1951, she was eighty-three years old.

Illinois public school records are required to be kept on file for sixty years. The only reference to Nella that remains in Chicago records cites her attendance at Coleman School, as a seventh-grade student, during 1903 and 1904. Her address is listed as 4538 South State Street. Peter Larson is identified as her father. The city directory for that year, however, does not mention him. No records of Anna's schooling in Chicago have survived for the same period of time. Nella is, however, identified for the 1907–1908 academic year as attending Fisk University's Normal School, as a third-year student. The listing in the university catalog identifies her as Nellie Marie Larsen.

It is not until the 1910 census that accurate information can be located for the Peter Larsen family. Although the family is listed in the Chicago city directory for 1908 as residing at 143 West 70th Place, during the 1910 census, Peter, Mary, and Anna are described as living at 43 West 70th Place. Their ages are forty-three, forty, and seventeen, respectively. Peter and Mary are identified as having been married for nineteen years. The most revealing piece of information from the census material applying to them is not the fact that Nella is missing but that Mary Larsen is identified as the mother of one child only. In the category listing such information ("Mother of How Many Children" "Number Here"), a one has been written. "Number Now Living" similarly indicates only one. Thus not only was Nella no longer living with them (she would have been nineteen years old at the time) but she was also written out of their lives.

My assumption is that Mary provided the information for the census taker, because as the housewife it would have been more likely that she was home when the material was collected. There are other inconsistencies, to be sure, but none as glaring as Nella's obliteration. The date for Peter's arrival in the United States is given as 1885, for Mary's as 1887. Under trade or profession, Peter is described as a conductor and Mary as a dressmaker, and these are their designated occupations on other later public documents. The property at 43 West 70th Place, a single-dwelling home, is described as being owned by the Larsens.

Was Nella living in Copenhagen with her relatives during the time of the 1910 census? Is that the explanation for her omission from the information devoted to her family? I think not. I have come to the conclusion that her Denmark years are a total fabrication, a fancy embroidery upon the tragedy of her early life. The registrar at the University of Copenhagen answered my queries by indicating that "we have not been able in the archives of the University of Copenhagen to find any signs showing that Nella Larsen was inscribed as a student or passed any examinations at the university."[3] Other records for the city show no indications of Nella's residence during the years that she claims, 1910–1912.

Assuming the possibility that Nella was in Denmark during this time and simply fabricated her attendance at the University of Copenhagen, possibly by attending a few lectures, I checked with the United States Department of State Passport Division only to learn that there are no records of her travel overseas for this period of time. A more revealing fact can be found on her 1930 application for a passport, when she was about to begin her Guggenheim year. On that application she wrote "never" in the space provided for an indication of earlier passports. The Department of State has assured me, in fact, that the 1930 application is her first and was followed by one renewal only, in 1932. In short, she was never in Denmark, except in her imagination.

When Nella began studying for her nursing certificate in 1912 at the Lincoln Hospital and Home in the Bronx, in New York City, she listed 43 West 70th Place, Chicago, as her address. Whether she considered that her home or simply the address of people who should be notified if there were an emergency, it is impossible to tell. Records for Lincoln Hospital and Home (the name was changed to Lincoln School for Nurses in 1927) are also incomplete. The information that has survived, however, states that Nella entered the program May 2, 1912, and completed her work May 13, 1915. Moreover, she reportedly "made an excellent record as a student and passed the State Board examination with an average of 94. The director of the school at the time stated that she had executive ability above the average."[4]

Nella's half sister, Anna, married George Henry Gardner November 8,

1913, while Nella was still attending Lincoln Hospital and Home. Their son, George Larsen Gardner, Jr., was born April 30, the following year. If the information on Anna's death certificate is accurate, the Gardners moved to California in 1917. If the date for their move to California on George, Jr.'s, certificate is the correct information, then the year was 1922. A friend of the family states that Peter and Mary Larsen followed shortly after the Gardners' earlier move, though she does not remember what year that was.

After Nella completed her nursing education at Lincoln in May of 1915, she worked as a supervisor at the hospital for a number of months. On October 15, she accepted the position of head nurse at Tuskegee Normal and Industrial Institute, Tuskegee, Alabama. In the 1915–1916 catalog for the institute, she is listed as holding this position. No other information remains in Tuskegee archives about her career there, though there is that odd statement in the Harmon Foundation's files about her friction with school authorities concerning her appearance, which resulted in their parting with "mutual disgust and relief." [5]

Was she too light-skinned for Tuskegee? Or was it her clothing, the way she dressed, her disdain of less "sophisticated" blacks? Both are possibilities, though equally likely was Tuskegee's isolated location. If the portrait of Helga Crane in Quicksand is autobiographical – and I believe that it is, particularly in the opening chapters – then Nella felt superior to the people around her. Not only was she lighter in color at a time in our history when great emphasis was placed on the degree of one's blackness, but she would have had a better education than many of her peers at the institute. Tuskegee was no place for someone as ambitious as Nella Larsen, nor for anyone who believed herself caught in a cultural morass.

So she left Tuskegee, and then she made her way back to New York City, possibly via Chicago. She returned to Lincoln Hospital and then somewhat later worked for the city's Department of Health. Somewhere along the way, she entered a faster track, met Elmer S. Imes, and began to cultivate the friends she would associate with during the Harlem Renaissance. Perhaps there was a period of poverty and disillusionment in Chicago after she left Tuskegee, in the manner attributed to Helga Crane in Quicksand, but I think not. Since she had former friends and connections in New York City from her Lincoln Hospital days, I suspect that it was a matter of renewing them.

This is not to imply that life was not difficult for Nella. It is simply clear that she had a flair for the dramatic and she knew how to use it.

One aspect of Helga Crane's situation in *Quicksand* has, I believe, major significance and may suggest what really happened to Nella in the Larsen household. Early in Larsen's novel, Helga is described as a "solitary girl with no family connections."[6] Her mother died when Helga was fifteen, and she is twenty-three at the beginning of the story. When Helga reaches Chicago, she seeks out her Uncle Peter, her mother's brother, who she believes will aid her financially. Uncle Peter is gone the day Helga tries to visit him. She is snubbed by Uncle Peter's wife, Mrs. Nilssen, who tells her never to come to their house again. The story is structured in such a fashion that some months later, a $5,000 check from Uncle Peter will come to Helga's rescue, but it takes a while, apparently, for Uncle Peter to learn that his wife has turned Helga away from their door.

The variations upon Nella Larsen's own life here are particularly revealing. As a novelist, Nella has split her real mother in two, by killing off Helga's mother and depicting Mrs. Nilssen as loathsome and bigoted. Furthermore, Larsen has taken her real stepfather (also named Peter) and turned him into the sympathetic character. Psychologically, Larsen the writer, who lived in a situation not so far removed from Helga's, suggests that her real mother is emotionally dead to her — no better than Mrs. Nilssen. Uncle Peter, by contrast, she depicts as "the one relative who thought kindly, or even calmly, of her. . . . Uncle Peter was different. In his contemptuous way he was fond of her . . . he had been extraordinarily generous with her."[7]

According to Mildred Phillips, Nella's mother was a hard, difficult woman to live with, while her stepfather, Peter, apparently had genuine affection for her. Her mother's contempt for her recalls Helga's statement to Axel Olsen about why she cannot marry him: "If we were married, you might come to be ashamed of me, to hate me, to hate all dark people. My mother did that."[8] The decision to remove Nella from the household — the tragedy of Nella's childhood — I attribute to Nella's mother and not to her stepfather. Why else would Mary Larsen deny her first child's existence on the census information? The situation in *Quicksand*, then, is further revealing because Helga feels twice abandoned: first by her biological father ("the gay suave scoundrel, Helga's father, [who] had left her"[9]) and second by her mother.

The portrait of Helga in the early pages of Quicksand would appear to be a thinly disguised picture of Nella herself. This is not simply the picture of a lonely, solitary girl who has no family connections, but an adult who has been unable to forget "her unloved, unloving, and unhappy childhood." [10] When she returns home to seek support for her troubles, she realizes that she has "no home," [11] no family at all.

To be sure, the situation in Quicksand is clouded with ambiguity, especially about Helga's feelings regarding her mother. Her affair with a black man is attributed to a romanticized fervor for life: "A fair Scandinavian girl in love with life, with love, with passion, dreaming, and risking all in one blind surrender." [12] The problem is with the later marriage "to a man of her own race, but not of her own kind – so passionately, so instinctively resented by Helga even at the trivial age of six." [13] The ambiguity is further clouded by Helga's feelings of illegitimacy. It is Mrs. Nilssen who tells her, "Your mother wasn't married, was she? I mean, to your father?" almost immediately adding, "And please remember that my husband is not your uncle." [14]

So what was the story of Nella's origins? I surmise that something like this happened.

Mary Hansen arrives in New York City sometime around the year 1888. Though she is twenty-one years old and an adult, she quickly discovers that America is not the land of promise she envisioned before she left Denmark. Unskilled, she is forced to accept menial jobs in order to guarantee her survival in the new world. Lonely and often intimidated by her difficulty with English, she retreats into herself, even after she acquires a steady position as a maid for a rich family. The one person who appears to take an interest in her is their chauffeur. Though he is black, she thinks nothing of this, since as a child in Denmark she grew up free of any racial prejudice.

To her delight, the relationship between the two of them develops. Suddenly she discovers joy and happiness in her life, for the first time since she has been in America. But all too soon the pleasure ends when she discovers that she is expecting a child. At the beginning of her pregnancy, she thinks little of the fact that her lover is a black man. It goes through her mind that she should have an abortion – as the man himself suggests – but she decides to bear the child and live with the consequences. Though she has concealed his identity from her employers, it is not until well into the pregnancy that she begins to worry about the question of race.

Arrangements are made for a midwife to assist at the delivery, thanks to her employers. They are tolerant of her situation — or so she believes, until the child is born. Though not nearly as black as her lover, the child, a girl she calls Nella, is dark. Immediately everyone in the household understands the situation. The chauffeur has, in fact, disappeared, and Mary discovers that her own departure would not be unwelcome.

She flees with her infant child to Chicago, where she has been told that the Scandinavian population is centered. Again, she accepts menial work, living with her child in a room and relying upon an old woman to take care of Nella during the days when she has to be away. The child is light-skinned enough that Mary believes her features will in time bleach completely away. She has been in the United States long enough to understand the lowly position permitted and attained by black people. She wonders, in fact, how foolish she could have been to accept a black man as her lover.

One day when Nella is half a year old, Mary attends a social function involving her countrymen. There she meets Peter Larsen, a man slightly older than she who is visiting friends in Chicago. The attraction is mutual and almost immediate. Fortunately, she has had the foresight to leave Nella with the old woman who looks after her. Peter proposes to her, but Mary is in a quandary about her child. Still, they sleep together before Peter returns to his home in Iowa, and Mary agrees to consider his proposal seriously.

Mary discovers herself in a second quandary almost immediately after Peter's departure. Hasn't she been a fool not to think of herself first before her child? Why didn't she abandon her child before starting all over in Chicago? Is it too late to give the child away to some adoption agency? Mary doesn't know what to do, though she realizes that her feelings about Nella have radically changed. How could she even have considered bearing a black man's child? All black people, in fact, she has begun to hold in contempt because they remind her of her fateful error.

When she misses her period, Mary believes that she is doubly cursed. Not only has she born a black child out of wedlock but now she has become impregnated by the man who would free her from her entrapment. What can she do? Give Nella up for adoption or abandon her? Abort the child in her belly? Start all over again somewhere else?

In her depression, she does nothing at all to escape her predicament. The child she leaves increasingly to the whims of the old woman, who seems genuinely fond of her. The letters that arrive from Peter she scans hurriedly and then destroys without answering. As the time of her confinement approaches, she often seems hysterical, aware of little around her. Somehow, even though she knows this is impossible, she fears that her second child will also be black. Fortunately for Nella, the old woman dotes upon her.

When the second child is born – another girl, whom she names Anna Elizabeth – Mary feels as if she has been released from her recent misery. She delights in the infant, often dazzled by her startling whiteness. She is relieved, also, that Peter's letters have become more infrequent. Perhaps they will completely stop and she will be able to begin her life again with at least one child she can truly love.

Life slowly improves for Mary, which is to say that the patterns of her daily activities become less confused, less troubled. Her work is drudgery, to be sure, but that she accepts, now that she has centered her life so totally upon Anna. As for the other child, well, she will simply have to wait and see. There are days when she believes that Nella's skin is visibly lightening.

Then one day, nearly a year and a half after their initial encounter, Peter Larsen reappears in her life. Ostensibly visiting friends in the big city, he has come in search of Mary to discover why she has answered none of his letters. When he finally locates the place where she lives, she is at work. Only the old woman is there with her charges, and Peter believes that he has tracked down the wrong Mary Hansen. Were all of his letters, in fact, sent to the wrong person? No wonder they were unanswered. But what of the person who claimed to be Mary Hansen? What happened to her?

He is about to leave when something tells him to stay, some inner feeling that all will be resolved if he will only wait until this Mary Hansen returns. He glances at the children – one of them a toddler and darker than the younger one, the other one just learning to crawl. Suddenly while he is looking at the younger child, he discovers that he is engulfed in emotion. Something tells him that he has come to the right place, that this Mary Hansen is the woman who has dominated his thoughts for more than a year.

He waits, hours it seems, for Mary's return, and then, just when he believes it has all been an error and that he should depart without seeing her, she returns. Emotion. Wonder. Surprise. Tears followed by laughter. It does not take long before they plan their future lives together. It is Peter who insists that they be married before he returns to Iowa to gather his belong-

ings. Outside, it is cold and there is snow on the ground. Later, in the evening as they walk through the darkness in search of a minister, Mary knows
that even though this man, this miracle of her life, says that he will raise
both of her children as his own, the darker one will always be her burden,
a reminder of her past. In time, she will have to discover a way to remove
Nella from their lives. But not yet, not now, while her heart is alive with so
much wonder.

Invisible Darkness

I do not really know myself, who I am, my selfhood, my spiritual
identity, or what I am. I have some information about it, but also
some misinformation, some understanding, but much illusion. Real
knowledge, real recognition, realization? No. What are my complex
motivations? What is my aim, assuming that I have but one aim? I do
not really know my wife, my child, my closest friends. I do not really
know anyone or anything.
— Jean Toomer, initial meeting with Gurdjieff, circa 1948 [1]

Why a career with such auspicious beginnings had such an
inauspicious ending has continued to perplex students of the Harlem
Renaissance. Many search for answers in the scattered fragments of
Larsen's biography, which reveal a delicate and unstable person.
— Deborah E. McDowell, "Introduction" to *Quicksand* and *Passing*, 1986

In recent years, there have been a number of biographies
which have told us more about the biographer than the subject, where the
writer's personality assumed center stage at the expense of the subject, who
was left standing in the wings. Fortunately, I am not able to write that kind
of biography — to tell you after all these pages something to the effect that
Nella Larsen was my grandmother. She was not. My fascination with Jean
Toomer and Nella Larsen grew out of a profound admiration of their work,
followed by a curiosity about their lives. I wanted to know what happened
to them after the Harlem Renaissance, when they appeared to be silent.

This is not to say, however, that my feelings about both Jean Toomer and

Nella Larsen have not been transformed. They have, which I believe is standard fare for anyone delving so completely into another person's life. You learn things you would just as soon not know. The admiration and respect that prompts one to undertake the study in the first place slowly gives way. I am content now that I never did meet Jean Toomer, though I regret that I never had the opportunity for such an encounter with Nella Larsen. I would like to know more about how she lived all those years alone in her studio apartment on Second Avenue. I would even settle for a fleeting glimpse of her walking down the street, or perhaps attired in her nursing uniform at Gouverneur Hospital, making her rounds as the supervisor, checking the other nurses.

As I researched their lives and discovered that Toomer and Larsen knew each other during that brief period of time when Jean led a Gurdjieff group in Harlem, I had a momentary fancy that I could bring them together in a revealing scene – a dual epiphany – that would once and forever shed light upon their true personalities. It would be the centerpiece of my biography. That was not to be, and I believe I am grateful for that now, also. Nella had enough trouble with Elmer to last a lifetime. It was her good fortune that she did not become another name on Jean's list of sexual conquests, though she shares an affinity with some of his victims. Victims? Should the word be as strong as that? Indeed, yes, as Mabel Dodge Luhan's pathetic letters to Jean reveal, or as Margery Latimer's brief marriage and awful death remind us.

We become what we want to become, we do what we want to do, some people say. The victim chooses his or her own tragedy. Perhaps, in some instances. Margery had a strong death wish much of her adult life, to be sure, but I doubt that she thought her life would end in the manner in which it did. Nancy Loughridge, who has researched her life extensively, does not blame Jean for the complications that developed during Margery's delivery, though she wonders if the midwife left because she had not been paid or had caught wind of a supposed interracial marriage. Loughridge also wonders if Margery, had she lived, would have taken the child and run in the opposite direction, once she realized what a cad her husband was.[2]

Toomer was a bit of a louse, at least where women were concerned. He went through them by the dozens, possibly by the hundreds. It was to the credit of his good taste or intuitive foresight that many of these women would subsequently become quite famous, and in some cases more well known than Jean himself. Margaret Naumberg, Mabel Dodge Luhan, Georgia O'Keeffe, and his two wives, to mention only five. In his book on the Harlem Renaissance, David Levering Lewis adds Edna St. Vincent Millay to the list of Toomer's possible conquests. Other names are frequently mentioned, although the validation of these relationships is often difficult. Dorothy Peterson's letters to Jean in the Beinecke Library at Yale remained sealed for many years, though her torrid relationship with Jean was well known at the time it occurred. Their affair prompted Carl Van Vechten to remark in one of his letters to her, "I think Jean Toomer's letters are also of the highest interest as a document. . . . His love-making I find rather algebraic. Was he more HUMAN in the flesh?" [3] Although this is an exaggeration, people who knew him say that no woman was safe once she entered a room where Jean was present. Thousands of women thought they were in love with him, one of his acquaintances informed me, extending the hyperbole even further.

"He loved to screw," [4] Jean's medical doctor bluntly told me, though he quickly added that Jean was not a rascal in most of his relationships. "He was very much a body type . . . charged with the mystery of life," [5] a magnetic and feeling sort of person with characteristics which women often found irresistible. Friends admit, however, that he used his blackness – at least the myth of his blackness – in his seductions. Certainly that perception of him is verified in Bona's thoughts in "Bona and Paul" in Cane. And it is supported in the more reflective picture Jean presents of himself in one of his much later unpublished novels, Eight-Day World. In the opening paragraph of that autobiographical work, Toomer describes his main character as "a man's man – yet all his life he'd done nothing but fool with women and mess them up as he messed himself [up]." [6]

Jean's sexual promiscuity was part and parcel of the times during which he lived and the people with whom he often associated, as well as his own prevailing bohemian attitude. It was also rooted in his ambivalent attitude toward his mother, that childlike waif who lived in P. B. S. Pinchback's household but was not permitted to grow up. When Nina finally did assert herself and remarry, she left her son with the feeling of abandonment, just as Jean's father had left her. It isn't difficult to see the pattern reemerging in his own adulthood in Jean's cavalier attitude toward women. The numerous unfulfilled relationships between men and women in Cane – in "Karintha," "Becky," "Fern," "Esther," "Blood-Burning Moon," "Avey," "Theatre,"

"Box Seat," "Bona and Paul," and "Kabnis" – appear to validate this way of life.

In a sense, Jean Toomer's wide-ranging sexual pursuits were nothing more than an extension of the opportunism that characterized so many of the activities and relationships throughout his life. Like his grandfather, who was an unconscious model for him, Jean perfected the art of taking advantage of the situations that prevailed. P. B. S. lived as a white man but claimed to be black whenever the situation could be turned to his advantage. Even Jean's father, Nathan, was not adverse to leaving a woman when monetary reward disappeared. One-upping his father and grandfather, Jean quickly mastered the art of living well at the expense of others. It was his grandfather, at first, who could always be relied upon for more money – until Pinchback's pocket was empty. During his student years, Jean sponged off the good will of his roommates' parents. Later, various women – Margaret Naumberg, Mabel Dodge Luhan, and his two wives – enabled him to avoid the drudgery of gainful employment. I am convinced that the prolonged illness late in Toomer's life was a manifestation of his fear that Marjorie would divorce him and leave him without a penny.

Jean's illness, centered in his abdomen, is psychologically revealing because it was also an unconscious repetition of his mother's and his first wife's illnesses. Both women suffered from prolonged periods of abdominal pain. Nina's pain was genuine, culminating in the complications of her appendectomy, though it had earlier been considered psychosomatic. Margery's pain was of unknown origin but considered to be part of her high-strung nature. It is easy to perceive Jean's similar complication as an indirect commentary on both of their deaths.

The question of Jean Toomer's blackness is closely related to his opportunism, so close that it is almost impossible to separate the two. For years, I thought there was no logical rationale for classifying Jean Toomer as an African American writer. If one believes that a few drops of blood define one's ethnic origins, then technically he was black. By analogy, then hundreds of thousands – if not millions – of so-called white Americans are black. Furthermore, if whiteness (and white blood) is such a powerful amulet for determining one's status in America, then shouldn't it be the other way around? The more likely scenario (and logic) tells me that three drops of white blood make one white. So it must be something else, though it is fairly obvious that there was dark blood in Jean Toomer's ancestors.

Toomer was raised as a white person. Sociologically and culturally that is what he considered himself to be until the 1909 conversation with his grandfather, when P. B. S. informed him that Eliza Stewart may have been of mixed heritage. Until that moment, he had apparently never seriously considered the possibility, though the effect of this knowledge so traumatized him that he altered it and called himself an American. There were the years following Nina Toomer Coombs's death, when Jean and his grandparents lived in a racially mixed neighborhood and he attended a predominantly black school. But as soon as he graduated from high school, he made a hasty withdrawal from this first foray into black life and skittered off to Wisconsin. His autobiographical writings make the significance of that location absolutely clear: if he continued to live in a racially mixed community, people might begin to regard him as a Negro.

Comparing Jean Toomer to Walter White – another Harlem Renaissance figure who was also Caucasian in appearance – is especially revealing. White was raised as a black person and thought of himself as such. Despite the irony of his name, he took great pride in his black heritage in a way that Toomer found impossible. White's career was an assertion of racial pride, at a time when great advantages became almost immediate if one crossed over the racial line. Jean Toomer, by contrast, did not demonstrate that pride and commitment to black heritage, except for the year or so while he was working on *Cane*.

The question that arises is whether or not Toomer knew that he was passing. If he didn't consider himself a black person, then how could he possibly believe that he was leading a life of such duplicity? Unfortunately, Toomer's dreams during the period of his Jungian analysis late in life tell us something quite different. They reveal a divided self, and they even hint at his acute regret at joining the white world instead of remaining black. And isn't it clear from Margery Latimer's letter to Blanche Matthias that she believed Jean was black?

Toomer's connection to and with the Harlem Renaissance might best be called an accident of time and place. If he had not told Waldo Frank and others that he was P. B. S. Pinchback's grandson, he might never have been connected with the Renaissance. If he had not used Waldo Frank's friendship and influence among New York publishers – blatantly, to his own advantage, it should be said – he might have remained unpublished. More likely, he would have found a publisher who would not have tried to promote him as a black writer, and today he would simply be regarded as another American author (like Waldo Frank, Sherwood Anderson, or even William Faulkner) who chose to write about black life in the United States. Clearly, by the time *Cane* saw print, Toomer deeply regretted being classified as a Negro author.

To his surprise and horror, the classification stuck. Why wouldn't it? *Cane* is one of the masterpieces of twentieth-century American fiction. Though its mixed form is often initially confusing, the statement it makes about ethnic pride through the nourishment of one's roots is absolutely indisputable. On a personal level, *Cane* is not simply about Jean Toomer's inability to accept his blackness but about America's failure to accept its Africanness. Still, people of differing ethnic origins have been proud to claim the novel, as if proprietary rights are a guarantee of artistic greatness. Fortunately, the work can stand on its own creative merit, with or without the ethnic claimants. Like *Huckleberry Finn* and *Light in August* and *Invisible Man*, Toomer's novel addresses one of the major issues of American life – racism in the United States. It is very much a social document about that specific American malady, yet its affirmation of blackness is never weighted down by the romantic sentiment of some of Toomer's contemporaries' work.

Instead, one might say that *Cane* catalogues the frustrations and psychoses of black life in a kleptomaniacal world, where one culture steals from another while simultaneously beating it down. In the jealousy that binds the two cultures together, Toomer discovers not only life and heritage but also poetry. *Cane* was Toomer's ultimate homage to black life, his praise song of a way of life he himself was unable to embrace.

The loss was his own. He decided that he wanted nothing to do with the Harlem Renaissance, once he had helped launch it. When writers of the movement began to regard him as one of their leaders, he turned his back on them and went on to something else. As Marjorie Content Toomer and others commented after his death, Jean never really thought of himself as part of the black renaissance because he never thought of himself as a black person. Small wonder that he could never write another *Cane*.

To do so, he would have had to make a bold commitment to what he clearly regarded as restrictive, limiting, denigrating, and he was too street-wise to do that. Expressed another way, Jean Toomer was afraid to continue his association with black life because he had observed too closely the ways in which black people in America are humiliated. And hadn't he already spent years of his life learning how to take advantage of the situation? Wasn't he doing quite well for himself by avoiding the racial question?

So he called himself an American and let people take him for what they would, while he turned to other subjects – which led to the collapse of his artistic talent. Rarely has a writer of such magnificent potential stumbled so completely. Almost all of the post-*Cane* writings read like so much gibberish. His spiritual quest – which was in part an attempt to prove to himself that his decision to abandon black life had been the correct one – clearly did not mesh with his creativity. Again and again, the subject of his subsequent fiction was linked to that quest. The characters are almost always thinly disguised versions of himself, as if he were his own greatest creation. In a haunting sort of way, Jean Toomer was like Joe Christmas in William Faulkner's *Light in August*. Their lives were controlled by the problem of race and not knowing what to make of it.

Toomer's own writing became a problem of distance. In *Cane* he wrote as if by possession about a way of life that fascinated yet threatened him. He had touched the forbidden subject yet managed to wriggle away. Thereafter, his subject was not a culture in all its song and movement but an individual turned in upon himself. The gobbledygook characters and situations in the post-*Cane* works, which were intended to be satirical, more often collapse under their ideological weight. As he pushed Gurdjieffian thought – forced it, one might say – into his fiction, his characters became one-dimensional and bloodless. Thus, race and Gurdjieff both ruined and propelled his work – race, because he couldn't accept his blackness after *Cane* was completed, and Gurdjieff, because the master's philosophy helped Jean to deny his former self.

Moreover, the situations he wrote about seemed to exist in some private world. *Cane* had been rooted firmly in a specific time and place sociologically, historically, and culturally. The later work almost exclusively ignored these issues, as if Toomer the writer had himself taken up residence in a vacuum. The trip to India is indicative of the situation. There was Jean on his spiritual junket (funded by his father-in-law), dragging his wife and child from ashram to ashram, oblivious of their discomfort or of the squalor all around him, even unaware, apparently, that a war was about to break out and that the three of them might end up in Japan as political prisoners. The trip was a failure, yet that didn't alter the course of Jean's action. He was determined to find himself, at the expense of family and, to a lesser extent, friends.

The lesson to be learned from this is an obvious one: creative expression only accidentally meshes with the hidden dimension of human fallibility. Furthermore, it can certainly be argued that if Jean Toomer never found what he was searching for, he aided many others in their own similar quests. *Cane* has not only been the inspiration for numerous black writers who followed him but for several generations of American readers who have been illuminated by the book's inspiriting assertion of cultural roots. As a Gurdjieff leader and as a Quaker thinker, Toomer's influence was also significant, though less demonstrable. If *Cane* lives on, as it does and will, what does it matter that the writer himself undergoes an inner death? Still, there are those roots. Like Kabnis in the final section of *Cane*, Jean Toomer was suspended above the soil that would nourish him. Voluntarily, he cut himself off, severed the cord that would connect him and nourish his creativity.

The displacement of his artistic talent can be summed up by a statement Toomer made in *Portage Potential*: "There are two kinds of people: those who wish to influence, those who wish to be influenced; those who dominate, those who are dominated."[7] In its original context, the quotation typifies the relationship between Jean and Margery Latimer, at least at the beginning of their experiment in communal living at Portage, Wisconsin. Moreover, the statement gives us a clue for understanding Jean's method of breaking down Margery's ego and dominating it by his own — browbeating her, subduing her will until he had remolded her into the person *he* thought she should be.

In a sense, it was ego that got into Jean's way. He wanted not only to find himself but to have others regard him as a great spiritual leader, one who walked in Gurdjieff's (or others') footsteps. Though there is no consensus on this, several of Toomer's friends have told me that he was not a very significant figure in the Gurdjieff movement. The end result was that both

Jean Toomer, circa 1960. Photo by Marjorie Content. Courtesy of Susan L. Sandberg.

his creativity and his spiritual trip were displaced by the advancement of his own ego. Yet the choice was his own, even if it was triggered by the conflicting parts of his personality. If he had lost control over his artistic imagination (and he seemed to realize this), he could at least acquire a new status through the guidance of others. Without making the discovery for himself—

and before he completed his own pilgrimage – he took it upon himself to be the teacher of others. Though she admitted that it was an unkind image of her stepfather, Susan Sandberg said that what Jean Toomer liked most was to be surrounded by his followers: the guru, encircled by his disciples.

While Jean Toomer enhanced his ego, Nella Larsen was engaged in a totally different relationship with her fellow travelers. While Jean undertook the dubious task of guiding their souls, Nella followed the humanitarian approach and attended to their bodies. In the eyes of Alice Carper, one of her coworkers late in life, Nella became an exemplary worker who instilled in others a sense of respect and admiration. "She really loved people," Carper said of her, "especially the sick. She would see that anything could be done to help them."[8] She was dedicated to her nursing career and quickly rewarded for her efforts by attaining the rank of supervisor, in charge of the nursing staff of Gouverneur Hospital.

That position and the subsequent one at Metropolitan Hospital in the last year or so of her life permitted her to survive. She threw herself into her work in order to forget the pain and misery of her previous lives: as a child, forsaken to the wind; as a wife, abandoned by her spouse; as a writer, rejected by the whims of the marketplace. She never missed a day of work. She was so admired by her coworkers that when she transferred from Gouverneur to Metropolitan, a number of other people went along with her. Although her death was unacknowledged by the newspapers and by the literary world (in part because she used the name Imes), her funeral was attended by forty or fifty colleagues.

She kept her misery to herself. She earned the admiration of her associates by being strict, by tolerating no infractions of the rules. If she caught any of the nurses nodding during the night shift, she woke them up and scolded them (Carper says that Nella herself took uppers to stay awake and possibly to conceal her unhappiness). Though she was liked by everyone with whom she worked, few people were aware of her acute depression. Away from the hospital, she was lonely and reclusive. The social life that she had was limited to contact with two or three of her coworkers. Without their attempts to draw her out, her life might have turned totally inward.

Without question, she certainly had reasons for her depression, beginning with the traumatic situation of her childhood. My speculation is that she was removed from the Larsen household sometime around the age of nine or ten, though it may have been later. It had to have been early enough for her sister, Anna Elizabeth, to forget about her completely. I fully understand Nella's reasons for rewriting her childhood when she became an adult. Why not cover the pain and trauma of rejection with the romantic account of three years in Copenhagen? Why not embroider it in *Quicksand* by placing Helga Crane in a culture free of racial prejudice – the exact opposite of the one in which she had grown up in America? If she could not escape the racism in her own life, she could escape it symbolically through her fiction.

Fortunately, she was talented and hard-working. The evidence is clear that she gave everything she had to her profession as soon as she began her training as a nurse – as she did to her careers as librarian and writer. It did not take long for other people to recognize her multiple talents. I can imagine her about the time when she completed her nursing degree, happy for the first time in her life. The happiness was of short duration, however, once she realized her error in seeking employment at Tuskegee. In *Quicksand*, she described the institution as a

> showplace in the black belt, exemplification of the white man's magnanimity, refutation of the black man's inefficiency. Life had died out of it. It was . . . now only a big knife with cruelly sharp edges ruthlessly cutting all to a pattern, the white man's pattern. Teachers as well as students were subjected to the paring process, for it tolerated no innovations, no individualisms. Ideas it rejected, and looked with open hostility on one and all who had the temerity to offer a suggestion or ever so mildly express a disapproval. Enthusiasm, spontaneity, if not actually suppressed, were at least openly regretted as unladylike or ungentlemanly qualities. The place was smug and fat with self-satisfaction.[9]

As one of the Talented Tenth, Nella loathed the Tuskegee goal of mediocrity.

She must have had a second period of happiness after she returned to New York City and married Elmer S. Imes. Her letters written during the early part of the 1920s certainly attest to this. Her new career as librarian and then as writer provided her with a momentary glimpse of fame and fortune, and there is no question that she derived a great amount of satisfaction as one of Harlem's elite. Parties, cabarets, literary soirées – Harlem was the place to be and she was very much a part of it. But then her marriage began to fail, as Elmer became interested in other women. What could be worse than the crushing humiliation that the other woman – the one Elmer left Nella for – was white?

As she watched their marriage deteriorate, Nella sought refuge in her writing. In one sense, Quicksand and Passing were cryptic pleas for help addressed to her husband, who no longer was interested in her. Even worse, by the time she was once again on her own and ready to start all over, the Harlem Renaissance had ended. The curtain had fallen across the decade, and black culture was no longer in fashion. It was as if the nation had played still another trick upon black people. Black artists had been permitted to sit at the table with white artists, without realizing that their moment of glory had contributed to their further pacification.

Nella tried to continue with her literary life, but the defeats, coming so close upon one another, made it impossible. It should be emphasized that she did not give up, that she did not go down without fighting, as has commonly been perceived. She wrote additional novels (at least three, if my calculations are correct) before rejection forced her to abandon the career of letters. The return to nursing was inevitable, perhaps, given the economics of the situation; yet it was not a defeat, since in the opinion of her associates she was a true humanitarian, dedicated to healing the wounds of others. Stated another way, Nella Larsen resolved the tragedy of her life and rose above it. Unlike Jean Toomer, she successfully managed a pattern for survival.

There were three major events that led to Nella's silence as a writer, that forced withdrawal upon her. The breakdown of her marriage with Elmer and their divorce was the first, and perhaps also the most psychologically damaging. As she told Carolyn Lane years later, "He broke my heart." [10] Elmer's rejection must have been even more painful than her family's, since Elmer had been her choice and her character misjudgment. So total was her sense of rejection that she never recovered from it and lived in a state of prolonged depression; yet the fact that she identified herself as Mrs. Imes and not as Nella Larsen tells us something about her belief in marriage as a necessary social convention.

Second was the public embarrassment of being accused of having plagiarized her story, "Sanctuary," in Forum. Though it can only have been an accident of fate – a curse upon her for having a photographic memory – she

Nella Larsen, circa 1929. Photo by Carl Van Vechten. Courtesy of Yale Collection of American Literature, Beinecke Rare Book and Manuscript Library, Yale University.

knew that her friends were talking behind her back. She had participated in some of the backbiting during the Renaissance, as her surviving letters demonstrate. But it was too much once the tables were turned. Perhaps the accusations of plagiarism, more than anything else, resulted in the severing of her relationships with Carl Van Vechten and others, who were, after all, still living in rather close proximity to her.

The coup de grâce was delivered by the publishers who rejected her work after *Passing*. Since the manuscripts to these later novels no longer exist, there is no way to determine their merit. It is difficult to believe, however, that they were inferior to *Quicksand* and *Passing*. It is impossible to believe that they were of lesser merit than the hurricane of undistinguished novels published every season. In part, it was a question of the times. The Harlem Renaissance played a cruel joke upon her, as it did upon numerous other writers. (By contrast, Jean Toomer might be said to have played a joke on the Harlem Renaissance.) Publishers no longer wanted books about black life. Readers had lost interest in black subjects. Rather than face obscurity, she tried to write to their dictates, to adjust to the changing market. There is one novel that she refers to as her "white" novel. No one knows how long she kept writing and sending out her manuscripts before she gave in to the humiliation of constant rejection.

Still, *Quicksand* survives as one of the major pieces of early twentieth-century American feminist fiction, a beacon cutting through the darkness and probing what is still a controversial subject – the black woman's fate in American society. The novel was clearly a precursor of subsequent works by other African American women – novels by Zora Neale Hurston and, somewhat later, by Toni Morrison, Alice Walker, Gayl Jones, Gloria Naylor, and Marita Golden. As a group, these women writers (and several others) have frequently created unflattering male characters and earned the rancor of their male contemporaries. In Mel Watkins's words, these writers have added to "the sometimes bitter antagonism between black men and women."[11] Larsen probed the subject before them, with considerable skill and psychological understanding. The survival of black culture in America, she warned, is dependent upon the mutual respect and admiration of black males and females.

Passing is a lesser novel than *Quicksand* but still a significant contribution to American culture. As a metaphor commenting upon racial attitudes and misconceptions, the novel continues to engage our attention. In narrative voice, Larsen was years ahead of her time. Readers today, accustomed to writers playing narrative tricks, still fail to understand that Irene Redfield is an unreliable commentator upon her situation and that the primary subject of the story is not passing but jealousy. The power of the novel lies in Larsen's psychological portrait of a woman driven to violence, out of fear that her husband is about to be taken away from her, that her family is about to disintegrate. Like Quicksand, Passing has just begun to receive serious examination by feminist literary critics.

Jean Toomer and Nella Larsen were about as different from one another as two people could be. Their similarities can be summed up in a sentence or two. Though both wrote about black subjects during the 1920s and then seemingly disappeared, darkness eluded Toomer as it stalked Larsen through the reclusive years of her singular life. Toomer was gregarious, a bit of a charlatan, and dependent throughout his entire life upon the good will of other people. Women especially were attracted to him – both because of his appearance and because of the mysteries of the universe, which they believed (and he believed) he could unlock. He spent most of his adult life searching for that elusive unknown which promises happiness and respect. There is little in his personal life that one can call admirable or worthy of emulation. He died in defeat, broken in body and spirit, cut off, one might say, from everything that had once nourished him.

Nella Larsen was a sad, beautiful, lonely woman – elegant, sophisticated, witty, cultured, modern, urbane. Tragedy and disappointment were the constants in her life. Yet, unlike Jean Toomer, she responded to these situations by working out a pattern of survival that permitted her to administer to the sick and the downcast, as she inched along her own lonely pathway toward obscurity and oblivion. As she effaced herself and became more reclusive, her professional life soared. She knew, even if she was not rewarded in kind, that the pain of the inner soul can be mitigated by others, and that invisibility is often one's only guarantee of survival.

Notes

ABBREVIATIONS

Amistad. Amistad Research Center, New Orleans, Louisiana.

Guggenheim. John Simon Guggenheim Memorial Foundation, New York City.

Harmon. Harmon Foundation Records, Manuscript Division, Library of Congress.

Howard. Alain Locke Collection, Howard University Library.

JTP. The Jean Toomer Papers, held at Fisk University from 1963 to 1985 and at Yale University in the Beinecke Rare Book and Manuscript Library since January 1986. Some of the Toomer papers originally given to Fisk were recatalogued after they were transferred to the Beinecke Library. For inconsistencies, the reader should consult the Beinecke catalog, which lists both the original Fisk numbering and the subsequent Yale numbering.

JWJC. James Weldon Johnson Memorial Collection/Collection of American Literature, Beinecke Rare Book and Manuscript Library, Yale University.

NAACP. Walter White Correspondence, NAACP Files, Library of Congress.

NYPL. Carl Van Vechten Collection, Manuscript Division, New York Public Library.

Pennsylvania. Waldo Frank Collection/Special Collections, Van Pelt Library, University of Pennsylvania.

Wisconsin. Margery Latimer Letters, University of Wisconsin Library, Madison.

INTRODUCTION

1. Washington, MS., 50.
2. Richmond Barthe to author, 5 Nov. 1985.

IN THE MIDDLE

1. Johnson, 146.
2. C. McKay, 175.
3. Johnson, 254.
4. Clayton, 44.
5. Ibid., 44–45.
6. Lewis, 90.

7. Locke, 9–10.
8. Huggins, 91.
9. Cripps, *Black Film as Genre*, 17.
10. Ibid., 17.
11. Cripps, *Slow Fade to Black*, 82.
12. Cripps, *Black Film as Genre*, 25.
13. Lewis.
14. Huggins, 13.

TOOMER

1. Toomer, *Wayward and Seeking*, 111. This book excerpts material from several of Jean Toomer's unpublished au-

tobiographies, which were written at various stages of his life. Except where noted, I use the term *autobiography* in a generic sense to refer to these works collectively.

2. Ibid.

3. Scruggs, 85.

4. Toomer, *Wayward and Seeking*, 113.

5. Ibid., 116.

6. Ibid., 119.

7. Ibid., 120.

8. Ibid., 121.

9. Ibid., 120–121.

10. Ibid., 123.

11. Toomer to Alain Locke, 8 Nov. 1921, Howard.

12. Toomer, *Wayward and Seeking*, 123.

13. Ibid.

14. Dillard, 5.

15. Toomer, *Wayward and Seeking*, 124.

16. Ibid.

17. John McClure to Toomer, 30 June 1922, in Benson and Dillard, 20–21.

18. Toomer, *Balo*, 282–283.

19. Toomer to Claude McKay, 19 Aug. 1922, in Bontemps, "Introduction" to *Cane*, viii–ix.

20. Sherwood Anderson to Toomer, Sept. 1922, in Benson and Dillard, 22.

21. Toomer to Sherwood Anderson, 28 Dec. 1922, in Benson and Dillard, 23.

22. Anderson to Toomer, 29 Dec. 1922, in Benson and Dillard, 24.

23. Ibid.

24. Toomer to Anderson, n.d., in Benson and Dillard, 25.

25. Toomer to Waldo Frank, Mar. 1922, Unnumbered letter, Waldo Frank Papers, cited in John Griffin, Jr.,

"Jean Toomer: American Writer," 119.

26. Ibid.

27. Toomer to Frank, 12 Dec. 1922, letter 800, JTP.

28. Toomer to Frank, 15 Jan. 1923, Pennsylvania.

29. Frank, Introduction to *Cane*, xi.

30. Ibid., vii–viii.

31. Horace Liveright to Toomer, n.d., letter 175, JTP.

32. Toomer to Liveright, n.d., letter 176, JTP.

33. Ibid.

34. Ibid.

35. Toomer to Claude Barnett, 29 April 1923, in Benson and Dillard, 33.

36. Toomer, *Wayward and Seeking*, 127.

37. Interview of Gorham B. Munson by India M. Watterson, recorded 27–28 June 1969, tape 1, side 1, transcript, 6, Amistad.

38. Ibid.

39. Ibid., 8.

40. Ibid., side 2, 7.

41. Durham, 41–45.

42. Armstrong, 26.

43. Review of *Cane*, *Boston Transcript*, 8.

44. Littell, 126.

45. Gregory, 374.

46. DuBois, "The Younger Literary Movement," 161–162.

47. Robert T. Kerlin, "Singers of New Songs," 162.

48. Lasker, 191.

49. Ibid.

50. Littell, 126.

51. For all of Waldo Frank's fame, *Holiday* didn't do that much better. Be-

tween 1923 and 1949, when it went out of print, the novel sold approximately 1,750 copies.

52. Turner, 2.

53. Bone, 81.

54. Toomer, *Cane*, 133. The Boni and Liveright, University Place Press, and Harper and Row editions of *Cane* share the same pagination.

55. Ibid., 161.

56. Ibid., 189–190.

57. Ibid., 1.

58. Ibid., 239.

59. Ibid., 119.

60. Ibid., 21.

61. Ibid.

62. Ibid.

63. Ibid., 150.

64. Ibid., 217–218.

65. Charles S. Johnson, quoted in Bontemps, "Introduction" to *Cane*, vii.

66. Toomer, *Wayward and Seeking*, 131.

67. Munson to Frank, 15 Feb. 1924, Pennsylvania.

68. James Moore, 126.

69. Travers, vii.

70. Quoted in Moore, 187.

71. Moore, 187.

72. Byrd, 50–51.

73. Quoted in Moore, 3. See also Lawrence's short story "Mother and Daughter," in which Gurdjieff is ridiculed as "The Turkish Delight [who] was sixty, gray-haired and fat . . . with short thighs, like a toad."

74. N. McKay, 191.

75. Ouspensky, 282.

76. N. McKay, 186.

77. Toomer, *Cane*, 19.

78. Ibid., 31.

79. In reproducing the plates of the original edition for the 1967 University Place Press hardback reprint and the 1969 Harper paperback, the publisher inadvertently omitted the first of these designs. The Norton 1975 new edition of *Cane* also omitted the first arc.

80. "Demonstrations," box 53, folder 26, JTP.

81. "The Second River," box 32, folder 556, 12, JTP.

82. Ibid., 13.

83. Ibid.

84. Ibid., 15.

85. Ibid.

86. Ibid.

87. Ouspensky, 67.

88. Ibid., 104.

89. Munson interview, tape 1, side 1, transcript, 12, Amistad.

90. Ibid.

91. Frank, quoted in Alan Trachtenberg, 107.

92. Ibid.

93. Bontemps, "Remembering *Cane*," 10.

94. "Gurdjieff: A New Group," box 66, folder 2, 1, JTP.

95. Hughes, 241–242.

96. Rudnick, 228.

97. Ibid.

98. Munson interview, tape 1, side 1, transcript, 15, Amistad.

99. Ibid.

100. Toomer, *From Exile into Being*, quoted in Fullenwider, 401.

101. *From Exile into Being*, fifth draft, n.d., box 15, folder 442, 122, JTP.

102. Ibid.

103. Ibid., 123.

104. Ibid., 125.

105. Ibid., 128.
106. Ibid., 139.
107. Ibid., 140.
108. Ibid., 145.
109. Ibid., 152.
110. Ibid., 155.
111. Ibid., 162.
112. Ibid., 176.
113. Ibid., 122.
114. Ouspensky, 324–325.
115. Ibid., 325.
116. Byrd, 86.
117. I have used the authorative text for "Winter on Earth" and "Mr. Costyve Duditch," as established by Darwin T. Turner in The Wayward and the Seeking, 172–173.
118. Ibid., 175.
119. Ibid., 180.
120. Ibid., 181.
121. Ibid., 185.
122. Ibid.
123. Ibid., 193.
124. Ibid., 196.
125. Ibid.
126. Ibid.
127. Toomer, "Reflections," 314.
128. Toomer, "White Arrow," 596.
129. Toomer, "York Beach," 39.
130. Ibid., 26.
131. Ibid., 74.
132. Ibid., 77.
133. Ibid., 12.
134. Ibid., 14.
135. Ibid., 78.
136. Toomer, Wayward and Seeking, 132.
137. Ibid.
138. Ibid., 133.
139. Ibid.

LARSEN

1. Thoms, 113–114.
2. Sylvander, 115.
3. Ibid.
4. Larsen, "Three Scandinavian Games," 191.
5. Larsen, "Danish Fun," 219.
6. Larsen, Quicksand, in An Intimation of Things Distant, 62.
7. Ibid., 63.
8. Allen Semi, "The Wrong Man," in An Intimation, 8.
9. Ibid., 3.
10. Ibid.
11. Ibid., 4.
12. Ibid., 5.
13. Ibid.
14. Ibid., 9.
15. Allen Semi, "Freedom," in An Intimation, 14.
16. Ibid., 16.
17. Ibid.
18. Ibid., 18.
19. Semi, "The Wrong Man," 4.
20. Horne, review of Flight, 227.
21. Larsen, "Correspondence," 295.
22. Horne, "Correspondence," 326.
23. White, "Correspondence," 397.
24. Charles Johnson to Walter White, 5 Aug. 1926, NAACP.
25. Larsen to Carl Van Vechten, 6 Aug. 1926, NYPL.
26. Larsen to Van Vechten, 11 Aug. 1926, NYPL.
27. Ibid.
28. Ibid.
29. Ibid.
30. Larsen to Van Vechten, 6 Oct. 1926, NYPL.
31. Ibid.

32. Ibid.

33. Larsen to Dorothy Peterson, Tuesday 2nd, JWJC.

34. Larsen to Peterson, 27 July 1927, JWJC.

35. Ibid.

36. Ibid.

37. Ibid.

38. Larsen to Van Vechten, 19 March 1928, JWJC.

39. Ibid.

40. Larsen to Van Vechten, 1 May 1928, JWJC.

41. Berlack.

42. Ibid.

43. Larsen, Quicksand, in An Intimation, 51.

44. Ibid., 36.

45. Ibid., 55.

46. Ibid., 56.

47. Ibid.

48. Ibid., 57.

49. Ibid.

50. Ibid., 33.

51. Ibid., 52.

52. Ibid., 47.

53. Ibid., 59.

54. Ibid., 77.

55. Ibid., 78.

56. Ibid., 79.

57. Ibid., 34.

58. Ibid., 86.

59. Ibid.

60. Ibid., 87.

61. Ibid., 103.

62. Ibid., 111.

63. Ibid., 112.

64. Ibid.

65. Ibid., 113.

66. Ibid., 122.

67. Ibid., 115.

68. Ibid., 125.

69. Ibid., 125–126.

70. Ibid., 140.

71. Ibid., 145.

72. Ibid., 148.

73. Ibid., 153.

74. Ibid., 156.

75. Ibid., 159.

76. Ibid., 43.

77. Ibid.

78. Ibid., 118.

79. Ibid., 35.

80. Ibid., 41.

81. Ibid.

82. Ibid., 97.

83. Ibid., 83.

84. Ibid., 59.

85. Ibid., 78.

86. Ibid., 77.

87. Ibid., 86.

88. Ibid., 112.

89. Ibid., 159.

90. Ibid., 160.

91. DuBois, "Two Novels," 202.

92. Ibid.

93. Yates.

94. Review of Quicksand, Amsterdam News, May 16, 1928.

95. Ibid.

96. Ibid.

97. Latimer.

98. Ibid.

99. Review of Quicksand, Saturday Review of Literature, 896.

100. Bradford, 522.

101. Review of Quicksand, New York Times Book Review, 17.

102. Edward Wasserman, Harmon.

103. George E. Haynes, Harmon.

104. Larsen fact sheet, Harmon.

105. DuBois, "Two Novels," 202.

106. Larsen to Van Vechten, 28 July 1929, JWJC.

107. Larsen, *Passing,* in *An Intimation,* 186–187.

108. Ibid., 187.

109. Ibid., 172.

110. Ibid., 197.

111. Ibid., 215.

112. Ibid., 216.

113. Ibid., 190.

114. Ibid., 223.

115. Ibid., 190.

116. Ibid., 219.

117. Ibid., 200–201.

118. Ibid., 213.

119. Ibid., 251.

120. Ibid., 258.

121. Ibid.

122. Ibid., 271.

123. Gloster, 145.

124. Larsen, *Passing,* in *An Intimation,* 271.

125. Ibid.

126. Ibid., 272.

127. Ibid., 272–273.

128. Ibid., 272.

129. The final paragraph of *Passing* reads as follows: "Centuries after, she heard the strange man saying: 'Death by misadventure, I'm inclined to believe. Let's go up and have another look at that window.'"

In one edition of Larsen's novels (*Quicksand and Passing,* in the American Women Writers Series [New Brunswick, N.J.: Rutgers University Press, 1986]), Deborah E. McDowell claims that this paragraph did not appear in the original Knopf edition, published in 1929. McDowell is in error. The

Rutgers edition of Larsen's novels was apparently based upon the Ayer Company's reprint of *Passing,* published in 1985. That edition, a photo reproduction of the third printing of Larsen's novel, omits the final paragraph of the novel. I am unable to determine if the ending of the Knopf third printing of Larsen's novel is an alteration suggested by Larsen or — as I suspect more likely — a matter of a dropped plate.

130. Larsen, *Passing,* in *An Intimation,* 267.

131. Book jacket of 1929 Knopf edition of *Passing.*

132. Ibid.

133. DuBois, "The Browsing Reader," 234, 238–239.

134. Ibid., 234.

135. Ibid.

136. Ibid., 249.

137. Seabrook, 1017.

138. Ibid., 1018.

139. Review of *Passing, New York Times Book Review,* 14.

140. Ibid.

141. Ibid.

142. Lewis Mumford, Harmon.

143. George E. Haynes, Harmon.

144. Walter White to Samuel Craig, 25 Sept. 1928, NAACP.

145. Larsen, Guggenheim.

146. Ibid.

147. Ibid.

148. Ibid.

ENDGAME

1. Bronz, 92.

LARSEN

1. Larsen, "Sanctuary," in *An Intimation*, 22.

2. Ibid., 27.

3. Harold Jackman to Countee Cullen, 27 Jan. 1930, Amistad.

4. Jackman to Cullen, 10 Feb. 1930, Amistad.

5. Jackman to Cullen, 28 Feb. 1930, Amistad.

6. Jackman to Cullen, 13 Mar. 1930, Amistad.

7. "Editor's Note," xli.

8. Ibid.

9. Larsen, "The Author's Explanation," xlii.

10. Ibid.

11. Ibid.

12. Ibid., xli.

13. Larsen to Van Vechten, 11 May 1930, JWJC.

14. Larsen to Van Vechten, 22 May 1930, JWJC.

15. Larsen to Van Vechten, 25 Aug. 1930, NYPL.

16. Elmer Imes to Van Vechten, 18 Sept. 1930, JWJC.

17. Larsen, *Passing*, in *An Intimation*, 212.

18. Larsen to Van Vechten, 30 Sept. 1930, JWJC.

19. Larsen to Van Vechten, 1 Oct. 1930, JWJC.

20. Larsen to Van Vechten, 12 Nov. 1930, JWJC.

21. Larsen to Van Vechten, 13 Nov. 1930, JWJC.

22. Larsen to Van Vechten, 12 Nov. 1930, JWJC.

23. Larsen to Van Vechten, 13 Nov. 1930, JWJC.

24. Larsen to Henry Moe, 20 Oct. 1930, Guggenheim.

25. Ibid.

26. Larsen to Van Vechten, 13 Nov. 1930, JWJC.

27. Larsen to Van Vechten, 25 Jan. 1931, JWJC.

28. Larsen to Moe, 31 Mar. 1931, Guggenheim.

29. Larsen to Moe, 11 Jan. 1931, Guggenheim.

30. Larsen to Van Vechten, 25 Jan. 1931, JWJC.

31. Ibid.

32. Larsen to Van Vechten, 22 Mar. 1931, JWJC.

33. Larsen to Moe, 31 Mar. 1931, Guggenheim.

34. Larsen to Van Vechten, 3 Mar. 1931, JWJC.

35. Larsen to Van Vechten, 7 Apr. 1931, JWJC.

36. Larsen to Van Vechten, 27 Apr. 1931, JWJC.

37. Larsen to Van Vechten, 3 May 1931, JWJC.

38. Larsen to Moe, 21 Apr. 1931, Guggenheim.

39. Larsen to Van Vechten, 11 May 1931, JWJC.

40. Ibid.

41. Ibid.

42. Larsen to Van Vechten, 4 June 1931, JWJC.

43. C. Abbott, reader's report on *Mirage*, 31 Aug. 1931, NYPL.

44. Larsen to Moe, 26 Sept. 1931, Guggenheim.

45. Ellison, 566.

46. Larsen to Van Vechten, 14 May 1932, JWJC.

47. Ibid.

48. Larsen to Van Vechten, 20 Apr. 1932, JWJC.

49. Imes to Van Vechten, 21 June 1932, JWJC.

50. Shockley, 438.

51. Larsen to Van Vechten, 12 May 1933, JWJC.

52. Larsen to Van Vechten, 27 June 1933, JWJC.

53. Larsen to Dorothy Peterson, 29 July 1933, JWJC.

54. Imes to Thomas Jones, 22 July 1933, Thomas Elsa Jones Papers, Fisk University Library, Nashville, Tenn.

55. Larsen to Peterson, 29 July 1933, JWJC.

56. Ibid.

57. Larsen to Peterson, 6 Sept. 1933, JWJC.

58. Ibid.

59. Ibid.

60. Van Vechten to James Weldon Johnson, 11 Oct. 1933, JWJC.

61. *Baltimore Afro-American*, 7 Oct. 1933.

62. Ibid.

63. Ibid.

64. Ibid.

65. Ibid.

66. Ann Allen Shockley states that after her divorce, Nella became assistant secretary of the newly formed Writers' League Against Lynching in December of 1933, but I am unable to verify this. Shockley, 438.

67. Nella Larsen Imes vs. Elmer S. Imes, *Final Decree*, in the First Circuit

Court for Davidson County, Tennessee, 30 Aug. 1933.

68. Imes to Van Vechten, 24 Feb. 1940, JWJC.

69. Imes to Van Vechten, 9 June 1941, JWJC.

70. Peterson to Van Vechten, 31 Oct. 1941, JWJC.

71. Peterson to Van Vechten, 9 Jan. 1942, JWJC.

72. Shockley, 438.

73. Alice Carper and Carolyn Lane to author, 18 May 1985.

74. New York City Certificate of Death, No. 156–64–107204, 31 Mar. 1964.

75. Carper to author, 18 May 1985.

76. Edward Donahoe to Grace N. Johnson, 16 Oct. 1965, JWJC.

77. Jean Blackwell Hutson to Louise Fox, 1 Aug. 1969, Schomberg Collection, New York Public Library.

78. Ibid.

79. Carper to author, 22 Feb. 1986.

80. Ibid.

81. Mildred Phillips to author, 19 Feb. 1986.

TOOMER

1. Margery Latimer to Blanche Matthias, n.d., beginning "I hope you are feeling much better," Wisconsin. Since the letters in this collection are undated, I have identified them by their first sentences.

2. Ibid.

3. Latimer to Ruth Ware, 5 July 1931, box 5, folder 7, JTP.

4. Latimer to Blanche Matthias, n.d.,

beginning "Thank you awfully for your letter and for the charming little sachet," Wisconsin.

5. Ibid.

6. Ibid.

7. Ibid.

8. Ibid.

9. Ibid.

10. "Jean Toomer Weds Novelist," *Daily News*, 26 Mar. 1932.

11. "Gossips Get Thrill from Novelist's Mate," undated newspaper clipping, box 64, folder 18, JTP.

12. Loughridge, 225.

13. "Elite of Portage Shocked by Tales of Toomer 'Cult,'" *Milwaukee Sentinel*, 20 Mar. 1932.

14. Toomer to Alfred A. Knopf, 28 Apr. 1931, JTP.

15. Foreword to *The Gallonwerps*, box 60, folder 4, JTP.

16. Box 32, folder 700, JTP.

17. *Essentials* (Chicago: Private Edition, 1931).

18. Ibid., unnumbered page.

19. Munson interview, tape 1, side 2, transcript, 15, Amistad.

20. *Essentials*, XIX.

21. Ibid., III.

22. Ibid., V.

23. Ibid., IX.

24. Ibid., XXIV.

25. Ibid., XXI.

26. Ibid., XXXI.

27. Ibid., XXXII.

28. Ibid., LI.

29. Ibid., XXIV.

30. Ibid., LXII.

31. Loughridge, 227.

32. "Racial Position," box 17, folder 9, JTP.

33. "Just Americans," *Time*, 28 Mar. 1932, 19.

34. Ibid.

35. Ibid.

36. *Milwaukee Sentinel*, 20 Mar. 1932.

37. Ibid.

38. Ibid.

39. "Toomer Cult Revelations Stir Chicago," *Milwaukee Sentinel*, 21 Mar. 1932.

40. Toomer to Nancy Cunard, 8 Feb. 1932, letter 387, JTP.

41. The pamphlet was published several years later with the altered title, "A Fiction and Some Facts," n.d., after Margery Latimer's death, when Jean had settled in Doylestown with his second wife.

42. Toomer, "A Fact and Some Fictions," in Benson and Dillard, *Jean Toomer*, 43.

43. Ibid.

44. Ibid.

45. Louis Fremont Baldwin, *From Negro to Caucasian* (San Francisco: Pilot Publishing Co., 1929).

46. *Time*, 28 Mar. 1932, 19.

47. Blanche Matthias, Introduction to *Margery Latimer Letters*, 3, Wisconsin.

48. Toomer, *Portage Potential*, 6, box 41, folder 2.

49. Ibid., 64.

50. Ibid., 24.

51. *Milwaukee Sentinel*, 21 Mar. 1932.

52. *Portage Potential*, 104.

53. Ibid., 113.

54. Ibid., 106.

55. Toomer to Harrison Smith, 27 Oct. 1932, letter 3014, JTP.

56. Toomer, *Caromb*, 174a, box 59, folder 2, JTP.

57. Ibid., 176.

58. Toomer, "Brown River, Smile," *Pagany*, 29.

59. Ibid., 30.

60. Ibid.

61. Ibid.

62. Ibid.

63. Ibid., 31.

64. Ibid.

65. Ibid.

66. Ibid.

67. Ibid., 32.

68. Ibid., 33.

69. Ibid.

70. Toomer, "The Hill," 297.

71. Georgia O'Keeffe to Toomer, in Lisle, 210.

72. Ibid.

73. Ibid., 211.

74. Munson interview, tape 1, side 2, transcript, 13, Amistad.

75. Griffin, *Pembroke*, 20.

76. Griffin, "Jean Toomer: American Writer," 385.

77. Sally Fell to author, 15 Nov. 1992.

78. Marjorie Content Toomer to author, 28 July 1984.

79. Ibid.

80. Griffin, *Pembroke*, 20.

81. Davenport, 6.

82. Griffin, *Pembroke*, 17.

83. Toomer to Harry Content, 22 Dec. 1936, box 1, folder 34, JTP.

84. Fisk University oral history interview with Mrs. Marjorie Content Toomer, Doylestown, Penn., 24 Oct. 1970, 9.

85. Davenport, 6–7.

86. Munson interview, tape 1, side 2, transcript, 15, Amistad.

87. Ibid., 18–19.

88. Toomer, "The Blue Meridian," in *Wayward and Seeking*, 222.

89. Ibid., 232.

90. Ibid.

91. Ibid., 215.

92. Ibid., 218.

93. Ibid., 223.

94. Ibid., 225.

95. Ibid.

96. Ibid., 226.

97. Ibid., 225.

98. Ibid., 226.

99. Ibid.

100. Ibid., 219.

101. Byrd, 163.

102. Toomer, in *Wayward and Seeking*, 215–216.

103. Byrd, 163.

104. Toomer to Harry Content, 24 Jan. 1938, box 1, folder 34, JTP.

105. Griffin, *Pembroke*, 22.

106. Ibid.

107. Toomer to Content, 13 June 1939, box 1, folder 34, JTP.

108. Content to Toomer, 14 June 1939, box 1, folder 34, JTP.

109. Toomer to Content, 18 June 1939, box 1, folder 34, JTP.

110. Griffin, *Pembroke*, 23.

111. Ibid.

112. Ibid., 24.

113. Toomer, "Bombay," India journal, 12 Nov. 1939, box 62, folder 1435, JTP.

114. Ibid., 24–28, Nov. 1939.

115. *The Angel Begori or Exile's Return*, 1, box 23, folder 563, JTP.

116. Ibid., 65.

117. Interview with Susan L. Sandberg, Doylestown, 23 Oct. 1985.

118. Sally Fell to author, 15 Nov. 1992.

119. Griffin, *Pembroke*, 24.

120. Kerman and Eldridge, 255.

121. "Why I Joined the Society of Friends," box 55, folder 1253, JTP.

122. Kerman and Eldridge, 256.

123. Ibid., 370.

124. Fell to author, 17 Oct. 1992.

125. Ibid.

126. "The Flavor of Man" (Philadelphia: Young Friends Movement of the Philadelphia Yearly Meetings, 1949), 3.

127. Ibid., 6.

128. Ibid., 7.

129. Ibid.

130. Ibid., 8.

131. Ibid., 32.

132. Lawrence Miller, Jr., to author, 21 Oct. 1992.

133. Frank K. Bjornsgaard to author, 4 Nov. 1992.

134. Otto, 8.

135. Munson interview, tape 1, side 2, transcript, 16, Amistad.

136. Ibid.

137. Toomer to Edgar Cayce, 19 Apr. 1943, in Griffin, "Jean Toomer: American Writer," 397.

138. Munson interview, tape 1, side 2, transcript, 17, Amistad.

139. Ibid.

140. Griffin, *Pembroke*, 25.

141. Ibid.

142. Sandberg to author, 29 Oct. 1992.

143. Bjornsgaard to author, 4 Nov. 1992.

144. Sandberg to author, 29 Oct. 1992.

145. Sandberg interview; Sandberg to author, 29 Oct. 1992.

146. Marjorie Content Toomer to author, 28 July 1984.

147. 29 June 1949, box 62, folder 1442, JTP.

148. Toomer to Douglas Steere, 15 Oct. 1949, box 7, folder 241, JTP.

149. 10 June 1949, box 62, folder 1442, JTP.

150. 10 Aug. 1949, box 62, folder 1442, JTP.

151. 21 Jan. 1950, box 62, folder 1445, JTP.

152. 30 Jan. 1950, box 62, folder 1445, JTP.

153. 10 July 1949, box 62, folder 1442, JTP.

154. 8 July 1949, box 62, folder 1442, JTP.

155. 17 Nov. 1949, box 62, folder 1444, JTP.

156. 11 May 1950, box 62, folder 1447, JTP.

157. 11 Sept. 1949, box 62, folder 1443, JTP.

158. 11 Sept. 1949, box 62, folder 1443, JTP.

159. Toomer to Parker Morgan, 13 Sept. 1950, box 4, folder 109, JTP.

160. Munson interview, tape 2, side 1, transcript, 2, Amistad.

161. Ibid.

162. Fisk University oral history interview, 10.

163. Ibid.

164. Ibid., 14.

165. Sandberg interview.

CHILDHOOD

TOOMER

1. Toomer, *Wayward and Seeking*, 30.
2. Ibid., 33.
3. Ibid., 28.
4. Ibid., 29.
5. Griffin, "Jean Toomer: American Writer," 13.
6. Toomer, *Wayward and Seeking*, 25. Darwin T. Turner states in a footnote that the senate seat was refused twice.
7. Ibid., 24–25.
8. DuBois, *Black Reconstruction in America*, 469–470.
9. Toomer, *Wayward and Seeking*, 31.
10. Ibid.
11. Ibid., 32.
12. Ibid., 33.
13. Ibid., 34.
14. Ibid., 36.
15. Ibid.
16. Ibid., 38.
17. Ibid., 39.
18. Ibid., 44.
19. Ibid., 48.
20. Ibid., 62.
21. Ibid., 61.
22. Ibid., 71.
23. Ibid., 73.
24. Ibid.
25. Ibid., 73–74.
26. Ibid., 75.
27. Toomer, *Autobiography*, "Book of Brooklyn and New Rochelle, 1906–1909 – Mother and Stepfather," 1–2, box 15, folder 6, JTP.
28. Toomer, *Wayward and Seeking*, 85.
29. Ibid., 90.
30. Ibid.
31. Toomer, *Outline of an Autobiography*, "Book of Family," 4, box 11, folder 3, JTP.
32. Ibid., 7.
33. Toomer, *Wayward and Seeking*, 22.
34. Toomer, *Outline of an Autobiography*, "P. B. S. Pinchback," 4, box 14, folder 6, JTP.
35. Ibid.
36. Ibid.
37. Toomer, *Wayward and Seeking*, 93.
38. Ibid., 31.
39. Ibid., 53.
40. Ibid., 91.
41. Ibid., 94.
42. Ibid., 95.
43. Ibid., 97.
44. Ibid.
45. Toomer, *Cane*, 82–83.
46. Toomer, *Wayward and Seeking*, 100.
47. Toomer, *Cane*, 134–135.
48. Ibid., 137–138.
49. Ibid., 145.
50. Ibid.
51. Toomer, *Wayward and Seeking*, 100.
52. Ibid., 102.
53. Ibid.
54. Ibid., 104.
55. Ibid., 105.
56. Ibid.
57. Ibid., 106.
58. Ibid.
59. Ibid., 107.
60. Ibid., 108.
61. Ibid., 109.
62. Ibid., 111.
63. Ibid.

LARSEN

1. Larsen, *Passing* (New York: Knopf, 1929), dust jacket.

2. Metropolitan Hospital Center, 1901 First Ave., New York, New York 10029. Application dated 2 December 1961.

3. Kobenhavns Universitet Administrationen, Arkiv-Og Dokumentationsafdelingen. 12 Dec. 1985.

4. The Lincoln Fund, 292 Madison Avenue, New York, New York 10017. 13 May 1986.

5. Award files, 1929, Harmon.

6. Larsen, *Quicksand*, in *An Intimation*, 40.

7. Ibid., 41.

8. Ibid., 118.

9. Ibid., 56.

10. Ibid., 62.

11. Ibid., 63.

12. Ibid., 56.

13. Ibid.

14. Ibid., 61.

INVISIBLE DARKNESS

1. Toomer, box 53, folder 26, JTP.

2. Nancy Loughridge to author, 1 June 1986.

3. Van Vechten to Dorothy Peterson, 3 Aug. 1942, JWJC.

4. Interview with William J. Welch, 13 June 1986.

5. Ibid.

6. Toomer, *Eight-Day World*, 1, box 60, folder 1, JTP.

7. Toomer, *Portage Potential*, 17, box 41, folder 2, JTP.

8. Interview with Alice Carper, 11 June 1986.

9. Larsen, *Quicksand*, in *An Intimation*, 39.

10. Interview with Carolyn Lane, 19 May 1985.

11. Watkins, 1.

Sources

TOOMER

This section lists only published works by Jean Toomer quoted in the text. I have not given separate entries for parts of Cane that were published prior to the publication of the novel itself. Nor have I listed other works by Toomer published late in his life, such as his essays for the Quakers. For those items, as well as for the unpublished manuscripts in the Yale collection, the reader should consult the following: Darwin T. Turner, "Jean Toomer: Exile," In a Minor Chord (Carbondale, Ill.: Southern Illinois University Press, 1971); John C. Griffin, "Jean Toomer: A Bibliography," South Carolina Review 7 (April 1975): 61–64; and Cynthia Earl Kerman and Richard Eldridge, The Lives of Jean Toomer (Baton Rouge: Louisiana State University Press, 1987).

BOOKS

Cane. New York: Boni and Liveright, 1923. Rpts. New York: University Place Press, 1967; New York: Harper and Row, 1969; New York: Norton, 1975.
Essentials. Privately published. Chicago: Lakeside Press, 1931.
The Wayward and the Seeking: A Collection of Writings by Jean Toomer. Ed. Darwin T. Turner. Washington: Howard University Press, 1980.

OTHER WORKS

Balo. In Plays of Negro Life, ed. Alain Locke and Gregory Montgomery. New York: Harper, 1927. Rpt. Westport, Ct.: Negro Universities Press (Greenwood Press), 1977.
"Winter on Earth." In Second American Caravan: A Yearbook of American Literature, ed. Alfred Kreymborg, Lewis Mumford, and Paul Rosenfeld, 694–715. New York: Macaulay, 1928. Rpt. in Wayward and Seeking, 166–181.
"Mr. Costyve Duditch." Dial 85 (Dec. 1928): 460–476. Rpt. in Wayward and Seeking, 182–196.
"Reflections." Dial 86 (April 1929): 314.
"White Arrow." Dial 86 (July 1929): 596. Rpt. in Wayward and Seeking, 202.
"York Beach." In The New American Caravan, ed. Alfred Kreymborg, Lewis Mumford, and Paul Rosenfeld, 12–83. New York: Macaulay, 1929.
"Brown River, Smile." Pagany (Winter 1932): 29–33.

"The Blue Meridian." In *The New Caravan*, ed. Alfred Kreymborg, Lewis Mumford, and Paul Rosenfeld, 107–133. New York: Macaulay, 1936. Rpt. in *Wayward and Seeking*, 214–234.

LARSEN

BOOKS

Quicksand. New York: Knopf, 1928. Rpts. Westport, Ct.: Negro Universities Press (Greenwood Press), 1969; New York: Collier Books, 1971; New Brunswick, N.J.: Rutgers University Press, 1986. Rpt. in *An Intimation of Things Distant: The Collected Fiction of Nella Larsen*. Ed. by Charles R. Larson, 29–162. New York: Anchor Books, 1992.

Passing. New York: Knopf, 1929. Rpts. New York: Greenberg Publishers, 1935; Westport, Ct.: Negro Universities Press (Greenwood Press), 1969; New York: Collier Books, 1971; Salem, N.H.: Ayer Company, 1985; New Brunswick, N.J.: Rutgers University Press, 1986. Rpt. in *An Intimation of Things Distant*, 163–275.

An Intimation of Things Distant: The Collected Fiction of Nella Larsen. Ed. by Charles R. Larson. New York: Anchor Books, 1992.

OTHER WORKS

"Three Scandinavian Games." *The Brownies' Book* (June 1920): 191.

"Danish Fun." *The Brownies' Book* (July 1920): 219.

[As Allen Semi]. "The Wrong Man." *Young's Magazine* (Jan. 1926): 243–246. Rpt. in *An Intimation of Things Distant*, 1–9.

[As Allen Semi]. "Freedom." *Young's Magazine* (April 1926): 241–243. Rpt. in *An Intimation of Things Distant*, 11–18.

"Correspondence." *Opportunity* (Sept. 1926): 295.

"Sanctuary." *Forum* (Jan. 1930): 15–18. Rpt. in *An Intimation of Things Distant*, 19–27.

"The Author's Explanation." *Forum* (April 1930): xli–xlii.

GENERAL BIBLIOGRAPHY

Armstrong, John. "The Real Negro." *New York Tribune*, 14 Oct. 1923, 26.

Baldwin, Louis Fremont. *From Negro to Caucasian*. San Francisco: Pilot Publishing Company, 1929.

Benson, Brian Joseph, and Mabel Mayle Dillard. *Jean Toomer*. Boston: Twayne, 1980.

Berlack, Thelma E. "New Author Unearthed Right Here in Harlem." *Amsterdam News*, 23 May 1928.

Bone, Robert. *The Negro Novel in America*. Rev. ed. New Haven: Yale University Press, 1965.

Bontemps, Arna. "Introduction" to *Cane*. New York: Harper and Row, 1969, vii–xvi.

———. "Remembering *Cane*." *Banc* 1 (May–June 1972): 9–10.

Bradford, Roark. "Mixed Blood." *New York Herald Tribune*, 13 May 1928, 522.

Bronz, Stephen H. *Roots of Negro Racial Consciousness*. New York: Libra, 1964.

Byrd, Rudolph P. *Jean Toomer's Years with Gurdjieff*. Athens: University of Georgia Press, 1990.

Clayton, Horace R. "Ideological Forces in the Work of Negro Writers." In *Anger, and Beyond*, ed. Herbert Hill, 37–50. New York: Perennial, 1966.

Cripps, Thomas. *Black Film as Genre*. Bloomington: Indiana University Press, 1978.

———. *Slow Fade to Black*. New York: Oxford University Press, 1977.

Davenport, Franklin. "Mill House." *Banc* 1 (May–June 1972): 6–7.

Dillard, Mabel Mayle. "Behind the Veil: Jean Toomer's Esthetic." In *The Merrill Studies in Cane*, ed. Frank Durham, 2–10. Columbus, Ohio: Charles E. Merrill, 1971.

DuBois, W. E. B. *Black Reconstruction in America*. New York: Russell and Russell, 1935. Rpt. New York: Atheneum, 1969.

———. "The Browsing Reader." *Crisis* 36 (1929): 234, 248–249.

———. "The Younger Literary Movement." *Crisis* 27 (1924): 161–162.

———. "Two Novels." *Crisis* 35 (1928): 202, 211.

Durham, Frank. "The Only Negro Member of the Poetry Society of South Carolina." In *The Merrill Studies in Cane*, ed. Frank Durham, 11–14. Columbus, Ohio: Charles E. Merrill, 1971.

"Editor's Note." *Forum* (April 1930): xli.

"Elite of Portage Shocked by Tales of Toomer 'Cult.'" *Milwaukee Sentinel*, 20 Mar. 1932.

Ellison, Ralph. *Invisible Man*. New York: Random House, 1952. Rpt. New York: Vintage, 1972.

Fisher, Rudolph, "The Caucasian Storms Harlem," *Mercury* 11 (1927): 393–398.

Frank, Waldo. "Introduction." *Cane*. New York: Boni and Liveright, 1923. Rpts. New York: University Place Press, 1967; New York: Harper and Row, 1969, vii–xvi.

Frank, Waldo, Lewis Mumford, Dorothy Norman, Paul Rosenfeld, and Harold Rugg, eds. *America and Alfred Stieglitz: A Collective Portrait*. New York: Doubleday, 1934. Rpt. New York: Octagon Books, 1975.

Fullenwider, S. P. "Jean Toomer: Lost Generation, or Negro Renaissance." *Phylon* 25 (Fourth Quarter, 1966): 396–403. Rpt. in *The Merrill Studies in Cane*, ed. Frank

Durham 66–74. Columbus, Ohio: Charles E. Merrill, 1971.

Gloster, Hugh M. *Negro Voices in American Fiction.* Chapel Hill: University of North Carolina Press, 1948.

Gregory, Montgomery. Review of *Cane. Opportunity* (Dec. 1923): 374–475. Rpt. in *The Merrill Studies in Cane,* ed. Frank Durham, 35–40. Columbus, Ohio: Charles E. Merrill, 1971.

Griffin, John C. "A Chat with Marjory [sic] Content Toomer." *Pembroke* 5 (1974): 15–27.

———. "Jean Toomer: American Writer." Ph.D. diss., University of South Carolina, 1976.

Horne, Frank. Review of *Flight,* by Walter White. *Opportunity* (July 1926): 227.

———. "Correspondence." *Opportunity* (Oct. 1926): 326.

Huggins, Nathan Irvin. *Harlem Renaissance.* New York: Oxford University Press, 1971.

Hughes, Langston. *The Big Sea.* New York: Knopf, 1940. Rpt. New York: Hill and Wang, 1963.

"Jean Toomer Weds Novelist." *Daily News,* 26 Mar. 1932.

Johnson, James Weldon. *Black Manhattan.* New York: 1930. Rpt. New York: Atheneum, 1968.

"Just Americans." *Time,* 28 Mar. 1932, 19. Rpt. in *The Merrill Studies in Cane,* ed. Frank Durham, 15. Columbus, Ohio: Charles E. Merrill, 1971.

Kerlin, Robert T. "Singers of New Songs." *Opportunity* (May 1926): 162. Rpt. in *The Merrill Studies in Cane,* ed. Frank Durham, 42–44. Columbus, Ohio: Charles E. Merrill, 1971.

Kerman, Cynthia Earl, and Richard Eldridge. *The Lives of Jean Toomer: A Hunger for Wholeness.* Baton Rouge: Louisiana State University Press, 1987.

Lasker, Bruno. "Doors Open Southward." *Survey,* 1 Nov. 1923, 190–191. Rpt. in *The Merrill Studies in Cane,* ed. Frank Durham, 29–30. Columbus, Ohio: Charles E. Merrill, 1971.

Latimer, Margery. Review of *Quicksand. New York World,* 22 July 1928.

Lewis, David Levering. *When Harlem Was in Vogue.* New York: Knopf, 1981.

Lisle, Laurie. *Portrait of an Artist: A Biography of Georgia O'Keeffe.* New York: Seaview Books, 1980.

Littell, Robert. Review of *Cane. New Republic,* 26 Dec. 1923, 126. Rpt. in *The Merrill Studies in Cane,* ed. Frank Durham, 32–33. Columbus, Ohio: Charles E. Merrill, 1971.

Locke, Alain. *The New Negro.* New York: Boni and Liveright, 1925. Rpt. New York: Arno Press, 1968.

Loughridge, Nancy. "Afterword: The Life." In *Guardian Angel and Other Stories,* by Margery Latimer. Old Westbury, N.Y.: Feminist Press, 1984.

McKay, Claude. *Home to Harlem*. New York: Harper, 1928. Rpt. New York: Pocket Books, 1965.

McKay, Nellie Y. *Jean Toomer, Artist*. Chapel Hill: University of North Carolina Press, 1984.

Moore, James. *Gurdjieff and Mansfield*. London: Routledge and Kegan Paul, 1980.

"Novelist Divorces Fisk Professor." *Baltimore Afro-American*, 7 Oct. 1933.

Otto, George Edward. "Religious Society of Friends." *Banc* 1 (May–June 1972): 8.

Ouspensky, P. D. *In Search of the Miraculous*. New York: Harcourt, Brace, 1949.

Review of *Cane*. Boston Transcript, 15 Dec. 1923, 8.

Review of *Passing*. New York Times Book Review, 28 April 1929, 14.

Review of *Quicksand*. Amsterdam News, 16 May 1928.

Review of *Quicksand*. New York Times Book Review, 8 April 1928, 17.

Review of *Quicksand*. Saturday Review of Literature, 19 May 1928, 896.

Rudnick, Lois Palken. *Mabel Dodge Luhan*. Albuquerque: University of New Mexico Press, 1984.

Scruggs, Charles. "Jean Toomer: Fugitive." *American Literature* 47 (March 1975): 84–96.

Seabrook, W. B. "Touch of the Tar-brush." *Saturday Review of Literature*, 18 May 1929, 1017–18.

Shockley, Ann Allen. *Afro-American Women Writers 1746–1933*. New York: Meridian, 1989.

Sylvander, Carolyn Wedin. *Jessie Redmon Fauset, Black American Writer*. Troy, N.Y.: Whitson Publishing Company, 1981.

Thoms, Adah B. *Pathfinders: A History of the Progress of Colored Graduate Nurses*. New York: Kay Print House, 1929. Rpt. New York: Garland, 1928.

"Toomer Cult Revelations Stir Chicago." *Milwaukee Sentinel*, 21 March 1932.

Trachtenberg, Alan, ed. *Memoirs of Waldo Frank*. Amherst: University of Massachusetts Press, 1973.

Travers, P. L. Foreword to *Who Are You Monsieur Gurdjieff?*, by Rene Zuber, v–vii. London: Routledge and Kegan Paul, 1980.

Turner, Darwin T. *In a Minor Chord: Three Afro-American Writers and Their Search for Identity*. Carbondale: Southern Illinois University Press, 1971.

Washington, Mary Helen. "Nella Larsen: Mystery Woman of the Harlem Renaissance." *MS.*, Dec. 1980.

Watkins, Mel. "Sexism, Racism and Black Women Writers." *New York Times Book Review*, 15 June 1986.

White, Walter. "Correspondence." *Opportunity* (Dec. 1926): 397.

Yates, Ruth L. Review of *Quicksand*. Pittsburgh Courier, 26 May 1928.

Index